Not Forgotten

Australian Catholic Educators
1820–2020

As we celebrate 200 years of Catholic Education in Australia, it is timely to reflect on the inspiring stories of the pioneers who shaped our story. *Not Forgotten* captures the rich tapestry of the legacy of those who had the vision, courage and conviction to ensure Catholic schools were an important part of the education landscape from the early days of colonial Australia. In their stories, we read of their commitment to forming young people in their faith, the importance of quality learning, the priority given to the formation of staff and the unfolding role of governance. Common in all the stories is the commitment to the young people in their care and the provision of an education that would give each child the opportunity to realise the gifts God gave them and live a life that is full. As we look to the future, *Not Forgotten* is a valuable resource for all in our Catholic schools and recommended reading for those shaping the future mission of Catholic education in our rapidly changing world. We stand on the shoulders of these great leaders and quiet achievers of Catholic education. It is with gratitude that we honour their stories and the contribution they made as we look to the future of our Catholic schools in Australia with hope.

Pam Betts
Executive Director
Archdiocese of Brisbane Catholic Education

An enduring and deeply-researched tribute to the forgotten heroes of Australian Catholic education, whose untiring labours created the possibility of an expanded mind and spirit for the generation of today.

James Franklin
Editor
Journal of the Australian Catholic Historical Society

This dictionary of the lives of Catholic educators who have made a significant or representative contribution to the development of Catholic education in Australia provides a collective biography of a diverse group with common cause. The editors, Anne Benjamin and Seamus O'Grady, are to be congratulated for producing this valuable historical resource which links individual lives to the wider historical processes in our history.

Dictionaries of biography are major collaborative research projects not undertaken lightly. As the General Editor of the *Australian Dictionary of Biography*, I appreciate the work that has gone into producing *Not Forgotten: Australian Catholic Educators 1820-2020*. The ADB welcomes this project and congratulates the editors, Anne Benjamin and Seamus O'Grady, on the publication of this valuable historical resource."

Melanie Nolan
Professor of History
Director, National Centre for Biography
General Editor, *Australian Dictionary of Biography*

Not Forgotten

AUSTRALIAN CATHOLIC EDUCATORS

1820 – 2020

Edited by
Anne Benjamin & Seamus O'Grady

COVENTRY
PRESS

Published in Australia by
Coventry Press
www.coventrypress.com.au
33 Scoresby Road Bayswater VIC 3153

ISBN 9780648725152

Compilation copyright © Anne Benjamin and Seamus O'Grady 2020
Copyright of individual chapters remains with the authors of those chapters.

All rights reserved. Other than for the purposes and subject to the conditions prescribed under the *Copyright Act*, no part of this publication may be reproduced, stored in a retrieval system, or transmitted in any form or by any means, electronic, mechanical, photocopying, recording or otherwise, without the prior permission of the publisher.

Catalogue-in-Publication entry is available from the National Library of Australia
http://catologue.nla.gov.au

Cover design by Ian James – www.jgd.com.au
Text design by Coventry Press
Set in Alegreya 11 pt

Printed in Australia

Contents

Foreword	Dermot Nestor	v
Preface	Edmund Campion	ix
Note on contributors		xiii
Chapter One	Introduction to the BDACE Online Project	
	Seamus O'Grady	1
Chapter Two	Catholic Educators 1820–2020	
	Seamus O'Grady	7
Chapter Three	1820–1880	15
Context	Charles McGee	15
Biographies		30
Farrell Cuffe (ca 1775–1848)		30
George Marley (1788–ca 1848)		33
Archdeacon John William McEncroe (1794–1868)		36
Andrew Higgins (1797–1859)		41
Brigid Dwyer (1808–1878)		44
Bridget Mary Magdalen McGuigan		
(Mother Mary Francis rsc) (1842–1923)		47
Reflection	Anne Benjamin	51
Chapter Four	1880–1960	63
Context	Janice Garaty	63
Biographies		76
Ellen Hogan (Sr M. Gabriel op) (1842–1915)		76
Mother Alice Anastasia Kennedy pbvm (1876–1960)		80
Mary Philomena Douglas fcJ (1897–1958)		83
Mother Mary Benignus Fitzgerald RSM		
(Elizabeth Fitzgerald 1890–1946)		88
Monsignor John Thomas McMahon OBE (1893–1989)		91
Mona Margaret Griffin		
(Mother Mary Xavier osu) (1897–1985)		96
Loretta Marie Slattery (Sr Clare sgs) (1900–1980)		99

	William John Graham msc (Fr 'Bill' Graham) (1912–1966)	102
	Lawrence George Carmody	
	(Br Aloysius Meldan fsc) (1916–1981)	106
Reflection	Graham English	112
Chapter Five	1960–2000	123
Context	Kelvin Canavan fms	123
Biographies		141
	Brother Ronald Edwin Fogarty fms	
	(Thomas Fogarty, 1913–2009)	141
	Fr Charles Fraser sj (1913–2004)	146
	Mother Loyola Fraser csb (1918–2008)	150
	Francis (Frank) Irenaeus McCarthy cfc oam face	
	(1920–2010)	155
	Sr Mary St Bernard fdnsc (1925–2016)	159
	Francis (Frank) Michael Martin (1928–2015)	162
	Margaret Toohey rscj (1930–2014)	167
	Ann Dennis Clark (1935–1997)	170
	Deirdre Rofe (Sr Mary Anne ibvm) (1943–2002)	175
	Sr Winifred Agnes Ryan mss (1915–2011)	179
Reflection	Brian Croke	183
Chapter Six	2000–2020	193
Context	Dr Lee-Anne Perry AM	193
Biographies		207
	Br Bernard Noel Bulfin fsp (1936–2018)	207
	Veronica Therese Ryan, rsj (1936–2008)	213
	Bishop Barry Collins (1938–2000)	217
	Barry Francis Dwyer (1938–2009)	222
	Ann-Marie Webb sm (1943–2008)	227
Reflection	+ Vincent Long	230
Epilogue	Brian Croke	241
Appendix A	Additional biographies	251
Appendix B	Entries by canonical status	253
Appendix C	Video interviews	255

Foreword

"Whereof one cannot speak, thereof one must be silent"

Ludwig Wittgenstein, *Tractatus Logico-Philosophicus*

The realm of ignorance is every bit as vast, complex and multifaceted as that of knowledge. With a handful of clear Cartesian exceptions, whatever someone may know, they can also and with equal measure, be ignorant of. The seeming inevitability of ignorance is not referenced here as an indulgence in the abstractions of philosophy (considered by some as the home of ignorance). On the contrary, it is noted as an affirmation of the faith that human thinking and action often spring from a dimension of our existence that is greater than human knowledge and which can only be experienced in humble acknowledgment of our ignorance. The recognition that all human knowledge emerges from and ultimately remains a corollary of ignorance also provides an appropriate frame for a learned work on the craft of education and the mission of Catholic educators in particular.

As the first hard-copy output from the wider *Biographical Dictionary of Australian Catholic Educators* project, this volume provides an enticing and readily digestible entrée to all that will follow. That wider project – originally conceived by Dr Brian Croke as a response to a critical gap in the documented history of Australian Catholic education – contains four elements: an extensive bibliography capturing the breadth of what literature is available on the topic of Australian Catholic education, a Living History digital repository which includes interviews with and testimonials from some of the most significant practitioners and leaders of Catholic education and a database relating to the project of Australian Catholic education since its inception. This volume represents the first hard-copy publication of the fourth and major element: a dictionary of biography. Extending well beyond a simplistic documentation of the facts of any particular life, the careful and studied analyses that decorate the pages of this volume animate the experience of those facts. Spanning the two hundred-year period between 1820 – 2020, this study captures the substance, the significance and the spirit of Catholic education in Australia in a way that few others ever have.

Enlightening, entertaining and always engaging, each chapter, and the wider work in which they sit, simultaneously functions at a more profound level. They show that while Catholic education was not always the preserve of religious or indeed of the Irish who settled here *en masse*, it has always been marked by its professionalism and a level of organisational dexterity that sets it apart even today. They also show that the history of this institution is not one ceaselessly punctuated by triumph and success. Rather it is one that betrays evidence of toil, of threat, and often, of tragedy. Between these poles however, and indeed at the heart of the entire mission are people; people whose commitment to the vocation of Catholic education, to the countless families and children it has supported and, to the Church they ultimately served, remained a constant. It is these people that are the history of Catholic education in Australia and to whom the authors of this work stand as heirs.

This is also a timely work. It provides a consolidated and contextualised account of Catholic education when all too often that story has been told in an unsystematic and heavily dispersed manner. Faced with the imminent decline and potential disappearance of the Religious Institutes who furnished Catholic education with its intellectual rigor and moral fibre, this work ensures that *memory* is something far more expansive and impactful than a mere knowledge of past things. The momentous contribution of laity that is acknowledged throughout this work emphasises one of the enduring yet unrealised principles of Vatican II: *participation*. Within the context of Pope Francis' call for an educational village that exhibits a renewed passion for open, inclusive and constructive dialogue this work also reminds us that education, and Catholic education in particular, has always been defined by service to and for the wider community; without calculation, without fear, but always with tenderness and with understanding.

Framing a work of this type and of such quality is no easy task. It requires a special kind of commitment which no sense of a deadline could ever instil. It is thus incumbent upon me to acknowledge the editorial efforts and singular contributions of Honorary Professor Anne Benjamin and Mr Seamus O'Grady. Their limitless energy and expository polish have ensured that the whole presented here is very much greater than the sum of its parts. A special note of thanks to my ACU colleague Professor Michael Ondaatje who, with guidance from the University's Arts and Culture Committee, provided initial support for this project within ACU. A special mention also to the Vice-Chancellor and President of ACU Professor Greg Craven AO GCSG whose sponsorship of the project gives concrete expression to the mission and value proposition of Catholic education.

Finally, I would like to express my deep gratitude to Anne and to Seamus for the invitation to provide a foreword to what is not just an important historical book but equally, a book of historical importance. It is an honour and a privilege to provide these words on behalf of the Australian Catholic University, an institution which is very much a part of the living history captured in these pages. It is now for you, the reader, to take up this volume, to position yourself in its story and to know again that which none of us should ignore.

Professor Dermot Nestor,
Executive Dean | Faculty of Theology and Philosophy,
Australian Catholic University

Preface

For centuries, education was a function of the church. Schools taught grammar, sums, maps, spelling but also what to believe in and how to live rightly. In Australia's early days, schoolhouses were also churches and government grants went to ministers of religion and schoolteachers. When church leaders went back to the old country to recruit helpers, they were looking for teachers as well as clergy. Out in the parishes these shared a dual ministry, although much of this history is now lost.

From the end of this first period, Jeremiah Crowley's story throws some light back onto this lost history. An Irishman, he came to Sydney in 1845 at the age of 16. Ten years later, Catholics in North Sydney petitioned government for a teacher in their church school and their petition was granted. Jeremiah Crowley came to the school a few years later, remaining there for more than twenty years. He quickly became a significant figure in parish life, speaking at parish meetings and serving Mass if need be – otherwise sitting in the same seat Sunday after Sunday, year after year, and always on time. He was auditor of parish accounts and became a confidant of the parish priests, travelling with them across the vast parish, which stretched from the Harbour to the Hawkesbury River and from the Pacific Ocean to the Lane Cove River.

Crowley was a correspondent of the Sydney Catholic paper, the *Freeman's Journal* and when the history of the parish came to be written at its centenary, it relied heavily on his dispatches. When state aid to church schools was stopped, he moved to a local government school, thus allowing the nuns to take charge of the Catholic school.

By the final quarter of the 19th century, it had become clear that Catholic schools must learn to survive without government funds. What could the Catholic community do? They turned to the religious orders of Europe, inviting them to come south and staff their schools. So they came from Famine-recovering Ireland and Germany's *Kulturkampf* and anti-religious France to teach the sons and daughters of the poor and to live in poverty themselves. Soon their heroism would attract many young Australians to join them.

Thus, the parish school became a centre of Catholic life with its need to build and maintain the fabric and to house and feed the teachers. Fund-raising for the school – raffles, house parties, fetes, car drives, dances and balls – welded parishioners together as much as their experience of Sunday Mass. As well, the unfair denial of state aid to their schools bruised ordinary Catholics' citizenship for over a century.

The crisis of the denial of state aid rallied the Catholic laity to want schools staffed by religious. In 1880, for example, Catholics in Araluen in southern NSW raised one hundred pounds and wrote to the archbishop in Sydney to send them some religious sisters – otherwise they would have to place their children in the government school. In response to such widespread demands, the bishops at a Plenary Council, in 1885, ordered that when a parish was opened, the first building was to be a school (where Sunday Mass could be said); later a church might be built. By contrast, the bishops of the United States, meeting in 1884, had decided that in a new parish or mission, the first building was to be a church.

By and large, parish schools were taught by religious sisters. The demand for their services was insistent, so much so that orders which had been founded for something other, such as social work, found themselves pressed into taking charge of schools, with obvious penalties. Nevertheless, in a time of crisis they kept the schools open; later generations would rediscover their founders' charisms.

In the poor classrooms of parish schools, nuns laid the foundations of a religious culture that endured into the 21st century. They were true makers of Australian Catholicism. In their schools, the certainties of the penny catechism were drummed into children's memories alongside a mathematical – 'How far can you go?' – exegesis of the Ten Commandments. Each Friday, this school religion reached its apotheosis at Benediction of the Most Blessed Sacrament with its expressive sights, sounds and smells, a touch of heaven on earth. Even if pupils later 'lost the faith', this schooldays culture remained as a rich residue in their lives.

As boys grew up, their schooling was transferred to the care of religious brothers, who launched them into manhood. The purpose of the brothers' schools, Dr Mannix said, was to work towards a future society in which 'Catholics might hope to secure, without fear or favour, their due and proportionate share of the good things that Australia has to offer'. This came at a high cost – Morris West's first novel, *Moon in My Pocket*, which he did not allow to be republished, showed how bleak the life of a brother could be. Nevertheless, they achieved Dr Mannix's expectations. Brother Barry Coldrey has written:

> In a way, the teaching Brotherhoods were working-class, self-help movements... Over the years they helped to propel droves of working-class Catholics into the middle class and the professions, offered a strong vigorous, hard-working model of masculinity and played an important role in assimilating migrants at a time when assimilation was socially crucial and in accord with government policy.

One should also point to some societal benefits of the Catholic schools in this period. Everyone knows that brothers' schools produced many football stars; but who is aware that they also fostered an equal number of good writers? Similarly, convent schools were often the only places offering a musical education in their district. Without them, the history of music in Australia would be somewhat reduced.

Ken Inglis told historians that they should write about people who did not know what happened next. For some in the Catholic educational world, the Second Vatican Council (1962-65) was a surprise. They had seen their schools, self-isolated in parishes, grow into a diocesan system. Once, the priest charged with overseeing schools in a diocese had been able to locate his 'office' in a suitcase under his bed. Now there was greater centralisation, if only to deal with governments and speak with one voice. So Vatican II happened in a changing culture of the schools. Among teachers, it loosened the hold religious orders had on individuals, many of whom went elsewhere.

At the same time, years at school were lengthened, which meant more teachers were needed. Would the Catholic school system collapse? The introduction of needs-based state aid for church schools in the 1970s came just in time. It meant that lay teachers could be hired and paid proper wages. It meant also that lay teachers had to take on the responsibility of handing on the tradition, of ensuring that Catholic schools continued to be Catholic. To meet this need, tertiary levels of religious education grew.

The *Biographical Dictionary of Australian Catholic Educators* is offered to this new generation of teachers. They are carriers of a long tradition who can learn from the past. Lord Acton wrote that studying history gives us a choice of what we today call role models. This dictionary is a vast collection of role models for Catholic educators. I say to each reader: choose your role model here.

Edmund Campion
Catholic Institute of Sydney

Note on contributors

Articles and editing

Dr Anne Benjamin has served Catholic education over many years as classroom teacher, teacher educator, curriculum designer, researcher and system leader including as Executive Director of Catholic schools in the Diocese of Parramatta. She has worked with Catholic educators across dioceses in Australia, as well as in Papua New Guinea and Tonga.

Br Kelvin Canavan taught large classes in Marist primary schools (1960-67) at the same time attending the University of Sydney as an evening student. In 1968, he was appointed Inspector of Schools in the Archdiocese of Sydney, aged 31, and for the next forty years was a major player in the development of the Archdiocesan System of schools funded progressively by governments.

Dr Brian Croke is an Honorary Associate at the University of Sydney with extensive experience as author, editor, presenter, reviewer and critic. He is passionate that Australian educators learn more about the unique history of Catholic Education and the people who made it happen. Educated at Macquarie, Oxford and Harvard Universities, he has published extensively on various topics in Roman and Byzantine history and historiography and modern historiography. He was Executive Director of the Catholic Education Commission NSW from 1994 to 2017 and contributed the chapter on Australia to the first International Handbook of Catholic Education (2007).

Dr Graham English spent forty-six years in Catholic education as a teacher in primary and secondary schools, a religious education consultant in Sydney Catholic Education Office and a lecturer in

Religious Education at Australian Catholic University. He has a BA (ANU), an MA (Lancaster) and an Ed D (Sydney).

DR JANICE GARATY was a humanities teacher for many years. Her doctoral thesis (ACU) is a contextual history of a Sydney Catholic girls' school and a commissioned work, Providence Provides: Brigidine Sisters in the NSW Province, was published in 2013. Her research interests include the contribution of individuals to Catholic culture in the 19th century.

DR DAMIAN JOHN GLEESON, an Irish-Australian history scholar, contributed several portraits. His acclaimed work, The Rock of St George (2017) received the prestigious Ron Rathbone Local History Award. Dr Gleeson's next work, a history of St Patrick's Parish, Mortlake (NSW) is due for publication in November 2020.

The Editors acknowledge the assistance of Dr Damian Gleeson in the review and editing of a number of biographies.

CHARLES MCGEE was educated by the Brigidine Sisters and Marist Brothers in Randwick NSW. He graduated in Arts at the University of Sydney and later completed a Diploma in Education at the Australian Catholic University. He spent forty-two years as a classroom teacher in a wide range of subjects, holding leadership positions including principal. As historian, Charles has researched and published extensively on the teachers and Catholic schools prior to 1880.

BISHOP VINCENT LONG VAN NGUYEN OFM CONV is the fourth Bishop of Parramatta. He came to Australia as a refugee and is Australia's first Asian-born bishop. He serves as the Chair of the Bishops Commission for Social Justice: Service and Mission. Bishop Vincent has been clear and outspoken on the need for reform within the Church especially following revelations about sexual abuse of minors in the Church. He is also a strong advocate for refugees and displaced people.

SEAMUS O'GRADY has had a lifetime engagement with Catholic schools – as student, Marist Brother, lay teacher, Religious Education Coordinator,

Principal, Consultant and Director (Religious Education and Curriculum). He holds qualifications in Science, Education and Theology.

Dr Lee-Anne Perry AM is the Executive Director of the Queensland Catholic Education Commission. She came to this role in 2015 after twenty-five years as a principal in Catholic schools, following a teaching career in state and Catholic schools both in New South Wales and Queensland. In her current role, Dr Perry advocates at both a State and national level on educational policy including funding, national reforms, school workforce leadership and planning, curriculum and assessment.

Biographies

Cecilie Amiet rscj
Anne Benjamin
Marlette Black pbvm
Maree Byron osu
Julian Casey fms
Mary Cresp rsj
Graham English
Gabrielle Foley RSM
Damian J. Gleeson
Elizabeth Hellwig op
Aengus Kavanagh fsp
Clare Keady csb
Jim Littleton msc
Carlos Lopez
Charles McGee
Elizabeth Murray sgs
Anne O'Brien
Seamus O'Grady
Gail Reneker sm
Carol Rosenhain
Robyn Scott
Helen Simpson fdnsc

Corrie van den Bosch mss
Bill Wilding cfc
Mel Williams osu

Photographs

We acknowledge permission to use photographs and materials generously provided by the following Religious Orders and Congregations

    Sisters of Charity
    Dominican Sisters of Eastern Australia and the Solomon Islands
    Sisters of the Presentation of the Blessed Virgin Mary
    Faithful Companions of Jesus
    Institute of Sisters of Mercy of Australia and Papua New Guinea
    Australian Ursuline Sisters
    Sisters of the Good Samaritan
    Missionaries of the Sacred Heart
    De La Salle Brothers
    Marist Brothers
    Society of Jesus
    Brigidine Sisters
    Christian Brothers
    Daughters of our Lady of the Sacred Heart
    Society of the Sacred Heart
    Institute of the Blessed Virgin Mary
    Missionary Sisters of Service
    Patrician Brothers
    Sisters of St Joseph of the Sacred Heart
    Marist Sisters

Note on Contributors

Due to space limitation we were unable to provide biographies from other Orders and Congregations involved in Catholic education in Australia. We expect to include them in future publications

- Augustinians
- Benedictines
- Carmelites
- Dominican Friars
- Oblates of Mary Immaculate
- Vincentians
- Salesians
- Franciscan Missionaries of Mary
- Holy Faith Sisters
- Poor Clares
- Sisters of St Joseph Lochinvar
- Sisters of Mercy Parramatta
- Sisters of Mercy North Sydney

If we have inadvertently omitted any group, we will rectify in future editions.

Similarly, we chose to publish one biography from each Order or Congregation even when we received multiple biographies from them. We will publish these online and/or in future publications.

Chapter One
Introduction to the BDACE Online Project

Seamus O'Grady

"Today we live; tomorrow we die and are quickly forgotten... who will care when you are gone?¹"

Some of you may be familiar with the reflections of Thomas a' Kempis in his centuries' old spirituality guide, *The Imitation of Christ*. Such sobering words were often read out in the refectory of convents and monasteries during meal times and clearly not intended to aid digestion! Perhaps we are more familiar with the Shakespearean quotation, 'the evil that men do lives after them, the good is oft interred with their bones'.² How can we tip the balance in favour of remembering the good?

Familiar to most Australians are the words of the Anzac anthem, Lest we forget. By regularly calling to mind these heroes of the past, they somehow stay alive for us. A recent novelist, Tess Gerritsen put it this way, 'Only the forgotten are truly dead!'³

Whatever the case, a recent article opined that the memory of nearly all of us will be erased within a hundred years of our death. Presumably, we Catholic educators are doomed to the same fate. Why should Catholic educators be especially remembered? Which of us deserves posthumous gratitude and for what reason?

---

¹ Thomas a' Kempis, *The Imitation of Christ*, Book 1, Chapter 23, v. 1.
² William Shakespeare, *Julius Caesar*, Act 3, Sc 2, 81-83.
³ Tess Gerritsen, *The Sinner*, (London: Bantam Press, 2003).

The Biographical Dictionary of Australian Catholic Educators (BDACE) is a brave attempt on the part of Catholic leaders in this country to bring into the contemporary world the life and times of people who – against the odds –established, maintained and developed Catholic schools that nourished the lives of countless Australians.

There are the forgotten lay teachers in colonial times who established schools bearing the name 'Catholic' in city and country. Then the Religious who came across the seas at the pleading of bishops to keep the schools alive particularly when governments abandoned their funding. Joined by plucky home-grown groups of women and men, they fostered a uniquely Australian brand of Catholic Education. Who are these people to whom we owe such a debt of gratitude?

Why such a project now? In 2020, Catholic education is a distinctive element in the life of the Catholic Church in Australia and in Australian society more generally. It is an integral part of the Australian social landscape lived out through its schools and tertiary institutions. It has influenced many Australian citizens and institutions and continues to do so. In the early 21st century, Catholic education is associated with high-profile professionalism and sophisticated organisations. Telling the story is important for society generally, but more importantly for the Church and Catholic educators of the present and future.

In fact, Catholic education has played a significant role in the life of Australia from the earliest days of the 1780s when Britain first established a settlement in this land long the domain of its indigenous peoples.

The story of Catholic education over more than two hundred years is a story of struggle, courage, imagination, faith, tragedy and persistence. Above all, it is the story of the women and men of faith who believed in the power of education for the children of this country and who worked, often heroically, to provide an education of mind and spirit. Histories of schools and churches are one thing, but stories of the flesh and blood people that built and maintained them for the good of their students and fellow citizens resonate with and inspire us even years after they have gone.

Chapter One Introduction to the BDACE Online Project

2020 is a significant year – the bi-centenary of plans to establish a Catholic school in Australia at Parramatta by Fr John Therry, although it is more likely that the school actually began in January 1821. Catholic schooling has continued in Parramatta until the present day. It is appropriate, then, that this first publication of the BDACE in print celebrates the faithful women and men educators of the first 200 years. From such humble beginnings, the existing edifice of over 2000 Australian Catholic schools is an extraordinary achievement.

As Catholics, we hold every human life as valuable and worth remembering. Every Catholic educator deserves a biography. Who are we to select and eulogise? Who fell out of favour and who – through dint of fate or weakness of character – failed to live up to this high calling? To whom were monuments erected and buildings named? Who is a worthy entry in the *Biographical Dictionary of Australian Catholic Educators*? We have grappled with these questions and come up with a selection of people from extraordinary leaders to humble workers, their numbers limited only by our time and resources for the task.

Why bother bringing them back to life? Is it that their existence and work has somehow fashioned the DNA of those of us who follow? That we want to extend their influence through our own lives as teachers in Catholic schools? What made them want to reincarnate the Jesus of Nazareth to enrich the lives of their pupils? What Spirit pervaded the lives of these Catholic Educators?

We are not alone in this quest. The BDACE is modelled on the *Australian Dictionary of Biography (ADB)* which, since its inception in 1966, has included more than one hundred entries for Catholic Educators. While these biographies have not necessarily focused on their role in Catholic Education, they do present a detailed record of its development over two centuries: church hierarchy (38 entries), clerics (7), religious priests (13), religious sisters (37), religious brothers (13) and lay teachers (4). The BDACE, at least initially, will not normally replicate these ADB biographies but provide a hyper-link to them. Later on, we will revisit some of these biographies from a clearer Catholic education perspective.

When first proposed by Dr Anne Benjamin and strongly endorsed by Dr Brian Croke (former Executive Director of the NSW Catholic Education Commission), the Project Team engaged with the staff of the ADB in Canberra for guidance and direction. Their ongoing interest and support have enabled us to proceed in an orderly and structured way which has won widespread confidence in the BDACE from those currently (and formerly) involved in Catholic education across Australia.

We have been overwhelmed and humbled by the responses to our request from religious congregations, Catholic schools offices, historical societies and individuals. Nearly all Congregations involved in Catholic schools in Australia have submitted biographies of deceased members, made suggestions regarding interviewing living members for our *Living Legends* element, sent valuable related documents and offered their support (some even financially). Unable to make contrasts on the relative worthiness of competing entries, we have left it to Congregations themselves to decide which of their members should be among the first to have entries in the BDACE.

We are fortunate that a Sydney historian, Charles McGee, has extensively researched the early beginnings of Catholic education in NSW and provided us with copies of his publications. Of particular relevance to the BDACE is his *The Forgotten Ones, Teachers in the Catholic Schools of New South Wales before 1880*. He has kindly submitted several biographies for these early teachers. Other historians have also submitted biographies of Catholic educators with whom they are familiar.

It was always the intention that the BDACE would be national in scope. The *Catholic Religious Australia (CRA) Assembly* in 2017 in Melbourne afforded us the opportunity to draw attention to our project and receive an excellent response to the survey we conducted with Catholic religious. From their suggestions we have established productive communication with Congregational leaders, archivists and secretarial staff.

This led to the return of more than 100 profiles of deceased religious and over 35 drafted biographies to proceed to the next stage. We have encouraged and accepted entries from Congregations whose works span state and territory borders, and even internationally.

Catholic Schools Offices have been no less supportive even though their own existence and archive development is of fairly recent origin. Dioceses and individuals have already submitted a sizeable number of biographies of lay people.

For ease of management we divided the contributions into three fairly clearly defined but overlapping periods in the history of Catholic schooling in Australia:

- Colonial era to 1880 (predominantly lay-run government-funded Catholic schools)
- The era of Religious Congregations founding and running Catholic schools 1880 – 1960 (no government funding)
- 1960 – present (movement to almost exclusively lay run Catholic schools with government funding)

To initiate the project, we have not focused on any one period but rather called for submissions across the eras.

The biographies are not meant to be lengthy treatises. They are typically between one thousand and fifteen hundred words and designed to engage the reader immediately. They elicit surprise, information and admiration but above all encourage the readers to find out more and to share with others.

We have interviewed people for the *Living Legends* section in Queensland, New South Wales, Victoria, South Australia and the ACT. To date, 30 Priests, Religious Sisters and Brothers have been video-interviewed for the *Living Legends* section of our project alongside 13 lay people. Further interviews are planned for the NT, Western Australia and Tasmania, and with more focus on regional and rural dioceses.

All the material we have collected is in a secure repository. The plan is to make available the materials online (subject to certain conditions) for researchers, teachers, students and interested members of the public.

Initial funding for the project was provided by the NSW Catholic Education Commission then maintained by Catholic Schools NSW over the past five years.

In 2020, the Australian Catholic University (ACU) became the sponsoring host and location for the BDACE. Given that the university itself grew out of the previous Teachers' Colleges conducted by Religious Congregations, ACU is a natural home for the BDACE. Like the ADB with host university ANU, the BDACE can be assured of longevity and prominence with ACU.

So, come with us on a journey through the annals of Catholic education as we encounter people like you and me who were inspired by Christ to bring good news to countless young Australians.

Chapter Two
Catholic Educators 1820-2020
Overview of the Introductory BDACE Volume

Seamus O'Grady

This volume is the first hard copy publication of the BDACE. It introduces the project which is neither a history of Catholic Education from colonial times nor a collection of naked biographies, but rather an anthology of selected biographies with contextualising pieces. It is unashamedly an attempt to whet readers' appetite for the BDACE so that they may be moved to contribute biographies, use the online version for research for themselves and their students, or just be inspired.

Above all, we want readers to get to know these wonderful people who gave their lives to Catholic Education and spread their stories far and wide.

We have divided the biographies into four notional eras: Colonial times to 1880, 1880-1960, 1960-2000, 2000-2020. We acknowledge that these divisions are somewhat arbitrary but nonetheless useful for grouping our biographies into recognisable time periods.

Colonial times to 1880

Essentially it was lay people who kept Catholic schools alive in this era with limited government financial assistance. Biographies are of pioneer priests, lay teachers and early Religious sisters and brothers who laboured to found and maintain Catholic schools. Charles McGee has provided an essay highlighting some of the context for the biographies. We have included six biographies:[4]

The biographies are complemented by an essay from Anne Benjamin on their relevance to contemporary Catholic educators.

- Cuffe, Farrell (ca 1775-1848). Scholar and Irish patriot.
- Marley, George (1778-ca 1848). Australia's first teacher in a Catholic school.
- McEncroe, Archdeacon John William (1794-1868). Priest and educator.
- Higgins, Andrew (1797-1859). Early teacher of Catholic children in Australia.
- Dwyer, Brigid (1808-1878). Australia's first native-born female teacher.
- McGuigan, Bridget Mary Magdalen (Mother Mary Francis rsc) (1842-1923). Prudent educator and administrator.

1880–1960

Around 1880, governments across Australia put an end to all financial aid to Catholic schools. There were already six congregations of Religious sisters working in schools (Good Samaritans, Sisters of Charity, Sisters of Mercy, Dominican Sisters, Loreto Sisters and Sisters

---

[4] A selection of biographies for this and following sections draws upon over 50 draft biographies submitted for inclusion in the BDACE at time of writing and several reworked from the *Australian Dictionary of Biography*. The editors have tried to strike a balance noting gender, location, congregational or clerical or lay, leadership/teaching, primary/secondary, tertiary, specialist, administration.

of St Joseph) and two congregations of Brothers (Marist and Christian). Facing the closure of Catholic schools as payment for lay teachers could not be maintained, some Bishops put out a call for more Religious Congregations to fill the gap. Thus began the era of Catholic schools almost totally staffed by Religious priests, brothers and sisters.

Extraordinary sacrifices were made by these men and women, recruited locally and overseas, often paid a pittance, yet dedicated to ensuring the survival and flourishing of Catholic schools. Faced with an enormous choice from this era, we have selected biographies of some wonderful people:

- Hogan, Ellen (Sr Mary Gabriel op) (1842-1915). Founder of an education system for the Catholic deaf.
- Kennedy, Alice Anastasia (Mother Ursula pbvm) (1876-1960). Pioneer in Catholic education in Queensland.
- Douglas, Kathleen (Mother Mary Philomena fcj) (1897-1958). Scholar, rigorous educator and visionary leader.
- Fitzgerald, Elizabeth (Mother Mary Benignus RSM) (1890-1946). Beloved educationist inspiring generations.
- McMahon, John Thomas (Monsignor) (1893-1989). First Director of Catholic education in Western Australia.
- Griffin, Mona Margaret (Mother Mary Xavier osu) (1897-1985). Gifted educator with a flair for literature and the creative.
- Slattery, Loretta Marie (Sr Mary Clare sgs) (1900-1980). Visionary Catholic educator.
- Graham, William John (Fr 'Bill' msc) (1912-1966). Priest, sportsman, teacher and sports master.
- Carmody, Lawrence George (Br Aloysius Meldan fsc) (1916-1981). Teacher, administrator, national and international leader.

This period of growth, conformity, liberation and change has been contextualised by historian Janice Garaty while academic Graham English reflects on the extraordinary impact these Religious had on Catholic schooling and their continuing relevance for Catholic educators today.

1960-2000

The sizzling sixties were revolutionary. There was Woodstock, the Beatles, protest movements, the Vietnam war... and Vatican II. The years that followed witnessed renewal in Religious life, liberation theology and the new catechetics but alarming for the mission of Catholic schools was the decline in religious vocations and church attendance. With burgeoning enrolments, the very survival of schools galvanised the campaign for state aid. The restoration of government funding following the 1973 Karmel report and the establishment of the Schools Commission heralded a new beginning for Catholic schools in Australia. The watershed Armidale Catholic Education conference set the groundwork for the emergence of Catholic education offices and the systemisation of schools. Religious teachers were progressively replaced by lay teachers and principals, and the training of lay teachers for Catholic schools accelerated.

In the early 70s, the bishops faced a dilemma: without government funding should they just commit to maintaining low fee-paying parish primary schools and leave secondary schools to the Religious congregations? In such a scenario, would access to the schools, particularly the secondary schools, be limited to those parents who could afford the higher fees? Or should the bishops fight for funding and provide both? A gruelling political fight ended in the granting of State Aid! As they say – the rest is history.

Coupled with the extraordinary changes flowing from Vatican II, it was fortunate that many Congregations had young Religious better qualified than their predecessors to move, in some cases prematurely, into the leadership of Catholic schools. Timely government funding enabled them to navigate Catholic schools through the massive changes taking place in church and society.

With government funding for Catholic schools relatively assured, apart from a brief hiccup with the unsuccessful challenge in the High Court by the *Defence of Government Schools* (DOGS) case, the laicisation of both leadership and staff of Catholic schools proceeded apace through this period. Structures such as Catholic education offices for the distribution of funding, administration and support of the schools reached maturity, resulting in stability and growth. By the turn of the century, Catholic schools were accepted as an integral part of the Australian schooling landscape.

The era was characterised by developments of more structured religious education curricula and the innovative appointment of Religious Education Co-ordinators in schools. While accountability for government funding was at least initially not excessive, there was growth in legislative requirements around child protection, registration and accreditation of schools and professionalism of teachers.

Br Kelvin Canavan fms, Emeritus Executive Director of the Sydney Catholic Education Office, was a key player in this era in NSW and provides the context for the biographies. And to glean what we have learned from these people in addressing our contemporary Catholic schools, we have the reflections of Dr Brian Croke. The biographies selected for inclusion in this section are:

- Fogarty, Thomas Edwin (Br Ronald fms) (1913-2009). Religious researcher and teacher-educator.
- Fraser, Charles (Fr Charles sj) (1913-2004). Disciplined scholarship graced by Christian humanity.
- Fraser, Joyce Eva (Mother Loyola csb) (1918-2008). In her, the love of God and of literature were beautifully blended.
- McCarthy, Francis Irenaeus (Br Francis McCarthy cfc) (1920-2010). Long-serving teacher and lover of art.
- Dent, Edna Ellen (Sr Mary St Bernard fdnsc) (1925-2016). No device will take the loving teacher's place.
- Martin, Francis Michael (Fr 'Frank') (1928-2015). Astute negotiator and visionary architect of a Catholic education system.
- Toohey, Margaret Mary (Sr Margaret rscj) (1930-2014). An educator ahead of her time.

- Clark, Ann Dennis (1935-1997). Visionary, charismatic, elegant and innovative leader.
- Rofe, Deidre Ann (Sr Mary Anne ibvm) (1943-2002). A quester by nature and a commander at need.
- Ryan, Winifred Agnes (Sr Agnes mss) (1915-2011). Founding congregational member and pioneer educator.

2000-2020

In the 21st century, Catholic schools continued to flourish but were increasingly populated by students of other faiths and none. Some bishops were concerned about the 'Catholicity' of the schools while parental support for the schools showed no sign of abating. Widespread surveys of parents confirmed that Catholic schools are still sought for their academic excellence and pastoral care/discipline within a school community embedded with Christian values. Provision of Religious Education falls well down the list but is nonetheless accepted and valued as integral to the mission of the Catholic school.

Catholic schools are now almost totally staffed by lay people. Government funding has continued to grow to the extent that many Catholic schools are funded to the same level as public schools (and a few beyond) causing a backlash from advocates for the latter. Increases in funding for capital works have enabled Catholic schools to update their facilities and to provide Catholic schools in new areas of city and country. With significant growth in the demand for accountability, transparency and proper governance, the schools and systems have increasingly turned to corporate management.

At this time, too, we are acutely mindful of the dreadful stories of shame that are part of our history. The *Royal Commission into Institutional Responses to Child Sexual Abuse* revealed that not a few of our forebears offended against children, their families, their faith and society. Their crimes should not, however, excise the stories of the faithful and true. No less now than ever, the champions of Catholic education in Australian should be celebrated. We have emerged more vigilant and wiser in the way we conduct our schools. Much hope has been placed in

Pope Francis for a humbler, forgiving church of service to all humankind and it is to this goal our contemporary Catholic schools aspire.

Writing about contemporary times can be problematic but we are fortunate to have someone familiar with contemporary Catholic schooling, Dr Lee-Anne Perry, Queensland Catholic Education Commission, to provide context; and a visionary Bishop, Vincent Long van Nguyen of Parramatta Diocese, to reflect on our current situation.

We have chosen five biographies in this recent era, educators who died in the past 20 years and who kept the flame of Catholic education alight in our contemporary Australian society:

- Bulfin, Edmund Noel (Br Bernard fsp) (1936-2018). Humble service and commitment.
- Ryan, Veronica Therese (Sr Veronica rsj) (1936-2008). Walking with Indigenous Australians.
- Collins, Barry (Bishop Collins) (1938-2000). Priest-Inspector of schools, Religious Education Director and Country Bishop.
- Dwyer, Barry Francis (1938-2009). An educator who kindled the Catholic imagination of children and young people.
- Webb, Ann-Marie (Sr Gerard Majella sm) (1943-2008). Stalwart of Catholic education.

Conclusion

The story of Catholic education for more than 200 years is a story of struggle, courage, imagination, faith, tragedy and persistence. Above all, it is the story of the women and men of faith who believed in the power of education for the children of this country and who worked, often heroically, to provide an education of mind and spirit.

The chronicling of the lives of selected Catholic educators protects an important legacy for the contemporary and future church and society, as well as providing tools for further study and understanding. This is the premise inspiring the *Biographical Dictionary of Australian Catholic Educators (BDACE)*, a project which aims to keep such stories alive to inspire current and future teachers and leaders in Catholic schools and become a great research tool that will bring honour to its host institution, *Australian Catholic University*.

This is the first printed publication of the *Biographical Dictionary of Australian Catholic Educators*, and it is anticipated it will be followed at intervals with subsequent volumes with specific themes.

Chapter Three
Developments in Catholic Education in Australia 1820-1880

Context

Hardships of a Dreary Winter[5]

Charles McGee

For many years, the dominant historical narrative about the creation of Catholic schools in New South Wales concentrated largely on matters of politics and administration and focused on the decision by the bishops to go it alone after the loss of state aid in 1882 to establish a separate and distinctive Catholic school system staffed largely by members of religious congregations. The heroes of this creation myth were the bishops, priests, sisters and brothers who prevailed against powerful opposition from the secularist legislators of the time.

The problem with this narrative is that it does not accord with historical reality. There is another set of heroes, who for one reason or another, have been largely excluded from the Catholic school story. From 1803 to 1882, over 150 elementary or primary schools were established in New South Wales by a remarkable group of pioneer

---

[5] In his *History of the Catholic Church in Australasia* (1895), Cardinal Moran devoted 37 pages out of 1003 to education and claimed that "the schools and religious teachers of today compared with those of 1897 are like the joys of the spring season compared with the hardships of a dreary winter".

priests and were staffed for the most part by lay men and women. Both priests and teachers were largely Irish-born or Australian-born of Irish descent.

If the priest and people were able to raise sufficient funds – a difficult task given the poverty of the Catholic community – part of an existing building was rented, or a small building of wood or stone was erected, that would serve as a chapel and school. Hundreds of men and women devoted themselves to these early schools for Catholic children, often labouring in the most difficult of circumstances. They bore the brunt of anti-Irish and anti-Catholic sentiment and later in the century faced the growth of liberal secularist ideology that placed the existence of their schools under severe threat. By providing elementary education and religious instruction to colonial youth, whose parents had received little or no education themselves and who had only a scant knowledge of their faith, these teachers kept Catholicity alive during the 1800s.

By the 1870s, many of the teachers who had devoted their lives to Catholic schools faced the bleak reality that when financial aid was withdrawn from their schools, they would no longer have a place in the Catholic educational landscape and would be forced to apply for positions in the public school system. By acknowledging the remarkable efforts of the early clergy and lay teachers in the foundation of Catholic schools, we create a richer, more diverse and more historically accurate creation myth and accord many who have been largely forgotten their rightful place in the story of Catholic education.

In 1820, two Irish emancipists, Patrick Kirk and Patrick Garrigan, provided a room in Hunter Street, Parramatta, where a school opened with an enrolment of twenty-four Catholics and seven Protestants. The teacher was George Marley, an accountant from County Meath, Ireland, who had been transported in 1814. In 1822 Andrew Higgins, a surveyor of roadworks from County Meath, Ireland, who had been transported in 1819, opened a school for Catholic children in the home of James Dempsey in Kent Street, Sydney. In 1824, work ceased on the original St Mary's Cathedral due to lack of funds. Despite this situation, Fr Therry was able to erect a wooden schoolhouse on the site. Thomas Byrne, the first native-born male teacher to serve in a Catholic school in Australia, began classes in the new building. Marley, Higgins and Byrne were decent, generous, educated men who endeavoured to provide some basic schooling for Catholic children. Their efforts failed because Fr Therry's defiance of government on many issues meant that they were unwilling to provide adequate financial support for Catholic educational endeavours. By 1830 not one chapel had been completed and only three schools were in operation.

A significant growth in the number of Catholic schools in the 1830s was largely due to the efforts of two Catholic laymen – Roger Therry and John Hubert Plunkett. Therry was from County Cork, Ireland, and was appointed Commissioner of the Court of Requests in New South Wales in 1829. Appalled by the state of the Catholic community, he persistently presented their case to Governor Bourke. As a result of his efforts, Bourke approved generous appropriations of funds for Catholic schools in the early 1830s. *The Returns of the Colony* for 1831, the year of Bourke's arrival, show that Church of England schools drew £2,500 and Catholic school payments were just £200. By 1834, grants to Catholic schools reached £800.

Plunkett, of County Roscommon, Ireland, arrived in 1832 as Solicitor General of New South Wales. He was largely responsible for the passing of Governor Bourke's *Church Act* which disestablished the Church of England and gave legal equality and financial assistance to the major denominations. This was soon extended to include their schools. Newly arrived clergy Fr John McEncroe, Fr William Ullathorne and Bishop John Bede Polding developed good relations with Governor Bourke and government was prepared to meet Catholic demands when approached in a respectful and proper manner. The first official salaries were approved for teachers in Catholic schools. By the end of the decade there were thirty Catholic schools conducted by lay teachers.

In 1848, Governor Fitzroy dramatically altered the face of education in New South Wales. He established two boards to control all schools. The Board of National Education had the power to set up National or Public schools and to acquire land and buildings for such enterprises. The Denominational School Board (DSB) would control Church of England, Presbyterian, Wesleyan Methodist and Catholic schools. It had the power to appoint and dismiss teachers, pay their salaries and conduct inspections. No financial assistance was available for purchasing land, building new schools or carrying out repairs.

From the outset, the DSB did not function well. It met infrequently, lacked clear direction and provided little, if any, effective leadership in the task of improving educational standards in Catholic schools. It left decision-making in the hands of Catholic authorities. A Catholic Education Committee was formed to deal with the DSB with Fr John McEncroe as chairman. At the end of 1848, he presented a claim to the DSB for a range of teacher salaries ranging from £80 to £20.

In 1849, Fr McEncroe raised the issue that financial grants to Catholic schools were not proportional to the current Catholic population and were being made on the basis of the 1841 census. A motion to grant an extra £800 to Catholic schools was passed in the Legislative Council. Some of this money was spent on books and £100 was set aside for teacher training. The bulk of the money was spent on substantially increasing the number of Catholic schools and not for increasing teacher salaries. Nineteen schools were placed in new localities with an annual teacher salary of only £30. The average salary of Catholic teachers dropped from about £44 to £37.

A Commission was set up in 1854 to report on the state of education. Instead of calling witnesses, it sent three commissioners to visit the schools. They noted that four Catholic schools were conducted in halls beneath churches, 23 in churches and 56 in houses or rooms with 14 of these made of bark or mud plaster with mud floors. Twenty-two schools had tolerable or moderate equipment, in 36 schools it was indifferent or bad and 10 schools were entirely without equipment. Several city schools had no playgrounds. Many schools were overcrowded – Charcoal Creek had accommodation for 30 and a daily attendance of 83. At Appin it was noted that the school building had become the priest's residence and school was conducted in a part of his stables. In general, the teachers in Catholic schools were described as being industrious, intelligent and zealous people of good principles. Public schools had the highest percentage of trained teachers and Catholic schools had the next highest.

Largely as a result of the findings of the Commission, a small band of Catholic teachers, deeply concerned about the circumstances in which they found themselves, formed the Australian Catholic Teachers Association. They endeavoured to raise issues of concern to Catholic teachers and approached the DSB concerning their salaries only to be informed that low government grants to Catholic schools meant that nothing could be done. They approached Polding concerning injustices inflicted by members of the clergy who demanded non-teaching services from them. Polding ruled in their favour and informed the clergy that the only work that should be expected of them was to be of an educational nature.

The teachers of the 1850s still laboured under difficult conditions. At Kent Street North, the roof was broken and rain regularly entered the building as there was no ceiling. The floor was perpetually damp, as it sat on the earth below. There were desks and maps but only a few mutilated reading books for over 100 children. In country areas, many of the schools were made of bark or mud plaster and had mud floors. School furniture was old or broken or was just a few stakes driven into the earthen floor with rough-cut logs laid on top. *The Wynyard Times* of 17 June 1862 observed that 'it is a fact patent to the public that an office so sacred as that of training the young mind is very poorly remunerated. The small sums offered are not equivalent to the wages of a shepherd or a bullock driver'.

In a letter to the DSB in 1860, Archbishop Polding claimed that many Catholic teachers still lacked adequate training 'our weak point is here – it was comparatively easy to obtain men possessed of sufficient knowledge. The grand difficulty lay in finding them practised in successful methods of teaching'. In 1861, he agreed that a building on the St Mary's site would become a training school for male teachers and would also provide courses for those already in service. *The Freeman's Journal* of 4 September 1861 declared his decision 'the most useful step taken in years for Catholic education'.

From 1861 to 1865, government grants increased steadily. In 1865, the grant to Catholic schools was £11,000. The number of Catholic schools increased rapidly over this period, from 87 schools in 1860 to 128 schools in 1865. Minimum salaries were set by the DSB for all denominational schools – £50 for teachers of infants and £60 for primary teachers. Greater allowances were to be paid to trainee teachers and larger schools were given assistant and pupil teachers. The DSB also proposed a classification system for teachers which was opposed by Fr McEncroe. In 1861 the DSB was able to pay for furnishing in some Catholic schools. Lack of residences at most Catholic schools still made it impossible for teachers and their families to maintain a respectable standard of living.

In December 1866, the *Public Schools Act* ended the dual board system and set up a Council of Education to control all schools receiving government financial aid. Such aid would only be granted to those Catholic schools that underwent inspection and met Council of Education standards. Council inspectors began moving through Catholic schools and actually certified all of them in the Sydney region to continue operation and thus receive aid. A concession was made in terms of teacher appointments with the Council allowing the Church to nominate teachers for their schools subject to approval by the Council. This provision remained for many years.

Early in 1867 Archbishop Polding stated that

> by the Education Bill, all control over school teachers, discipline, books is taken out of the hands of the bishops. We have still opened our schools with the exception of four not having the number of scholars required; but at the end of the year a large proportion will follow.

Later that year, he instigated his last initiative in Catholic education – the Catholic Association of the Archdiocese of Sydney for the Promotion of Religion and Education. Its aims were to raise the funds necessary to assist schools that had lost their certification to remain open, to contribute to teacher salaries, to erect new schools and to invite religious congregations from Europe to conduct schools in the Archdiocese.

Council inspections of Catholic schools also caused bitterness and worsened relations with Catholic authorities. Frequent complaints were made to the Council about the behaviour of their inspectors.

William Wilkins, secretary of the Council, claimed that the inspectors always conducted themselves in an unbiased manner and that most of the problems arose not from the Catholic teachers but from the tone and attitude of the clergy during the inspections. Inspectors were accused by Church authorities of neglecting to visit Catholic schools to approve the teacher, thus denying them a salary. In the Fish River District in 1868-1869, Bishop Quinn had established 12 provisional schools. Only two teachers were inspected and received salaries and it took six months for these two schools to be visited even though the inspector was based in Bathurst.

Salaries for Catholic teachers continued to remain low. *The Sydney Morning Herald* of 1 January 1870 noted that at the Goulburn Public School the teacher's salary was increased from £60 to £72 whereas at the Grabben Gullen Catholic school, with more pupils, the teacher's salary was £48 and would be reduced to £36 if numbers fell. *The Sydney Morning Herald* of 21 January 1870 pointed out how head teachers in large Catholic schools were exploited as they were expected to pay their assistant teachers from their own salaries and that many pupil teachers received no salary for considerable periods of time. The Council was also reluctant to increase the number of Catholic trainee teachers. The Catholic training school at St Mary's had closed in 1866, although it continued as a primary school, and all teachers trained at the Fort Street Public School. The Council used this shortage of teachers to close three Catholic schools early in 1868 because the Council had transferred the teachers and claimed no replacements were available.

Teachers in Catholic schools began to feel that the constant conflict between church authorities and the Council of Education was not in their best interests. Edward Kevin, the Catholic teacher at Jamberoo, wrote to the Council in 1867:

> Perceiving the unreasonable opposition of the heads of my denomination to the Public Schools Act, and the probability of its continuance, I would be doing an injustice to myself and my family confining my professional prospects to such an uncertainty.

Kevin left teaching and established a business at Albion Park. John Rooney, the teacher at Queanbeyan in 1866, was served a notice of dismissal by the local priest for not signing a petition against the *Public Schools Act*. Rooney claimed that he had not been asked to sign and refused to leave. He gathered much sympathy from the parents and other influential residents. The Council of Education intervened, and he was appointed to a public school in 1867. He later became an inspector.

Three Irish bishops arrived on the scene in the 1860s – Bishop Matthew Quinn at Bathurst, Bishop James Murray at Maitland and Bishop William Lanigan, who had been in the colony since 1859, and became Bishop of Goulburn in 1867. They owed their appointment to the influence of Cardinal Paul Cullen of Dublin and brought his ideas on education with them. Cullen was a fierce opponent of the Irish National schools in which the children were together for general instruction and separated for religious doctrine. He vigorously pursued a policy of replacing lay teachers with religious. In 1800, there were 120 female religious in Ireland and by 1870 there were 3,700. The number of Christian and Patrician Brothers also increased substantially.

All three bishops endeavoured to replace lay teachers with religious as soon as possible. Bishop Quinn brought Irish Sisters of Mercy with him who immediately assumed control of the girls' school at Bathurst. He added Sisters of St Joseph in 1872. By 1878, he had ninety nuns at work in his diocese. Bishop Murray replaced the Good Samaritan Sisters who had been at Maitland since 1864 with Irish Dominican sisters in 1867. Bishop Lanigan already had Irish Sisters of Mercy at Goulburn and a new convent was opened at Albury in 1868.

In contrast to Archbishop Polding, the Irish bishops were belligerent in their public remarks on education. In 1867 Bishop Quinn stated:

> I disbelieve in an infidel education and as I would shed my blood sooner than relinquish my belief in the Trinity, so would I shed my blood for Catholic education.

They believed that the only role for the laity was to donate what little they had to support Catholic schools. The lay teachers of the time became aware that they had no future in Catholic schools if the influence of the Irish bishops prevailed.

Individual teachers in Catholic schools were poorly treated during these years. Edmund Flannery and his wife Ellen, both trained teachers from Ireland, arrived in 1860 and were appointed to the Catholic school at Yass. They were praised by inspectors and gained the esteem of the people of the town. Despite the fine state of the school, Flannery received the lowest salary given to any teacher in Catholic schools. They were forced to take in boarders and conduct evening classes. During 1867, the local priest criticised him at Mass because Flannery insisted on using the books specified by the Council of Education. Reluctantly he was forced to apply for a teaching position in a Public school and instead of being appointed to a school he was made an inspector.

The physical state of Catholic schools was still the responsibility of the Church authorities. The 1875 reports by Council of Education inspectors on Catholic schools in the Sydney district indicate that many of them were in very poor condition. St Mary's Boys: 'The interior of the schoolroom presents an uninviting appearance, the walls and floors being very dirty, and the furniture is old, cumbrous and in disrepair.' Parramatta Street: 'The schoolroom is in a dilapidated state as nearly all of the windows are broken, and the interior presents a dingy, uninviting appearance.' Surry Hills Boys: 'The classroom into which some eighty infants were packed is badly lighted and ventilated.' During the same round of inspections many positive comments were made about the quality of the teaching. At The Haymarket it was noted that 'in most respects the discipline is good', at Newtown 'the instruction is imparted with earnestness and is painstaking', at Pyrmont 'the children are under healthy and effective discipline' and at Waterloo 'the instruction is imparted with earnestness and ability'.

An injustice that faced many Catholic teachers was the lack of teacher residences and the refusal of the Council of Education to pay them a rental allowance. It was pointed out in *The Sydney Morning Herald* of 15 July 1880 that:

A teacher in a Public school with under 200 children received £336 in salary and £100 rent allowance. A teacher in a Catholic school with over 200 children received £240 in salary and no rent allowance.

Despite many appeals to the Council of Education, no allowance was ever paid. When church authorities were approached about providing residences at their schools, the teachers were informed that no funds were available.

The situation of the Catholic teachers had become so dire that in *The Sydney Morning Herald* of 5 March 1880 it was claimed by a correspondent that:

> the teachers of the denominational schools have nothing to fear from the closing of their schools and everything to dread from keeping them open. The promoters of denominational schools (the Catholic Church) are expected to provide all necessary school buildings, including teachers' residences. The teachers of these schools have been unjustly treated by their denominations. I can quote at least a dozen instances where the teacher has gone to the wall because he refused to be made a convenience of by the priest who has trumped up some complaint and had the teacher censured or removed.

Religious teachers were taking over more schools conducted by lay teachers. From 1861, the Sisters of the Good Samaritan took over the girls' school at Sussex Street and in 1862 they began teaching at Balmain, St Mary's Cathedral and at their own convent in Pitt Street. They taught at West Maitland from 1864. From 1866, Sisters of Mercy taught at Bathurst and at Church Hill in Sydney. Dominican Sisters took over at West Maitland in 1867. By 1869, Sisters of Mercy were teaching at Albury and Raymond Terrace. In 1872, Marist Brothers opened a school at Harrington Street in The Rocks and took over lay-controlled schools at Parramatta and Parramatta Street in Chippendale. By 1875, Good Samaritan Sisters had taken over from lay teachers at Wollongong and

Windsor. In *The Freeman's Journal* of 3 August 1872, Polding did concede that the lay teachers being replaced had been doing their job 'in a fair measure' and that 'there were some good and accomplished teachers that had been long with us'.

It has been claimed by some historians that the better teachers in Catholic schools transferred to Public schools during the 1870s and that those who remained were lacking in professional competence. Given the fact that it was difficult for Catholic teachers to obtain a high classification under the Council of Education, teacher records indicate a significant number of Catholic teachers with such classifications remained in Catholic schools until the early 1880s. There have always been dedicated Catholic lay people who have opted to work in Catholic schools in difficult circumstances and for less remuneration than what they could obtain elsewhere and the 1870s were no exception.

Archbishop Vaughan and the Irishmen Quinn, Murray and Lanigan sunk their differences in 1879 and began a fierce debate over Catholic schools and state aid by issuing a Joint Pastoral in which they condemned Public schools as being 'seed plots of future immorality, infidelity and lawlessness'. This document represented a significant change of position for Vaughan and was followed up by five other pastorals during the remainder of the year. In these he stressed the power and beauty of schools conducted by religious congregations compared with those of lay teachers: 'parents know the advantage of bringing their children into direct contact with teachers who were living examples of highest sacrifice'. Commenting on the Joint Pastoral in *The Record* of 1 January 1880, Bishop Quinn claimed that 'the Archbishop wrote it, but I signed it and every word of it was mine'. In *The Catholic Standard* of April 1884, Bishop Lanigan stated that 'the Archbishop was several times urged to take some course. The words were his but the principles were from all of us'.

The *Public Instruction Act* of 1880 ended financial aid to Catholic schools effective from the end of 1882. Catholic teachers were clearly informed of the provisions that would operate as regards their employment in Public schools when financial aid ceased. They were guaranteed employment and would not be made redundant. Despite these assurances, they must have experienced a sense of trepidation as to what lay ahead. Would they be treated fairly in examinations for promotion? Did they have realistic chances of promotion given their background in Catholic schools? Would they be appointed to remote schools and be subject to frequent transfers? Would their years of service in Catholic schools be recognised at the end of their careers?

In 1880, there were 196 Catholic teachers (including trainee and pupil teachers) conducting 80 Catholic schools. Church authorities did little for them other than confirming that they would withdraw from the government system at the end of 1882 and would staff their schools with members of religious congregations as soon as possible. Few places would remain for lay teachers. There was little consolation in *The Freeman's Journal* of 25 February 1882:

> But now, that the grant is to be withdrawn from our schools, the place of the efficient lay teachers in charge of them must be supplied and this can only be adequately effected by a religious brotherhood.

Sympathy for the plight of the lay teachers was expressed in correspondence to *The Freeman's Journal* of 21 August 1880:

> We hope timely provision will be made to retain our Catholic teachers who have through good report and evil report been loyal to the cause of religious education, at considerable sacrifice to themselves.

Church authorities endeavoured to portray the loss of state aid and the removal of the lay teachers from their schools in a positive light. *The Freeman's Journal* of 1 May 1880 reported Archbishop Vaughan's words at the opening of the Forest Lodge School:

> Public schools, and I say it as my opinion, Denominational Schools under the Council – though in less extent – have been weakening and impoverishing the vigour of the faith.

In *The Freeman's Journal* of 13 January 1883, he claimed that 'the withdrawal of state aid would be the greatest blessing God could bestow on the Church' and that 'the Church getting complete control over her schools was worth far more than the money they had received from state aid', and what must have been very disheartening for Catholic teachers 'the withdrawal of the state schoolmasters and the replacing of them by Brothers and Nuns was an immense advantage to the Catholic body'.

The Irish bishops left no doubt in the minds of their people where they stood on their Catholic schools now conducted by religious. *The Maitland Mercury* of 11 October 1883 noted that:

> At Temora last Sunday, Mr James, a highly respected townsman was ordered to leave the Catholic Church during divine service because his children attended Public schools.

In the Archdiocese of Sydney in 1883, Marist Brothers conducted five schools, Sisters of Charity eight schools, Sisters of the Good Samaritan seventeen schools, Sisters of Mercy five schools and· Sisters of St Joseph fifteen schools. Clearly female religious greatly outnumbered their male counterparts. By 1885, the only lay teachers still in Catholic schools in and around Sydney were Valentine Ellery at Redfern, Mrs Murphy and Miss Power at Randwick, Mr O'Driscoll at Paddington, Mr Hughes at Woollahra, Mr Dunphy at Windsor, Mr Kent at Balmain, Miss Mulholland at Botany and unnamed teachers at Cook's River, Forest Lodge and Menangle. *The Freeman's Journal* of 11 October 1884 noted:

> State aid ceased 20 months ago but in the Archdiocese of Sydney there are now 105 schools, 370 teachers and 12,363 pupils. Nearly the whole body of our teachers belong to religious orders. The unbought labour of these Christian teachers is the highest value to Catholic education. There is also a small number of lay teachers and they are giving satisfaction.

Select Bibliography

Austin, A. G. *Australian Education 1788-1990*: church, state, and public education in Colonial Australia. Carlton Vic: Pitman, 1961.

Fogarty, R. *Catholic Education in Australia 1806-1956*, 2 Vols. Melbourne: Melbourne University Press, 1957.

Haines, G. *Lay Catholics and the Education Question in Nineteenth century New South Wales: the shaping of a decision*. Sydney: Catholic Theological Faculty, 1976.

Historical Records of NSW including *Colonial Secretary Papers* (Colonial Returns 1828-1857), *Denominational Schools Board* Reports and Minute Books (1856-1866), *Council of Education Papers* (Correspondence, Examination results, Denominational Schools Returns), *Teacher Rolls* (1869-1908)

MacDonald, Ian. *A School of their Own. The story of Parramatta Marist 1820-2000*. Parramatta: self-published, 2000.

Mahon, James. "Lay Teachers in Government-Aided Catholic Schools in NSW, 1848-1880". A revised version of a paper read to the Australian Catholic Historical Society, October, 1978.

McGee, Charles. "The Hardships of a Dreary Winter. Catholic Authorities and Lay Teachers in Nineteenth Century New South Wales." Sydney: Catholic Education Office.

McGee, Charles. *The Forgotten ones, Teachers in the Catholic Schools of New South Wales before 1880*. Sydney: Catholic Education Office Sydney, 2012.

Moran, F. P. Cardinal. *History of the Catholic Church in Australasia*. Sydney: Frank Coffee & Co, 1895.

Newspapers such as but not limited to: *Australasian Chronicle* 1839-1943, *Australian* 1824-1848, *Empire* 1850-1870, *Maitland Mercury*

1843-1870, *Sydney Morning Herald* 1842-1884, *The Freeman's Journal* 1850-1885.

O'Brien, E. *The Life and Letters of Archpriest J. J. Therry*. Sydney: Angus & Robertson, 1922.

O'Farrell, P. *The Irish in Australia 1788 to the present*. University of Notre Dame USA: University of Notre Dame Press, 2001.

Sweeney, B. *Bishop Matthew Quinn and the Development of Catholic Education in New South Wales 1865-1885*. Bathurst: Diocese of Bathurst, 2016.

Ullathorne, W. *The Catholic Mission in Australia*. Autobiography. London: Burns and Gates, 1891.

BIOGRAPHIES

Farrell Cuffe (ca 1775–1848)

Scholar and Irish patriot

Damian Gleeson

Rarely acknowledged as a Catholic penal educator, Farrell Cuffe, a 'defender' during the 1798 Irish revolution, brought his impressive teaching experience from Co Offaly (Kings County, Ireland) to become one of the colony's first teachers. Cuffe, who agreed to 'voluntarily exile' arrived per the Minerva in 1800, but his subsequent association with a minority of Irish subversives added to his issues. A scholar as well as an Irish patriot, Cuffe's penal experiences mirrored his homeland. After being caught with Irish revolutionary leaders in the colony, Cuffe was subject to an extraordinary 500 lashes and banished to Norfolk Island, where again he was never far from seditious rumblings, although mainly using his writing skills as his attack weapon.

Nevertheless – or perhaps as a result of – Norfolk Island, Cuffe on return to Sydney in 1806 was granted a town allotment in Pitt Street, Sydney, between Market and Parks Streets. In mid-1807 Cuffe established a school in 'Upper Pit's Row' or 61 Pitt Street. Unlike most schools that survived only a short duration – sometimes only months – Cuffe successfully operated his day school for at least 16 years, a record for the colonial era.

In 1809, when his common-law wife prepared to leave the colony (and again in 1815), Cuffe placed newspaper advertisements asking parents to pay any outstanding debts so as to 'enable him to adjust his Affairs to the Satisfaction of Mrs [Maria] Lane, who intends shortly to quit the Colony for England'. "Mrs Lane" does not appear to have returned after her second voyage.

In addition to operating his non-denominational 'Day School', Cuffe, in 1817, opened an afternoon/evening school for 'Grown Lads who have no apparent means to pay for their Education … and they will be carefully and charitably attended to'. It is possible this later school *might* have been associated with an unofficial recalcitrant Catholic chaplain, Fr Jeremiah O'Flynn. Otherwise, during his long career as a schoolmaster in Sydney and at Richmond, Cuffe operated his schools on an independent basis.

In 1819, Cuffe added a Sunday School. His financial support to the Benevolent Society and the Bible Society, amongst others, reflected a pragmatic ecumenical approach. His two wives – some writers have suggested three – were English Protestants.

In 1820, Cuffe married recidivist Bridget Crack, which might explain why he also became a licenced victualler. By 1826 they had removed to Richmond, where he again operated a school. Cuffe had a disarming Irish humour as evidenced in 1840, when Bridget was charged with drunkenness and disturbing 'divine worship' at Richmond. In a letter to the Protestant Minister, Cuffe said:

> Pardon my intrusion in sending these few lines to you, extremely sorry to hear that you were offended by the bearer, my wife. She is a native of England and still a prisoner, much disturbed in mind, her son came here to visit her, they are of the Protestant profession.
>
> I taught English learning and manners to "all religious persuasions for sixteen years in Sydney", then an arduous task. Pray Sir, please to forgive, "they know not what they do". (Highlighted in original)

Farrell Cuffe, aged about 73, and one of Australia's first Catholic educators, was buried in an unmarked grave at the old Catholic Cemetery, Windsor, in 1848.

Select Bibliography

Commercial Journal and Advertiser, Sydney, 1840.

Convicts Indent & records, State Records of New South Wales.

McGee, C. *A Touch of the Green: Sydney's first Catholic schools and their sites*, Sydney: Catholic Education Office, 2012.

New South Wales General Musters and Census, 1806-1841.

Sydney Gazette and NSW Advertiser, 1807-1830.

Whitaker, AM, *Unfinished Revolution: United Irishmen in New South Wales, 1800-1810* Darlinghurst NSW: Crossing Press, 2012.

George Marley (1788–ca 1848)

Australia's first teacher in a Catholic school

Damian Gleeson

Australia's first teacher employed in an identifiable Catholic school was an emancipist who had been transported to the penal colony seven years earlier. In 1813, at the age of 36, George Marley (Morley or Marlay) was convicted of embezzling money from his employers in Navan, Co. Meath, Ireland. He arrived on the *Three Bees* along with 210 prisoners into Sydney Cove on 6 May 1814.

Assigned to Captain William Campbell, Marley demonstrated good conduct which facilitated a petition in 1817 for a reduced sentence. In 1820, Marley, having completed his seven years' sentence, became Free by Servitude (FBS) and submitted a memorial for a small grant of land. The colonial government on 28 April 1821 awarded him a small grant of land.

Through the efforts of Fr John Therry, George Marley commenced a small Catholic school in Hunter Street, Parramatta, where he, Marlay, owned at least one home. The school's exact commencement date has been debated by historians. A reference to starting in October 1820 – based on a later statement by Fr Therry – has been too literally accepted. First reported operating in January 1821, the school had 31 students, 7 of whom were Protestants, and this date is a more accurate estimate of the school's commencement.

While the initial records are sparse, Mr Marley received one penny per student per week. On 10 October 1822 Marley applied for financial assistance as a schoolmaster. It appears to have gone unanswered, for on 22 November 1822 Marley made the following memorial to the Colonial Secretary:

> I have as of yesterday been directed by Captain Fennell [Aid-de-Camp to Governor Brisbane] to apply at your office respecting a provision for me as teacher of a catholic

[sic] schools in the town of Parramatta by His Excellency the Governor, and having reached town [i.e. Sydney] early enough to attend you at your public depot embolden me to the take the liberty of waiting on you at your private residence for such information as you may have the goodness to communicate.

George Marley's initiative in waiting at the Colonial Secretary's personal residence does not appear to have been successful. In March 1823, the "Colonial Fund" contained no allocation for a 'Roman Catholic Schoolmaster' at Parramatta, though such a position existed in Sydney and that teacher (probably Andrew Higgins) was paid £3.15 per annum. The Parramatta school remained in abeyance for several years. Ironically, Higgins taught there for a short while around 1825; from 1826-1828, James Cassidy was the resident schoolmaster.

After Marley left the Parramatta School in early 1823, he took up employment with John Macarthur at Camden, where he is listed as a clerk in the 1828 Census. While he clearly signed his name Marley, colonial officials mistakenly recorded it as Morley. The exact date of his death has yet to be confirmed but may have been 1852. George Marley has the distinction of being Australia's first teacher in a Catholic school.

Select Bibliography

Belfast Newsletter, 5 March 1813. Irish Newspapers Collection, NLA.

Canavan, K, fms. Bicentenary of Catholic Schooling in Australia – No 1 & 2, 2019. MSS.

Convict indents; Correspondence to Colonial Secretary; Inquest Series, SRNSW.

Lamb, B. *The history of the "Roman Catholic School" at Parramatta from its origins in Hunter Street Parramatta in 1820-21 to its passing to the management of the Marist Brothers in 1875*. Toowoomba: Marist Brothers, 1987, SLNSW.

Sydney Gazette & New South Wales Advertiser, 1821-1823.

O'Brien, E. *The Life and Letters of Archpriest J.J. Therry*, Sydney: Angus & Robertson, 1922.

McDonald, I. *A School of their Own – The Story of Parramatta Marist, 1820-2000*, Parramatta Marist, 2000.

Luttrell, J. *Worth the Struggle*, Sydney: Catholic Education Office, 1996.

Archdeacon John William McEncroe (1794–1868)

Priest and educator

Damian Gleeson

John McEncroe is fondly remembered for his devoted service to convicts, anti-transportation, as a newspaper editor in America and Australia, temperance advocate, friend to the poor, ecumenist but steadfastly pro-Irish, almost universally well-liked in an era of deep sectarianism, and loved by working class Irish, particularly those from his home province of Munster.

Born in the townland of Ardsallagh, near Cashel in County Tipperary on 26 December 1794, John's parents were William McEncroe, a landowner, and Mary D'Arcy. William died in a racecourse accident when John, their eldest, was 2 years of age. John attended Flynn's Grammar School, a step above a hedge school, and then undertook clerical training at St Patrick's Maynooth, where his influential lecturers included Fr (later Archbishop) John MacHale (or McHale). The national fervour of MacHale – described by the great Daniel O'Connell as the 'Lion of St Jarlath's – had a lasting legacy on McEncroe. A conscientious and diligent seminarian, McEncroe was ordained by Archbishop Daniel Murray on Trinity Sunday (1819) and almost immediately appointed a professor at St Finian's College, Navan, where he displayed a common touch within a scholarly disposition.

Three years later, McEncroe took up his first missionary challenge in the diocese of Charleston, South Carolina (USA), where he was an admirable lieutenant to its first bishop, Corkman John English. Due to contracting 'yellow fever', McEncroe returned to Ireland after seven years' service and became private secretary to the Archbishop of Cashel. Yearning though for further missionary work – greatly inspired by his American bishop – McEncroe volunteered for the Australian mission and fortuitously a passage became available with the influential John Hubert Plunkett who would become a lifetime friend, though they differed on several key policies.

Along with Polding and Fr John Joseph Therry, McEncroe became the third member of a triumphant group of pioneer Australian priests. From his arrival as official Catholic chaplain in 1832 until his death in 1868, McEncroe had a clear vision for the colony, which included educating the poor Irish. McEncroe was an ethical pragmatist. He had personally favoured the establishment of a non-denominational national system of education, as per the Irish model and his experience of Catholic and Protestants working together in the United States, but Sydney posed a unique challenge: to overcome blatant discrimination against Irish Catholics, McEncroe swung behind state aid to denominational schools as the preferred model. In 1848, when the NSW colonial government formalised arrangements for both church and national (government) schools, Polding appointed McEncroe as his 'correspondent' or interface with the powerful Denominational School Board (DSB), which had little sympathy to Catholic interests.

McEncroe undertook this large representative job. He was a lobbyist and meticulously prepared hundreds of submissions and petitions documenting the status of current schools, reviewing the merits of teachers and finances, and proposing new schools. He also skilfully utilised the [Australian] *Freeman's Journal* – which he had founded – to promote equality for Catholics who represented more than one third of the population.

As early as 1833, McEncroe sought to secure several Presentation (i.e. Christian) Brothers to come to Australia. However, Edmund Rice thought the Australian mission too distant. McEncroe systematically approached other Irish religious orders, and achieved success when the Mercy Sisters and Marist Brothers came to the colony.

As the first 'Chief Inspector of Catholic Schools', McEncroe was acutely aware of the paucity of experienced native-born lay teachers, and while unafraid to move on poorly-performing teachers, he empathised with their struggles, including meagre pay and paltry conditions. In 1857, he wrote: 'Much pains [sic] have been taken during this period to improve the class of teachers... 12 trained teachers have been introduced from Irish National Schools, and a marked improvement has been the result'.

McEncroe worked tirelessly to improve and expand Catholic education. He established the first Catholic teachers' training college in Kent Street, Sydney, in about 1849 and supported the formation of the Australian Catholic Teachers Association in 1856.

But success brought problems also. Polding continued to believe that the Archdiocese of Sydney could be centralised under the Benedictine umbrella. To this end, Polding overtly thwarted recommendations for McEncroe – although very well-liked by clergy and laity – to become a bishop. Polding also overlooked McEncroe for the position of Archdiocesan Vicar General, despite the latter's astute and wise management of the archdiocese while Polding was overseas. Polding's appointment of an inexperienced autocrat, Henry Gregory osb, raised hackles within the strongly Irish community. Upon Gregory's dismissal, Polding, somewhat reluctantly, again turned to McEncroe, to work with colonial authorities; the latter welcomed the return of a competent, meticulous, and down-to-earth Catholic representative.

Polding needed McEncroe, though the latter could have been given the opportunity to lead a diocese in Australia, Ireland or America. In the words of Sr Moira O'Sullivan rsc: 'McEncroe was never given the recognition that he deserved because he had not agreed to become a Benedictine'.

Polding, however, elevated McEncroe to the anachronistic Protestant title of Archdeacon – an insult for any fair-minded Tipperary man. Polding's criticism of McEncroe as 'timid' and 'excessively cautious' belies all of McEncroe's remarkable achievements as well as loyalty to Polding. Without such loyalty, Polding's long reign would surely have ended much sooner. The collective Benedictine community could never muster the support from the largely Irish-Australian community that McEncroe and Therry were able to do.

McEncroe's education portfolio was demanding given his multiplicity of other positions. He showed enduring patience with both state and church, including his immediate colleagues, Therry and Polding, both of whom – for starkly different reasons – lacked McEncroe's broader perceptive and calmer temperament. McEncroe played the ball, not the person, and successfully established a solid basis for Catholic schools.

Up until the end, McEncroe continued to negotiate for Irish lay and religious teachers to come to teach in colonial schools, often in rural areas. McEncroe personally agreed to sponsor new teaching staff. In 1868, McEncroe took ill at his parish church, St Patrick's in the Rocks, where he died on 22 August. Many thousands mourned his death and his funeral was reported to be the largest in the colony's history. In the panegyric for Archdeacon McEncroe, Monsignor John Rigney said: 'Well may the youth of the colony mourn— they have lost an enlightened and zealous patron of education'. Fittingly, John McEncroe is now buried alongside Therry and Polding in Sydney's St Mary's Cathedral Crypt.

McEncroe Publications

McEncroe, John. *Compendium of Irish Grammar*, Dublin 1822.

McEncroe, John. *The Wanderings of the human in, 'in searching the scriptures'* (Short title), Sydney, 1841. Second edition, Dublin 1859.

Select Bibliography

Birchley, D, *John William McEncroe*, PhD Thesis, University of Queensland, December 1983. (Mitchell Library, Sydney).

Birchley, D, *John McEncroe: colonial democrat*, Studies in the Christian Movement Manly, 1986).

Campion, E. "Archdeacon John McEncroe: an architect of the Australian church" *Journal of the Australian Catholic Historical Society 2018.*

Denominational Schools Board, Correspondence, State Records New South Wales.

Freeman's Journal, selected issues

O'Sullivan, M. "Archbishop Polding and the Catholic Church – another view", *The Sydney Papers*, Spring 1995.

Phillips, P. K. "McEncroe, John (1794-1868)", *Australian Dictionary of Biography*, vol. 2, 1967.

Rigney, R. *An Account of the Life and Missionary Labours of the Late Archdeacon McEncroe*, Sydney 1868.

Andrew Higgins (1797–1859)

Early teacher of Catholic children in Australia

Charles McGee

Andrew Higgins was born at Navan, County Meath, Ireland, in 1797. He was tried at Kildare in 1819 and received a life sentence. It was noted at his trial that he was a land surveyor and overseer of roadworks. Transported on the Daphne, he arrived at Sydney in September 1819, and became one of a large number of convicts forwarded to Liverpool for road construction.

In 1822, Fr John Therry petitioned the Colonial secretary asking that Higgins might be assigned to him as a teacher for a Catholic school in Sydney. His request was granted and on 3 April 1822, he again wrote to the Colonial Secretary:

> Permit me to recommend Andrew Higgins, Schoolmaster of Kent Street, who teaches sixty children, half of which number are instructed gratis, as he is a sober, attentive and moral young man, to solicit for him the usual weekly allowance of provisions from His Majesty's Stores.

On 20 April 1822, Therry was informed that

> for the encouragement of education among children of the lower orders, I am directed by His Excellency to acquaint you that he will allow you a penny per week for every child regular in attendance on Andrew Higgins, schoolmaster in Kent Street, such attendance from daily class rolls open to public inspection.

Higgins' school may well have been located, initially at least, in premises owned by James Dempsey, in Kent Street, near Erskine Street. Dempsey was born in Wexford, Ireland, and transported in 1802 for his role in the 1798 Irish Rebellion. He worked as a stonemason and built houses, the hospital and the first bridges across the Tank Stream. He was held in high esteem by colonial authorities and was granted an absolute pardon in 1809. For many years, his home was the Catholic centre of Sydney and a shelter for the poor and needy.

Robert Muldoon of Ballymahon, Ireland, was only seventeen years of age when he received a seven-year sentence at Newgate, Dublin, and transported to Sydney on the *Almorah* in 1820. Muldoon was also assigned to Fr Therry and assisted Higgins at the Sydney school.

The school appears to have moved later in 1822 as Higgins placed a notice in *The Sydney Gazette* to the effect that it was now in Castlereagh Street and the course of education consisted of Reading, Writing, English Grammar, Geography, Mathematics and Modern Book-keeping.

In December 1823, he married Mary Jackson who had been transported to the colony in 1822. In 1824, they assumed control of the Parramatta school after the loss of George Marley.

In 1827, Higgins was back in Sydney and employed as a clerk by James Lamy in George Street. He also became very involved with Fr Therry's financial dealings, particularly those concerning the construction of St Mary's. In 1828, Higgins was described in *The Sydney Gazette* of 18 June as being 'a clerk to the Rev. Mr. Therry'.

In the 1830s, Higgins was a property-seller at Petersham and moved on to purchasing and selling hotel licences. In 1840, he received his "Absolute Pardon". In 1842, he became the licensee of the Cheshire Cheese Hotel in Elizabeth Street.

The Sydney Morning Herald of 22 August 1859 announced the death of Andrew Higgins in California (his "Absolute Pardon" permitted him to leave the colony): 'He was formerly of Sydney, a very old and respected colonist whose death is much regretted by a large circle of friends'.

Andrew Higgins has received little recognition for a life devoted to the early Catholic community of Sydney and in particular for his opening, with Fr John Therry's backing, of a school for Catholic children in 1822.

Select Bibliography

Colonial Secretary Index, 1788-1825, https://www.records.nsw.gov.au/archives/collections-and-research/guides-and-indexes/colonial-secretary/indexes

Corrigan, U. *Catholic Education in NSW*, Sydney: Angus and Robertson, 1930.

McGee, C. *The Forgotten Ones – Teachers in the Catholic Schools of New South Wales before 1880*, Sydney: Catholic Education Office, 2012.

McGee, C. *People of Faith and Generosity – The Catholic Teachers of New South Wales before 1883*, McGee Publishing, 2017.

McGee, C. *The Forgotten Beginnings of Catholic Education in New South Wales*, McGee Publishing 2018.

Mayberry, P. *Irish Convicts to Australia*, http://members.pcug.org.au/ ppmay/cgi-bin/irish/irish.cgi

Murray, F. *Educating Emancipists' Children*, http://www.frankmurray.com.au/superceded-incorrect/research-notes-higgins-and-muldoon-school

O'Brien, E. *The Life and Letters of Archpriest J. J. Therry*, Sydney: Angus and Robertson, 1922.

Brigid Dwyer (1808–1878)

Australia's first native-born female teacher

Charles McGee

Michael Dwyer, known as the "Wicklow Chief", was born in 1772 at Camera, Wicklow, Ireland, and joined the Society of United Irishmen in 1797. He married Mary Doyle in 1798. Following the collapse of the United Irish forces at the Battle of Vinegar Hill, Dwyer and his men retreated to the Wicklow Mountains and continued guerrilla raids against the English. His bravery captured the imagination of the Irish people and he became something of a folk hero.

He surrendered in 1803 in anticipation of being sent to America, but the English reneged on this, and in 1806, with his wife Mary and two of his six children, he was deported to New South Wales as an unsentenced exile. He was allocated 100 acres of uncleared land facing Cabramatta Creek. Arrested in 1807 by Governor Bligh, he was tried for sedition and, although acquitted, he was exiled with Mary to Norfolk Island. In 1808, he was moved to Van Diemen's Land where Brigid was born.

In 1810, the family was back at Cabramatta and Michael became a constable in the Georges River district. By 1820, he was the chief constable at Liverpool and conducted an inn on his property. Bankrupted, he was forced to sell most of his assets and he died in 1825.

After his death, finding themselves with no means of support, Mary Dwyer with Brigid and her younger sister Eliza, moved to Sydney to keep house for Fr John Therry in a residence he had built for himself on the St Mary's site. It was here that they were reunited with the four family members who arrived from Ireland in 1828 — John, Peter, Esther and Mary Ann.

Brigid became a governess and subsequently a teacher at the Chapel School with Thomas Byrne. From 1828, her sister Esther became an assistant teacher with her. Brigid also taught at the Castlereagh Street School.

Brigid received no fixed salary from Government during her first eight years of teaching but was granted a half-penny per day for every pupil in actual attendance. A salary of 20 pounds was paid to her in 1834

In 1837, Brigid Dwyer married John O'Sullivan. He arrived in Sydney in 1828, on the same ship as her siblings, and resided with Fr Therry and the Dwyer family at St Mary's. They settled in Goulburn and Mary Dwyer came to live with them. John O'Sullivan was one of the outstanding Catholics of the early days and a trusted friend of priests and bishops – from Fr Therry and Archbishop Polding down to Bishop Lanigan. He was business adviser and closest friend of Fr Therry.

Brigid and John lived in Goulburn for thirty years and their home was an open house to the itinerant priests who rode across vast areas of the country. They were the friends of every priest who worked in Goulburn and John was largely behind the bringing of the Sisters of Mercy to that town. He provided lodgings for them until the first part of the convent was completed.

Brigid and John retired to Hunter's Hill in 1866 where John died in 1870 and Brigid in 1878. They are buried together along with three of their four children in the historic Mortis Street Cemetery at Goulburn. *The Freeman's Journal* of 7 September 1878 notes, 'Mrs O'Sullivan endeared herself wherever she went by kind and generous acts. However, the best consolation for her family will be the noble lesson of her life of rectitude and sterling Piety which she has left them'. She is also remembered as the first native-born female teacher.

Select Bibliography

Gahan, D. *The Peoples' Rising, Wexford 1798*, MacMillan, 1995.

McGee, C. *A Touch of Green – Sydney's First Catholic Schools and their Sites*, Sydney: Catholic Education Office, 2013.

McGee, C. *People of Faith and Generosity – The Catholic Teachers of New South Wales before 1883*, Sydney: McGee Publishing, 2017.

O'Brien, E. *The Life and Letters of Archpriest J. J. Therry*, Sydney: Angus and Robertson, 1922.

O'Brien, J. *The Men of '38 and other Pioneer Priests*, Donvale: Lowden Publishing, 1975.

Bridget Mary Magdalen McGuigan
(Mother Mary Francis rsc) (1842–1923)

Prudent educator and administrator

Carlos Lopez

Mother Mary Francis McGuigan was a gifted Catholic educator and skilful administrator. She was elected as the first Australian-born Superior General of the Religious Sisters of Charity of Australia in 1882 and remained in this position until 1920. Under her leadership, the Congregation grew exponentially, from 44 to over 400 members, allowing the order to expand its teaching and nursing apostolates in New South Wales, Victoria and Tasmania.

Bridget Mary Magdalen McGuigan, known in religious life as Sister (later Mother) Mary Francis McGuigan, was born on 16 January 1842 at Braidwood, New South Wales. She was the second of ten daughters born to John McGuigan, a pioneering pastoralist of the Monaro District and his wife Ellen McGuigan, née Foran. As told by Sr Mary Teresa Roper, the McGuigans were pious Catholics who often hosted the visiting district priest who used the family home at Norongo as a "station" for the celebration of Mass.

In 1856, Bridget and her older sister Mary were sent as boarders to be educated by the Benedictine Sisters at the Convent of the Presentation of the Virgin, Subiaco, Rydalmere. At Subiaco, Bridget encountered Sister Mary Alphonsus Unsworth, a Sister of Charity who was convalescing at Subiaco, and who later influenced Bridget's decision to join the Order. On 22 July 1861, Bridget McGuigan entered the Sisters of Charity at St Vincent's Convent, Potts Point, and was professed on 21 April 1864 taking the religious name of Sr Mary Francis.

During her novitiate, Sr M. Francis was sent to train and teach at St Vincent's Primary School (Victoria Street Roman Catholic School, Potts

Point), then under the management of its two founding teachers, Sr M. Aloysius Raymond (Headmistress) and Sr M. Alphonsus Unsworth (Infants Mistress). The Freeman's Journal of 1914 recounts that her aptitude for teaching was quickly recognised and she was appointed as the first assistant to Sr M. Aloysius. In 1865, she became Headmistress of St Vincent's School (following the withdrawal of Sr M. Aloysius due to ill health), continuing in this role until 1881. She maintained the school at a high standard, ensuring ongoing recognition and financial support from the Council of Education.

At the 1882 General Chapter, Sr M. Francis McGuigan was elected Superior General of the Sisters of Charity. This coincided with the removal of State Aid funding from non-government schools in New South Wales, which threatened to undermine the work of the Sisters in their schools. Mother M. Francis, responding to the call of Archbishop Roger Vaughan and aided by several junior Sisters who had trained and worked as teachers prior to entering the Congregation, staffed six parochial schools in addition to the five schools already under the Sisters' care. This was made possible through the financial support provided by the opening of St Vincent's Ladies College, a fee-paying boarding and day school at Potts Point in 1882, following Papal approval in 1879, to accept payment. This new college incorporated the old St Vincent's Primary School and offered both junior and senior schooling. Over the next 36 years, more than 20 Schools were staffed or established by the Sisters across Sydney and as far away as Bega and Bombala. Of note were the Garcia School of Music and St Vincent's Training College, a college for female primary school teachers, both established in 1896 at Potts Point.

The contribution of Mother M. Francis McGuigan and the Sisters of Charity to Catholic education in Australia, was however, not confined to a single state. Her own diary entries record that in 1889, five Sisters were sent to Melbourne, in response to a request made in 1888 by Archbishop Thomas Carr for the assistance of the Sisters in supporting Catholic schools in inner city Melbourne and for the establishment of a hospital. The Sisters undertook the staffing of St Patrick's School, East

Melbourne, and over the next 13 years staffed a further six parochial schools and established two senior schools.

The success of the Sisters in providing a sound Catholic education to their students resulted in further requests made to Mother M. Francis. In 1889, she noted in her diary that she had to deny an appeal from Bishop Higgins of Rockhampton who had requested eight Sisters to educate up to 1000 children, as 'the Sisters could not be spared... and the expense is great'. She also received further appeals from Melbourne and New Zealand for foundations, but again Mother M. Francis noted that she declined. These decisions were made in the context of negotiations, begun in 1888, for the amalgamation of the Hobart community of Sisters (separate from 1847) with those on the mainland which was achieved in 1890.

Tall, with an expressive countenance and stately deportment, Mother M Francis radiated a strong presence both as a junior Sister and as Superior General. Her authority was firm but gentle, guided by her strong sense of piety and justice. In 1914, she celebrated her Golden Jubilee, the first Australian born Sister of Charity to do so, before being succeeded in 1920 by Mother M. Berchmans Daly. After a short retirement, she succumbed to heart complications on 27 October 1923, and was laid to rest in the Lady Chapel of St Vincent's Chapel, Potts Point. The Catholic Press reported that Archbishop Kelly spoke at Mother M. Francis McGuigan's funeral and noted, 'The small seed sown in far-off days by the pioneer sisters of charity [sic], was under her guidance to grow and flourish'.

Mother M Francis McGuigan oversaw and guided the Sisters of Charity through a period of great change and growth. Despite being constrained by limited resources, further divided between the teaching and nursing apostolates, she was able to establish and staff schools and hospitals throughout New South Wales, Victoria and Tasmania. She prudently denied requests for further foundations which might overextend the Congregation, instead focussing on those already under her care. Mother M Francis McGuigan played a significant role in supporting Catholic education in Australia both as teacher and as an administrator, however, this was only possible owing to the support and work of the many unsung Sisters of the Congregation.

Selected writing

McGuigan, Mother Mary Francis, Diary, 1888, SER/01674/011, Congregational Archives of the Sisters of Charity

Select Bibliography

"Advertising: Monaro District for Positive Sale." *Queanbeyan Age*, 19 October 1871. http://nla.gov.au/nla.news-article30582261.

Cannell, Josephine. *To the Beckoning Shores: Urged on by the Love of Christ*. Hobart: N.P., 2007.

Donovan, Margaret M. *Apostolate of Love: Mary Aikenhead 1787-1858 Foundress of the Irish Sisters of Charity*. Melbourne: The Polding Press, 1979.

"Festival of Memories," *Freeman's Journal*, April 16, 1914. http://nla.gov.au/nla.news-article111292801.

Frappell, Samantha. *St Vincent's College Potts Point 1858-2008: 150 Years of Catholic Education*. Sydney: Kingsclear Books, 2009.

"Granting the petition of the Sisters of Charity to accept fees and to conduct boarding Schools. Given at Rome by Pope Leo XIII, 4 December 1879." 31 January 1880, SER/01720/002, A104/11, Congregational Archives of the Sisters of Charity.

"Mother Mary Francis McGuigan Dead: Solemn Requiem Mass." *The Catholic Press* (Sydney, NSW), November 1, 1923. http://nla.gov.au/nla.news-article106414201.

Roper, Sister Mary Teresa Joseph. *Short Sketch of the Life of Mary Francis McGuigan: Superior General of the Sisters of Charity of Australia*, 1923, SER/01710/008, Congregational Archives of the Sisters of Charity.

"The Cardinal at St Patrick's: A Flood of Memories." *Freeman's Journal*, 3 March 1900, 16, http://nla.gov.au/nla.news-article111310265.

REFLECTION

At the far end of the world...
Looking back to Colonial Catholic educators

Anne Benjamin

On my phone (and my watch), I have a photograph of my mother as a small child. It was probably taken around 1915 and she is with 40 other children, including her brother and older sister, all students of St Patrick's School at Millers Forest. Millers Forest is a rural settlement not far from Maitland in New South Wales. St Patrick's opened its doors as a school in 1887 with the Sisters of Mercy and the original 1880s school was a simple structure built from the red cedar famous in the area.

Millers Forest is a fertile area just across the broad sweep of river at Raymond Terrace, where the Hunter and Williams Rivers converge. Raymond Terrace is about 26 kilometres north of the port of Newcastle in New South Wales and the surrounding areas were important because of the strategic role of the rivers as transport routes at the time.

The European penal colony pitched its tents on the lands of the Eora people, and subsequently spread out through the lands of other nations. The Indigenous peoples were treated appallingly.[6]

Catholics, too, comprising many of the convicts, were on the peripheries of the new society. Priests were regarded with suspicion as purveyors of "papism". The early schools and their teachers struggled to get the necessary funds to educate the children of convicts who were largely destitute and illiterate. Writing to Pope Gregory XVI in 1841, Archbishop Polding wrote about the 'heretics who are bitterest enemies

---

[6] Archbishop Polding, Letter to E. Deas Thomson, 12 January 1844, in *The Letters of John Bede Polding osb*, Vol II, ed. Sr M Xavier Compton sgs et al, (Glebe: Good Samaritan Sisters, 1996), 2.

of our religion working to entice as many (youth) as they can from us'.[7] In 1850, Catholics from Raymond Terrace asked for more support for their school in

> a letter signed by eighteen Catholics, heads of families at this place, stating that forty-five children are attending the Catholic School there, and some eight or ten going to schools where they cannot receive any instruction in the tenets of the Catholic Church — and complaining of the injustice they suffer in not getting any public aid towards the support of their school.[8]

Whether or not as a result of this, it appears that the first Catholic school in Millers Forest was opened in 1852, predating the St Patrick's school attended by my mother by about 30 years. With two teachers, Thomas O'Brien and J. Devoy, it appears to have had a reasonably large enrolment.

In a Report of the Denominational School Board for 1857,[9] we read of provision being made for teachers' residences for the Catholic schools in Millers Forest and Raymond Terrace.[10] The estimated cost of each teacher's residence was 100 pounds. The teacher's salary was probably 30 pounds a year and the assistant teacher's 15 pounds.

At this time (1857), there were already 72 Catholic schools in the colony from a total number of 200 active schools (the others being 100 Church of England, 18 Presbyterian and 10 Wesleyan).

---

[7] Archbishop Polding, Letter to Pope Gregory XVI, circa June 1841, in *The Letters of John Bede Polding osb*, Vol I, ed. Sr M Xavier Compton sgs et al, (Glebe: Good Samaritan Sisters,1994), 176.
[8] "The Catholic School at Raymond Terrace", *Freeman's Journal*, 22 August 1850. https://trove.nla.gov.au/newspaper/article/115765806?
[9] Parliamentary Paper, "Report of the Denominational School Board for the Year 1857," reported in *Maitland Mercury* Thursday 10 June 1858, https://trove.nla.gov.au/newspaper/article/18639626?
[10] Parliamentary Paper. (This reference was in a report on Roman Catholic Schools from Fr John McEncroe which was appended to the Denominational School Board Report.)

Although the Catholic grants from the government were generally less than those to other denominations, the poverty of the early Catholic community was well-known.[11] The load of education was shared by parents, with those who could not afford to pay being educated without fees – a characteristic of Catholic schools that continues (admirably) to this day.

Tensions between lay people and clergy were sometimes part of the climate when it came to questions of funds to establish and run Catholic schools. When the good Catholics of Raymond Terrace had complained about their need for educational support in 1850, *The Freemans' Journal* reported that they had also insinuated that it 'is owing to the neglect of the Catholic Clergy that they do not receive Government aid as well as others for education'.

The paper (with which at one time the Rev. John McEncroe was associated) was at pains to correct this, arguing that the clergy had

> by "petitions and entreaties" endeavoured to procure from the Legislative Council a just sum, in proportion to the number of Roman Catholics in the colony, towards the support of Catholic Schools, but in vain! And during the last week, a Member of Council brought in a Bill for the purpose, amongst other things, if carried, of getting one of the Catholic Clergy punished by fine and imprisonment for daring to charge the honorable member with being instrumental in procuring a casting vote against an additional sum of £800 which the Government placed on the estimates for Catholic Schools for 1851.[12]

The fault, the paper berated, lies not with the clergy but the people that Catholics have voted into the Legislative Council. And concludes,

---

[11] Ronald Fogarty, fms, *Catholic Education in Australia 1806-1950*, Vol I, "Catholic Schools and the Denominational System", (Melbourne: Melbourne University Press, 1957), 59.
[12] *Freeman's Journal*, August 1850.

if the Catholics of the colony wish to bring up their children in the faith of their Irish and English forefathers, who suffered the loss of everything dear in this world, but preserved the "Faith", let them take care to vote for no candidate at the next election who will not pledge himself to see justice done to them, in this regard. We want no favours, we seek for justice, and we shall not rest satisfied until full justice, be done to us and to our children.[13]

This cry for justice in funding has echoed down through 200 years. And the divisions between school sectors right from the beginning set a tone that lives on. Disputes about funding might be conducted in a more civilised way, but the early divisions are evident in the regular debates about mechanisms for government funding of Australian schools.

In 1860, the 90 or so students at the Millers Forest school underwent the usual half-yearly examination.[14] This was conducted by the local priest, Reverend Luckie with the assistance of their teacher. Their teachers at this time were Mr Timothy O'Callaghan and Miss O'Callaghan. The report they received was very positive, with compliments directed to their teachers. The children were reportedly 'neatly dressed, and appeared in excellent health', displaying 'smartness and intelligence'. (It is pertinent to the conditions in the colony even in 1860 that the children's health and dress were factors to be remarked upon in a school report.) It was observed that reading is an area in 'which children are remarkably deficient'. In this instance, however, reading by the little Catholic children in Millers Forest was 'well executed and so sensibly withal that one must be impressed with the gratifying conviction that they fully understood what they read'. Furthermore, not just in literacy, but also in 'Mental Arithmetic, many of the children displayed a quickness of perception that was very interesting; as was specially

---

[13] *Freeman's Journal.*, August 1850
[14] The account that follows is taken from "The Catholic School Miller's Forest," in *The Freeman's Journal*, 1 February 1860.
https://trove.nla.gov.au/newspaper/article/114837499.

evinced in replies to extempore questions put to them by their rev. examiner'. (NAPLAN in another form?)

The greatest praise from Reverend Luckie was reserved for the children (and their teachers') achievements in religious education, or more precisely, "Christian Doctrine and their knowledge of Fleming's Historical Catechism".

'At the conclusion of the examination, there was no distribution, as at other times, of prints and books as prizes, but instead there was a plentiful spread of tea, cake, and buns, &c, to which, it is needless to say, the little ones did ample justice.' The article included a cameo of one of the teachers in the school:

> Miss O'Callaghan, to whom, on account of her amiable disposition, the children are much attached, attended to them with the solicitude of a mother, and took care that none were in want of the good things supplied. At the usual hour the innocent and merry school children dispersed to their homes, delighted with their school duties and their feast.[15]

The description of Miss O'Callaghan's solicitude for her students might sound a little quaint to our ears, but the care it describes is intrinsic to every teacher in Catholic schools. To be accurate, we should say, it is intrinsic to the work of all teachers, in all schools. In Catholic schools, however, there is an explicit set of values and public commitment to the ethos of care that should make it a defining hallmark.

The article concluded with a thoughtful postscript that contemporary administrators would surely honour: 'The examination of the school at Raymond Terrace has been postponed to Easter next, owing to the short period the present teacher Mr. D. O'Leary, has been in charge of the school. Miller's Forest, January 24th, 1860.'[16]

---

[15] "The Catholic School Miller's Forest," in *The Freeman's Journal*, 1 February 1860. https://trove.nla.gov.au/newspaper/article/114837499.

[16] *Freeman's Journal* February 1860.

In his article, Charles McGee refers to there being 196 lay teachers working in 83 Catholic schools in New South Wales in 1880.[17] Janice Garaty recounts that 'in 1880 there were about 800 lay (non-religious) teachers working in Catholic schools in the Australian colonies; most were Irish'.[18]

The biographies in this section suggest that early teachers were not without their flaws and idiosyncrasies. Some were untrained or inadequately trained. The competence, character and commitment of some teachers was problematic. Yet, the Thomas O'Brien and J. Devoy who taught the Catholic children at Millers Forest in the 1850s, the O'Callaghans who taught there in the 1860s, Michael Myers who taught there sometime in the 1870s, the Sisters of Mercy who followed at the "new" school at St Patrick's (and who taught my mother a love of poetry) and the others, many unknown, are all part of a great legacy of committed Catholic teachers who saw a need here at the end of the earth and were willing to respond, despite poor salaries and conditions.[19]

Even the small payment for the teachers' services was not always forthcoming. In a system antipathetic to Catholics, especially Irish Catholics, and sometimes exacerbated by the spikiness of priests like Fr Therry, payment for a long time was substantially less than that paid to teachers in non-denominational schools. This appears to be why George Marley's time in the Parramatta school was so short-lived. Andrew Higgins was not trained as a teacher but, at 25, he stepped forward to take on responsibility for children in a Catholic school, half of whom could afford no fees. Likewise, Brigid Dwyer, who for eight years received a halfpenny a day for each child attending. (If rolls are important now, then even more so then.) These teachers are just a few of many who responded to the poverty of Catholics, their exclusion from

---

[17] See this book, page 27.
[18] See this book, page 65.
[19] Charles McGee, in this book, pages 16-28. Also, *The Forgotten ones, Teachers in the Catholic Schools of New South Wales before 1880*, Sydney: Catholic Education Office Sydney, 2012; "The Hardships of a Dreary Winter."

society's benefits and their determination to preserve their faith, which in the case of the Irish was integral to their culture.

Gradually, members of religious congregations were introduced to take up the challenge of teaching in the growing number of Catholic schools.

A young South Australian woman of Scottish heritage, Mary MacKillop, who famously lived by the dictum, 'never see a need without doing something about it' bridges the shift from lay teachers to religious in Australian Catholic schools of the 19th century. Beginning her teaching as she did in 1860 as an eighteen-year-old lay Catholic woman who responded to the needs around her, Mary MacKillop provides direct continuity between the early Catholic educators, who were mostly lay, mostly Irish, and the following period in which Catholic education was predominantly in the hands of members of religious congregations. While many (if not most) of the other lay Catholic teachers moved into the public schools, Mary, as is well-celebrated, followed her calling into religious life and sainthood.

Catholic leaders of vision, such as Fr John McEncroe, saw the needs of the children of the poor Irish and imagined an educational solution that included the necessity of teacher training and the need to work within the political and bureaucratic circumstances in which Catholics in colonial Australia found themselves. Relations with the Government of the day with respect to funding, quality of teaching and curricula were complex and as fraught as they were necessary, with the Catholic voice often being divided on the preferred way forward.

Through the period of the mid-1830s to 1877, the bishop of the colony was John Bede Polding. When the English Benedictine arrived in Sydney, convicts still formed about 38% of the total population of just under 72,000. Bishop Polding was vigorous in assuming leadership; he was forthright and bold in acting on his judgments, even if burdened by the rigours of administration. Even before he left London in 1834, he had written to the Secretary of State for the Colonies, arguing, amongst other things, for the establishment of more schools for Catholic children of convicts, the establishment of a school of liberal education for middle classes (an idea that was never successful), money to purchase books and other equipment for the schools and properly qualified teachers.

He wrote strong letters to *The Australian* on education and the place of religious instruction in education.[20] He argued for access to proper funding for Catholic educational institutions and for a school system which permitted Catholic children the full culture, not just withdrawal for Religious Instruction.[21] In a petition to the Legislative Assembly in 1863, he wrote that 'any compulsion, direct or indirect, tending to throw Catholic children into schools not taught by Catholics would be a most injurious assault upon their religious liberty'.[22] Not all Catholics agreed. It is helpful to recall that, just as now, the church (both among its hierarchy and laity) was not of one mind on the proposed changes to education.

In response to the withdrawal of government funding from denominational schools (in 1882 in NSW and variously in other states), and the concomitant strategy of the bishops to bring in teachers from religious congregations, by 1880 the number of lay teachers in Catholic schools had reduced almost completely. Fast forward nearly another 100 years when, in the 1960s and 1970s, religious were leaving schools and teaching: lay people were once more needed to pick up the challenge. Once again, in the early 1960s-1970s, they often did so on very poor wages and under less-than-ideal conditions. If the parish priest or religious community was short of funds in a given week, many times a lay teacher simply had to wait to be paid.

Revisiting the lives and times of those first Catholic teachers in Australia offers a perspective on our own time. In the 1960's, 100 years after the O'Callaghans were teaching at Millers Forest, my own school would join other Catholic schools in the Hunter region to take part in massive celebrations for St Patrick's Day. We would travel to a

---

[20] Polding, *Letters* Vol I, 78-79.
[21] Polding, *Letters*, Vol II, 233.
[22] Archbishop Polding, Petition to the Legislative Assembly, 6 August 1863, in *The Letters of John Bede Polding osb*, Vol III, ed. Sr M Xavier Compton sgs et al, (Glebe: Good Samaritan Sisters, 1996) 123

central place, such as Maitland, and there make a grand procession down the length of High Street, attracting crowds, drums pounding and banners flying. Afterwards, there would be a picnic and a general sense of holiday. (Much more than for St Joseph, whose feast day falls just two days later, and who, one would have thought, commands a more significant role in the life of faith.) I realise now the significance of these triumphant demonstrations. While colonial Catholics also included English, Scottish, German, French, Italian and other nationalities, it was the deep scar of being second-class colonials worn by the Irish convicts and their free-born children that was still being excised. St Patrick's Day parades, 100 years on, were making unsubtle points to society about Catholicism and Catholic schools: we are still here. We *have* survived – despite you.

For many reasons – not least that Irish-Australians are a small minority in our schools and society – St Patrick's Day parades of this heroic kind no longer have a place. More importantly, that kind of church triumphalism is undesirable in a contemporary church, whose credibility is under severe question. The question now is not a matter of Catholics being the dregs of society, but an understandable response to the scandalous abuse of children by too-many Catholic churchmen and the dereliction of church leaders in the way they handled this abuse.

One remarkable aspect of the story of early Catholic educators in Australia is the rate at which schools were opened. It seems as though, wherever the people went, as the country opened up, a school was soon demanded and established. In 1833, there were 11 Catholic schools across the country; in 1848, 48; in 1858 with funding being available, 174.[23] Today there are 1746. Do we continue to keep multiplying schools? Or do we ask: where is the mission needed today? What is the particular demand that a Catholic education can meet? What is the mission Catholic schools should meet in fidelity to the gospel?

For the colonial teachers, education was seen as an essential tool to protect the cultural self-identity and faith of early Catholics. For the Irish, the culture and faith were largely interchangeable. Most of those

---

[23] Ronald Fogarty, *Catholic Education in Australia*, Vol 1, 38, 53-54.

early Irish Catholics were extremely poor. They too included in their outreach others who were in need, such as a young lay teacher, Mary MacKillop, from South Australia, who while working as a governess for her aunt and uncle's children, reached out to other children in poverty with a special regard for Aboriginal children in the area.

In a long letter to Lord Stanley, Her Majesty's Principal Secretary of State for the Colonies, in 1841 Archbishop Polding described the situation of the "Native Tribes of New Holland" as 'deplorable in the extreme and getting daily far beyond the reach of remedy'. His letter referred to Aborigines being despoiled of their natural inheritance, being persecuted, of their resources being depleted by the expansion of sheep stations and by the destruction of indigenous animals. He wrote of the deadly animosity between "Natives and Settlers", of bloodshed and how contact with 'European colonisation has been a prolific source of misery to the native population, a curse instead of a blessing'.[24]

What would Polding say today? So many years later, it is an indictment on our nation that the condition and well-being of Aboriginal Australians remains as it does. Peripheral.

In today's world of technology, communications and travel, Australian Catholic educators no longer need have a sense of being at the far end of the world. However, we are still called to "go to the peripheries". Inheriting a legacy from women and men teachers who, at personal cost at times, were themselves on the edges of society on this island at the far end of the world, we are well-placed to respond empathically to this challenge.

It is good to remember that in Australia Catholic schools enjoy a privileged position, vis-à-vis our colleagues in other parts of the world, such as the USA, UK, Sweden, Pakistan and other places where Catholic schools do not enjoy the freedom or the funding that we do here. As Brother Kelvin Canavan frequently reminds us, we can never take that privileged position (of government funding) for granted. It is good to see how the conditions for teachers has improved over the years so that they are paid in accord with colleagues in government

---

[24] Polding, *Letters*, Vol I, 185.

schools. It is wonderful to see the high-quality facilities where they teach. It is heartening to know of the qualifications of our teachers and of the commitment to learning that is part of every teacher's own responsibility. They are all to be celebrated.

The teachers we honour in this book and in the *Biographical Dictionary of Australian Catholic Educators* project responded by taking education to the peripheries of their societies. We must ask ourselves: where are the peripheries in Australia where Catholic education could open a welcoming door? Who are our neediest children? Who are our poor? Who the most vulnerable?

In the words of Bishop Vincent Long, reflecting with Catholic school leaders on Pope Francis' call to 'go to the periphery':

> How do our school communities personify the powerlessness and the compassion of Christ? How do we balance the need for recognition and success on the one hand, and the fundamental Christian ethos of care for the weakest on the other?[25]

It is perhaps just a little harder when our Catholic schools have become as successful as they have. Yet the same commitment and dedication that inspired our earliest teachers is alive in teachers across our schools, with many additional advantages of resources and training. Understanding where we have come from might help us discern the way forward.

Select Bibliography

___ "The Catholic School Miller's Forest," in *The Freeman's Journal*, 1 February 1860.
https://trove.nla.gov.au/newspaper/article/114837499.

---

[25] Bishop Vincent Long, "The call to go to the peripheries", Address at System Leadership Day, Parramatta, 25 January 2017, http://catholicoutlook.org/bishop-vincent-address-system-leadership-day-ceo/.

___ "The Catholic School at Raymond Terrace", *Freeman's Journal*, 22 August 1850. https://trove.nla.gov.au/newspaper/article/115765806.

Campion, Edmund. *Rockchoppers. Growing up Catholic in Australia.* Ringwood: Penguin, 1982.

Fogarty, Ronald. *Catholic Education in Australia 1806-1950*, Vol I, "Catholic Schools and the Denominational System", Melbourne: Melbourne University Press, 1957.

Long, Vincent. "The call to go to the peripheries", Address at System Leadership Day, Parramatta, 25th January 2017, http://catholicoutlook.org/bishop-vincent-address-system-leadership-day-ceo/.

Mahon, James. "Lay Teachers in Government-Aided Catholic Schools in NSW, 1848-1880". A revised version of a paper read to the Australian Catholic Historical Society, October 1978.

McGee, Charles. "The Hardships of a Dreary Winter. Catholic Authorities and Lay Teachers in Nineteenth Century New South Wales." Sydney: Catholic Education Office.

McGee, Charles. The Forgotten ones, Teachers in the Catholic Schools of New South Wales before 1880. Sydney: Catholic Education Office Sydney, 2012.

Parliamentary Paper, "Report of the Denominational School Board for the Year 1857," in *Maitland Mercury* Thursday 10 June 1858, https://trove.nla.gov.au/newspaper/article/18639626.

Polding, John Bede. *The Letters of John Bede Polding osb*, 3 Vols. Edited by Sr M. Xavier Compton, et al. Glebe: Good Samaritan Sisters, 1994-1996.

Scholastica, Mother. "Origins of Catholic Education in Australia," Paper read to Australian Catholic Historical Society. Volume 1:1, 1954. 3-16.

Chapter Four
Developments in Catholic Education in Australia 1880-1960

Context

... a helping hand to the little children of St Patrick's at the Antipodes[26]

Janice Garaty

The *NSW Education Act* of 1961 which incorporated recommendations of the 1957 *Wyndham Report* signalled a revolutionary change in the entire organisation and delivery of secondary education in that state, a pivotal reform. It bookends one end of this overview of the major steps in the advancement of Catholic education in Australia, the other being the NSW 1880 *Public Instruction Act* and the various similar acts which preceded it in other Australian colonies during the 1870s. South Australia, with a very small Catholic population, had introduced similar legislation as early as 1851, Tasmania and West Australia in 1871. Victoria had withdrawn state aid from denominational schools in 1872 and South Australia and Queensland followed suit in 1875. At the heart of some 80 years of struggle and sacrifice to follow was the overwhelming confidence of the bishops and other leaders of the Catholic community in the Catholic schools as the surest and most effective means of providing religious education.

---

[26] Archbishop Moran's letter to Reverend Mother at Callan, March 1884.

In 1880, there were about 800 lay (non-religious) teachers working in Catholic schools in the Australian colonies; most were Irish. Some were poorly trained, some were indifferent to their profession, but the majority were diligent and committed Catholics paid by the state. The early orders of religious women in Australia had embraced social work as their chief mission; this was particularly aimed at adults. After 1880, increasingly their work would be teaching as the bishops demanded their contribution. In Sydney, there were only five schools run by religious orders in the 1870s. It wasn't until the turn of the century that religious were in a position to replace completely lay teachers and that would then remain unchanged until the post Vatican 11 years with a quite-sudden drop in vocations, increasing population pressures and longer secondary school retention rates.

The Irish-born suffragan bishops, Matthew Quinn of Bathurst, James Murray of Maitland and William Lanigan of Goulburn were already building their own educational systems before 1880 but looked to Archbishop Vaughan of the Sydney Archdiocese to assume the mantle of leadership in responding to NSW Premier Henry Parkes' proposed legislation in 1879. After heated debate over several months in the NSW Parliament, the 1880 *Public Instruction Act* was to make education compulsory, non-sectarian and supposedly free. It would end government payments to all denominational schools (church-run) by December 1882. Archbishop Vaughan admitted that Sydney had been a 'little sleepy in matters of education' in a speech he gave on 12 October 1879.

The Australian bishops had published a joint pastoral letter, highly inflammatory in substance in 1879, and Catholics were threatened with denial of access to the sacraments if they sent their children to non-Catholic schools when a choice was possible. The answer to the so called 'Education Question' of the future of Catholic schools without state aid which had hovered since the 1860s would now become one of survival in the face of enormous obstacles.

Archbishop Vaughan never envisaged that religious (mostly women) would be the only teachers in Catholic schools, believing the withdrawal of state aid would inflict 'a temporary strain'. Bishop Quinn of Bathurst believed justice would be done. The 1880 Act resulted in the transfer of the management of Catholic schools from lay persons (a gradual move in most cases) to consecrated religious (nuns, brothers and priests) under the supervision of the bishops and their parish priests. Power struggles over ultimate authority of the invaluable human resources of the religious congregations had begun in earlier decades but after 1880 became exacerbated. The bishops prioritised Catholic schools within their pastoral planning and expected the religious orders to accede to this priority. Religious congregations, originally founded to carry out works such as nursing or care of the poor, often found that a bishop had insisted on them establishing a school as a condition of working in a diocese.

Struggles over authority between religious superiors and bishops were many. The Patrician Brothers from Mountrath, Ireland, had arrived in the Maitland diocese in 1883 at the invitation of Bishop Murray but left in 1888 because Murray was determined to enforce diocesan control. In 1891, they opened a boarding school (Holy Cross College) at Ryde in Sydney where they were welcomed by Cardinal Moran who did not have problems accepting congregations who wished to retain centralised, non-diocesan control.

Eminent historian Marcus Clarke saw the exclusion of church schools from the public purse by colonial governments as one of the most momentous decisions and probably the most disastrous in Australian history. It meant a permanent division within Australian educational systems into Catholic, Protestant and State schools. The Protestant denominational schools quickly decided to disband; after all, religion was mandated to be taught in the so-called secular state schools but Catholic priests were forbidden to enter state schools to give instruction.

Catholic schools would not disappear as most politicians had thought would soon happen. The enormous sacrifices demanded by Catholic parents and the religious teachers, who were absolutely key to the continuation of Catholic education over the next 80 years, left Catholics as an aggrieved minority. The cessation of government aid to church schools would remain a running sore in Australian society. Its cost was great, both in terms of human and financial sacrifices; it was achieved at the price of social isolation for the Catholic community and a continuing atmosphere of sectarian distrust. The construction in 1881 of the large gothic styled Blackfriars State School immediately adjacent to St Benedict's School at Abercrombie St Chippendale, an inner Sydney suburb, on land resumed from the Broadway parish by the government, was a very visible example of these frictions.

St Benedict's was divided into separate schools, the boys taught by the Marist Brothers and the girls by the Good Samaritans. They had been founded by Archbishop Polding in 1857 as the Sisters of the Good Shepherd, the first truly Australian Religious order and renamed to distinguish them from the French Institute of the Good Shepherd which had arrived in Melbourne in 1863. The 'Good Sams', as they were called, were leaders in this intense period of building and staffing Catholic schools and had been early pioneers, entering the Catholic denominational school system in 1861. The bishops were insistent no pupils should be turned away from a parish school and large class numbers occupying cramped unpleasant spaces and lack of basic resources made teaching extremely difficult; yet they were expected to compete with the new state schools. In 1900, St Benedict's had an enrolment of 978, the largest Catholic school enrolment in the colony.

Archbishop Vaughan made the Catholic school the symbol of Australian Catholicism and he spent the remainder of his life recruiting religious teachers. After travelling to England in 1883 for that purpose, he died within months. His successor, Patrick Francis Moran (soon Cardinal), would embrace Vaughan's strategy and for the next three generations it was nuns (mainly) and brothers who kept the Catholic education system working. Moran told his priests to build a school first, a building which could be divided into classrooms during the week and be used for devotions at the weekend; the church-schools were to be built by parishioners' donations and fund-raising. Unfortunately, the Australian clergy had little previous experience of religious communities and jealously guarded their authority as managers of the local school. Prominent Catholic historian, Edmund Campion, has said that 'in their drive to establish a total Catholic system the Irish bishops spared no one' and the Catholic school system was the Irish bishops' greatest monument. They were ruthless in demanding that Catholic parents ensure their children's attendance at them. It was elemental to the forging of a strong identity which in the 19th century was based on common religious, ethnic and economic circumstances.

In November 1895, the second Plenary Synod of Australia stated schools were to be the continuing priority. Between 1880 and 1900, the number of nuns in Australia increased from approximately 800 to over 3,000. The number of teaching Brothers increased from 80 to 380. The Sisters would ever remain the majority element in the staffing of Catholic schools. In 1884 in Sydney, there were 78 Brothers and 252 Sisters responsible for 11,000 pupils. By 1911, this had increased to 220 Brothers and 1374 Sisters teaching 24,477 pupils.

Cardinal Moran had set out to establish a Catholic system which would teach everything the State system taught and teach it just as well, plus Religion. His policy which was practical, pragmatic and political, was to put a Catholic primary school in every parish. An editorial in the *Freeman's Journal* in 1885 indicated the laity's belief in the need for Catholic schools to be subjected to 'independent examination' stating the 'Church must know that her schools are up to the mark'. The Second Plenary Council decreed the same Catechism should be used in all Australian dioceses, an order repeated by the Third Plenary Council. Competence in the teaching of Religion was the principal justification for the existence of religious (consecrated) teachers in a separate system.

In 1890, Cardinal Moran introduced his own competitive written exams for all fourth and fifth class students in the diocesan schools. Fourth class was the end of what we now know as primary education and the fifth class was the end of today's junior secondary years. Following this, primary education became more formalised. These diocesan exams had a profound influence by encouraging an excessive emphasis on written examinations and the wide publication of results led to competition within and between teaching orders. Examination success became an important marketing tool and the ability to prepare students for the various examinations was emphasised in advertisements and prospectus. Rewards for successful students were prizes and the most coveted of these was a diocesan scholarship (paid for by the teaching orders themselves) to continue onto secondary school. These would be replaced after 1911 by State bursaries. The diocesan inspector was paid to ensure the curriculum was taught adequately in the parish schools and his report was taken very seriously. Where an order owned their school property, they were independent of diocesan interference. The Parramatta Sisters of Mercy entered students of their day high school in the public examinations in 1889 as soon as their independent school was established.

These decades at the turn of the century saw accelerating change. In Queensland, two institutes, the Christian Brothers and the Sisters of Mercy had had almost monopolistic control of education in the capital Brisbane. Bishop Duhig, appointed co-adjutor in 1912, introduced 13 new teaching orders to Brisbane and oversaw a remarkable building program. The Christian Brothers had opened a boarding school at St Joseph's Nudgee in 1890 and established four other colleges in major Queensland cities. Invited to Bishop Higgin's Rockhampton diocese, the 'Good Sams' arrived at the inland Queensland town of Charters Towers in 1900 to staff a school of 700 children with 30 boarders. The 12 Sisters were all Australian-born and replaced the Sisters of Mercy who had struggled there for 17 years since 1882.

Of the 1000 religious in Australia in 1880, more than half would have been Irish born; there were some French and fewer still were German. The Irish bishops naturally turned to Ireland to provide the teachers they needed so desperately. The Sisters of Mercy were particularly pressured to send women to the Antipodes. It was fortunate that this period of intense recruitment coincided with the revival of Catholicism in Ireland itself and much increased numbers of religious vocations. The next few decades would see an influx of religious teaching orders to answer the bishops' call: Sisters of St Joseph (1880), Sisters of the Sacred Heart (1882), Poor Clares (1883), Daughters of Our Lady of the Sacred Heart (1885), Sisters of Mercy (Parramatta) (1888), Loreto (1892), Dominicans (1894), Brigidines (1901), Marist Sisters (1908), Presentation Sisters (1911) and Ursulines (1929) entered the Sydney diocese to fill the great need there. The speed at which they expanded was outstanding. The Josephites, who began at Penrith in 1880, within five years staffed 27 Sydney schools. There were 65 foundations of Josephites in NSW by 1910 as well as three in the Rockhampton diocese.

Cardinal Moran's Australasian Catholic Congresses of 1900, 1904 and 1909 sponsored the presentation of papers by both lay and religious women. This was indicative of Moran's personal interest and of the bishops in general in the higher education of girls; to them 'the home is the child's first school; its mother its first teacher'. By 1910, there were over 200 Catholic secondary schools for girls in Australia, 96 in NSW, 53 in Victoria, 15 in SA, 22 in WA and Queensland and 4 in Tasmania. By 1890, there were 18 boys' secondary schools in Australia and this number increased to 33 by 1910. The various education acts of this decade would have a 'toning-up' effect on Catholic secondary schools generally.

The *Bursary Endowment Act* of 1912 (NSW) provided bursaries for students in all schools but to be eligible they had to be students entered by a registered school for the Bursary Examination and pass a means test. Candidates had to sit for the Intermediate and Leaving Certificate exams set on prescribed syllabuses and attend schools inspected by government authorities. This Act was to have profound effects particularly on girls' education. An 'English' education designed to train young girls in cultural and feminine skills would no longer suffice. Most of the old congregations like the Dominicans and the Religious of the Sacred Heart saw this as resulting in a uniformity and standardisation which was detrimental to 'true education' but others like the Good Samaritans and the Sisters of Charity embraced the opportunities now offered. All the states passed similar legislation during this time to make more equitable provision for pupils in non-government schools.

The 1905 *Victorian Registration of Teachers and Schools Act* resulted in the founding of teacher-training colleges by religious institutes. An early involvement of the Loreto Sisters who had arrived in Ballarat, Victoria, in 1875, was in teacher-training in Ballarat and then in Melbourne. The Central Catholic Training College established by Archbishop Carr at Albert Park was staffed by Loreto Sisters at his invitation. The Good Samaritans established their own training college at St Scholastica's, Glebe, in Sydney, staffed by 12 Sisters and 12 visiting lecturers. The Sisters of St Joseph also established a teacher-training college at North Sydney in 1913. Both of these institutes had Sisters teaching in Victorian schools.

The 1916 *Public Instruction Act* (amendment) required Catholic schools to be inspected by Department of Education inspectors but the Archdiocese of Sydney retained its own system of priest-inspectors. After World War I, there was a large expansion of secondary education. Outstanding teachers united to launch the Catholic Secondary Schools Association (NSW) which organised annual conferences, seminars and its committees drew up syllabuses. It was 'professional and autonomous'.

In most country towns where there was no Catholic secondary school, the local parish school also provided commercial classes for young people of the district as well as the music universally taught and absolutely vital for financial viability. Catholic primary and secondary schools were a much loved and appreciated element of Australian life outside the major urban centres, part of the local economy and adding to the cultural as well as the spiritual resources of these towns.

Archbishop Sheehan, co-adjutor (1922-1937), had asked for power to establish a state-wide Catholic education authority in NSW. Father J. Thompson was brought from Strawberry Hill College, London and given the title of NSW Director of Catholic Education. He circulated a syllabus for teacher-training but the scheme hardly got off the ground, and when Sheehan resigned in frustration, any reform of teacher-training was stymied and the orders continued to operate their own training arrangements.

In the relatively stable inter-war period, the bishops came closest to the ideal of making a Catholic elementary education available to every Catholic child. In 1910, in Australia, there were 717 parochial schools serving 376 parishes. They were to increase to 1199 schools in 993 parishes by 1940. It was common for a school to begin as an elementary school and in time add on secondary classes mostly to intermediate level.

The new century demanded a new education system; an emerging nation required a more able and flexible workforce, capable of implementing technological change. The Catholic Church, under the enlightened leadership of Cardinal Moran, was also cognisant of these emerging demands. The orders of teaching religious had indicated their willingness to adopt educational reform and their determination to facilitate beneficial changes in the teaching environment, within the scope of funds and personnel. The Christian Brothers opened a technical high school in Paddington in 1903 which existed until 1966. The Marist Brothers were the pioneers in this field operating a technical college at Sydney's Church Hill from 1892 to 1962.

In Victoria, Archbishop Mannix approved the recommendation that religious teachers teaching in the Melbourne Archdiocese be paid a minimum annual stipend of 40 pounds. Compared to the Commonwealth basic wage of 213 pounds per annum then, it was hardly a living wage, and stipends for religious women would remain below that of religious men until the 1960s. Archbishop Mannix established the first state Catholic Education Office in Victoria in 1932. The seventh commandment of the Church (to send Catholic children to Catholic schools) was added after the 1937 Plenary Synod of the Australian bishops, most likely in response to the teaching of Pope Pius X1 in his encyclical *Divini Illius Magistri* (*On Christian Education*, 31 December 1929). It stressed that trained and competent teachers were essential. As a result, in 1931, the bishops of NSW set up a Board of Registration, chaired by Father Thompson. A similar board was established in SA in 1941.

With Australia suffering from economic depression through the 1930s, there were moves to make secondary education more practical in preparing students for employment. In 1937, the Marist Brothers School at St Benedict's Broadway became an Intermediate Technical High School and the Sisters opened St Benedict's Business College. In 1947, both schools were full, with nearly 600 on site although contact between the boys and girls was still kept to a minimum. The Primary Final Examination was introduced that same year; managed by the Catholic Education Office, it was modelled on the NSW State Bursary

Examination, another example of the Catholic system keeping up with public schools. It would be phased out in the late-1960s.

The most rapid population growth since the Gold Rushes saw 100,000 more children enrolled in Australian Catholic schools between 1953 and 1955. It was a result of the post-war 'Baby Boom' plus the beginnings of an influx of migrants. Many of these government-sponsored immigrants were displaced persons from the war in Europe and many of them came from Catholic countries. Governments were encouraging immigration to provide labour for large infrastructure projects like the Snowy Mountains Scheme and economically vital industries like steel making and ship building. In Whyalla SA, between 1956 and 1966, the population trebled and included 59 nationalities as its secondary industries grew.

With the building of the BHP Steelworks at Port Kembla in New South Wales, there was an explosion of numbers in the Catholic schools in the area. A class size at the Good Samaritans' Fairy Meadow school in 1962 was 80 plus. In the kindergarten, there were over 100 pupils, only 10 of whom spoke English. The Cowra Migrant Centre was opened in 1947 to house the families of men employed on jobs across NSW. At the Brigidine Sisters' Cowra primary school, 105 newly-arrived non-English speaking migrants enrolled in 1951. Sisters who had no training in teaching English as a Second Language (this was still to be developed as a discipline), let alone any suitable teaching resources, had to cope with extremely stressful conditions. Every Sunday they conducted outreach work at the centre after Mass, teaching English to the adults as well as the Catechism.

The Soviet Union's launch of Sputnik terrified Western Governments and would directly lead to Federal Government involvement in resourcing Catholic schools. The Australian Labor Party split in 1957 politicised the long-standing Catholic notion of the injustice of no state aid for denominational schools particularly in NSW. In 1958, the Catholic Teachers College (CTC) at North Sydney began the training of female lay teachers to be placed in Catholic primary schools. The Sydney diocesan inspector, Monsignor Slowey, had been a member of the committee chaired by the Director General of Education, Harold Wyndham, which reported in 1957. Slowey was in no doubt that the proposed extension by one year of secondary education in NSW and the mandatory teaching of science and other specialist subjects in the junior secondary years would require many more teachers and resources. These early graduates would be appointed by the Sydney Catholic Education Office, which had been established in 1949. Paid by the parish priest, often these pioneering lay teachers were not paid for the school vacation periods. Initially, at the CTC they were forbidden to speak to the religious trainees and a wall separated the two groups in the lecture room.

In 1960, the cost of Catholic schools was borne almost completely by the Catholic community. In 1963, some 77% of all teachers in NSW Catholic schools were religious and the religious orders could still exert some control over their schools through their leadership positions within their schools. The future of Catholic education had relied on increasing religious vocations. Beyond anyone's imagination was the effect on religious life of the Vatican Council which Pope John XXIII had announced in 1958. Some 50 years later, two-thirds of the schools in the Sydney Archdiocese which were founded by religious congregations were staffed and administered by lay persons. The 1960s would see almost insurmountable obstacles to the continuation of a separate and viable Catholic education system.

Select Bibliography

Barcan, A. *A History of Australian Education*. Melbourne: OUP, 1980.

Campbell, C. and Proctor, H. *A History of Australian Schooling*. Sydney: Allen and Unwin, 2014.

Campion, E. *Rockchoppers: Growing up Catholic in Australia*. Melbourne: Penguin, 1982.

Campion, E. *Australian Catholics: The Contribution of Catholics to the Development of Australian Society*. Melbourne: Viking, 1987.

Canavan, K. *St Benedict's School, Broadway: a history of a Catholic school 1838-2012*. Sydney: Catholic Education Office, 2014.

D'Orsa, J. *Monsignor John Slowey: Servant of Education, Facilitator of Change.* Sydney: Catholic Education Office, 1999.

Duffy, C. J., "What Decided the Direction of Catholic Education in NSW" in *Journal of the Australian Catholic Historical Society*, 7 (1981): 28-34.

Foale, M. T. *The Josephite Story: The Sisters of St Joseph, their foundation and early history 1866-1893.* Sydney: St Joseph's Generalate, 1989.

Foale, M. T. *Never See a Need: The Sisters of St Joseph in South Australia 1866-2010.* Hindmarsh SA: ATF Press, 2016.

Fogarty, R. *Catholic Education in Australia, 1806-1950*, 2 vols., Melbourne: MUP, 1959.

Garaty, J. *Providence Provides: Brigidine Sisters in the New South Wales Province.* Sydney: UNSW Press, 2013.

Hogan, M., *The Sectarian Strand: Religion in Australian History.* Melbourne: Penguin, 1987.

Luttrell, J. *Worth the Struggle: Sydney Catholic Schools 1820-1995.* Sydney: Catholic Education Office, 1996.

Luttrell, J. and Lourey, M. *St Mary's to St Catherine's: Catholic Schools of the Archdiocese of Sydney 1836-2006.* Sydney: Catholic Education Office, 2006.

Mahon, J. 'Lay Teachers in Government-aided Catholic Schools in NSW, 1848-1880' in *Journal of the Australian Catholic Historical Society* 6 (1979): 3-17.

MacGinley, M. R. 'Irish Women Religious and Australian Social History' in *Journal of the Australian Catholic Historical Society* 17 (1996): 56-66.

MacGinley, M. R. 2nd ed., *A Dynamic of Hope: Institutes of Women Religious in Australia*. Darlinghurst: Crossing Press, 2006.

O'Brien, A. *God's Willing Workers: Women and religion in Australia*. Sydney: UNSW Press, 2005.

O'Donoghue, M. X. *Mother Vincent Whitty: Woman and Educator in a Masculine Society*. Melbourne MUP, 1972.

O'Farrell, P. J. *The Catholic Church and Community in Australia: A History*. Melbourne: Nelson, 1977.

Ryan, M. *Foundations of Religious Education in Catholic Schools: An Australian Perspective*. Melbourne: Thompson/Social Science Press, 2005.

Walsh, M. *The Good Sams: Sisters of the Good Samaritan 1857-1969*. Melbourne: John Garratt Publishing, 2001.

Zimmerman, B. *The Making of a Diocese: Maitland, its bishop, priests and people 1866-1909*. Melbourne: MUP, 2000.

BIOGRAPHIES

Ellen Hogan (Sr M. Gabriel op) (1842–1915)

Founder of an education system for the Catholic deaf

Elizabeth Hellwig op

In July 1875, a tiny Irish woman disembarked in Sydney from the Ellora. Ellen Hogan, known as Sister Mary Gabriel, was deaf, but despite her disability, or perhaps because of it, this indomitable lady, then aged 31, was destined for an uncommon greatness. She is remembered with reverence and deep affection as the founder of an education system for the Catholic deaf that would become internationally renowned. She spoke no words, but the power of her communication skills and her ability to hand these on to young people who lived in the-then separate world of the 'deaf and dumb', were her gift. Furthermore, Sr M. Gabriel broke down barriers with hearing people to such an extent that she readily obtained the patronage necessary to create a viable, life-giving institution for those who could not 'speak' for themselves.

Ellen Hogan was born in Dublin in August 1842. Her parents were John Hogan and Mary McMahon. At about age eight, Ellen contracted scarlatina and its high fevers left her profoundly deaf from about 1850. Early years of hearing gave her language on which to build when the spoken word could no longer reach her. Ellen began her schooling at St Mary's Dominican School for the Deaf at Cabra in Dublin on 1 December 1851. She was appointed an assistant teacher in 1856, aged just 13. Two letters survive, written in 1862, attesting to her fine style of writing, both in English and French. She remained at Cabra until 2 October 1864.

Ellen wished to devote her life to God, but deafness seemed too great an obstacle as she could not take part in the liturgical requirements of nuns, nor could she pronounce her vows publicly. Pope Pius IX was consulted, and readily approved of her being accepted. She took vows as Sr M. Gabriel at the hands of Cardinal Cullen of Dublin on 26 August 1867, the first religious Sister with a disability permitted to take solemn vows.

In 1871, Patrick Sullivan, from Rock Forest, approached St Mary's Convent, Maitland NSW. He asked for a Catholic education for his daughter. This was no ordinary request since 12-year-old Catherine was deaf. The 28 Sisters in Maitland were sympathetic and some, having attended high school in Dublin in the neighbourhood of Cabra, were familiar with the Irish one-handed signing as distinct from other versions of signing used in the UK and the USA. They accepted Catherine and immediately wrote to their Sisters in Ireland asking for a trained teacher to be sent to NSW.

When the call came to Cabra in Ireland, Sr M. Gabriel volunteered. On arrival in NSW, she was sent to Star of the Sea Convent, Newcastle, where Catherine, now sixteen, and Elizabeth Rewault, aged ten, awaited her. Numbers grew slowly. Only 30 hearing-impaired students were admitted between 1875-1885. Sr M. Gabriel and her young pupils worked in a small cottage on the property.

By 1886, increasing numbers and limited space required a new school, and a new image. Sr M. Gabriel wrote to Cardinal Moran and asked that he and the bishops take a serious look at the number of Catholic deaf children in the wider community who were not receiving a Catholic education. New pupils arrived from all States and New Zealand. Suitable land was found in Waratah, Newcastle and a beautiful building was erected by the Sisters, fully supported by the Australian Catholic hierarchy. Sister M. Gabriel ran the school, and designed much of the new building, but needed others to be its public face. Sr M. Columba Dwyer joined Sr M. Gabriel in 1889 and was trained by her, alongside other capable deaf students, like Marianne Hanney, an early boarder and great friend.

At that time, education for the deaf had consisted of pure manualism – sign language, fingerspelling, writing and reading. Debate about the best methods had raged throughout the deaf world for many years. In

1880, a congress of teachers of the deaf in Milan decided that all schools for the deaf should use oralism – that is, lip reading, speech reading and writing. Sr M. Gabriel was informed by her bishop in 1892 that a new teacher, Sr M. Mechtilde Corcoran, an Irish Sister, trained in oralism in England, would be joining the staff. In the *Waratah Report* of 1888, Sr M. Gabriel expressed concern and appealed to allow manualism to remain the preferred method in the school. Such was her passion that she expressed a desire to return to Ireland if oralism was introduced. The bishop did not change his mind, writing that he would accept whatever decision she took, and he would pay her fare home if necessary. Sr M. Gabriel stayed with her deaf children. For the next 20 years, speech was taught to some of the children. Oralism was not adopted fully until the 1950s. The arguments about method continue today.

In 1910, Sister Gabriel's general health broke down. Her friend and fellow teacher, Marianne Hanney, remained by her side as nurse and constant companion. Sr M. Gabriel and Marianne travelled to Sydney in 1914 one last time for a reunion with former pupils.

Sr M. Gabriel, surrounded by her sisters, Marianne and other pupil friends, died on 25 November 1915, and was buried in Sandgate Cemetery, Newcastle. She was deeply mourned.

Select Bibliography

Annals of St Mary's Convent Maitland, 1871 (*Maitland Annals*) DAS.

Archives of the Dominican Sisters, Cabra Ireland.

Australasian Catholic Directory.

Burke, J. "The History of Catholic Schooling for Deaf and Dumb Children in the Hunter Valley." MA Thesis, University of Newcastle, 1974. Dominican Archives Strathfield (DAS).

Congregational Register of the Dominican Sisters, DAS.

Congregational Register, Dominican Sisters of Eastern Australia and the Solomon Islands DAS.

Dominican Sisters of Eastern Australia and the Solomon Islands. *Congregational Register*, unpublished manuscript 1867– DAS.

Dominican Sisters of Eastern Australia and the Solomon Islands. Personnel Files, DAS.

Dominican Nuns Maitland. *Report of the Deaf and Dumb Institution*, Waratah, NSW, 1888, 1890, 1901, 1915. DAS.

Dooley, A. *To Be Fully Alive: A Monograph on Australian Dominican Education of Hearing-Impaired Children*, unpublished manuscript, 1990. O'Hanlon, M. Assumpta. *Dominican Pioneers*. Published for the Dominican Nuns Strathfield by the Australasian Publishing Company, Sydney 1949. DAS.

Egan, Sr M. Madeleine. *A History of Catholic Deaf Education in Australia. 1875-1975.*

Monograph published on behalf of the Dominican Sisters, Holy Name Province, Waratah NSW. 1975. DAS.

Moran, Cardinal Patrick. *History of the Catholic Church in Australasia*, (Sydney: Frank Coffee and Company), 1896.

O'Hanlon, Sr M. Assumpta, *Dominican Pioneers in New South Wales*, (Sydney: The Australasian Publishing Company), 1949.

Newcastle Chronicle, 24 June, 1873; 2 September, 1875.

Report of the Deaf and Dumb Institution, Waratah, NSW, 1890.

Mother Alice Anastasia Kennedy pbvm (1876–1960)

Pioneer in Catholic education in Queensland

Sr Marlette Black pbvm (RIP)

Alice Anastasia Kennedy was born in Daylesford, Victoria, on 21 January 1876, the ninth of twelve children born to Laurence Kennedy and Mary Agnes (nee Cummins). Alice's parents – of Tipperary heritage – followed the Irish tradition of naming her after a deceased older sister.

Alice attended St Michael's Daylesford School and from 1892, Holy Cross High School founded by Presentation Sisters, whose foundress, Nano Nagle, believed teaching the poor would enable them to rise out of poverty. While at Holy Cross, Alice successfully competed in the Matriculation Exams for Melbourne University.

Aged 19, Alice entered the Novitiate of the Presentation Congregation at Wagga Wagga on 26 April 1895, taking the name of Sister Ursula. She made her Religious Profession on 13 November 1897. She was one of five volunteers chosen by the Wagga Congregation to found a school in Longreach, Queensland. Arriving there on 13 February 1900, the sisters taught girls and boys of primary age until, in 1902, a building housing Convent, boarding facilities for girls and a high school, was opened. Sr Ursula became Principal Teacher of Our Lady's College.

Sr Ursula believed in respect for the individual and their abilities. Outside evaluations and the gaining of qualifications were seen as useful benchmarks, or as necessary for future employment. In the Primary School, State School Education Department Inspectors visited annually from 1900. From 1902, Sr Ursula entered students for the Junior Public Examinations of Sydney University and from 1911 for the Junior (and later Senior) Public Examinations of Queensland University.

Other students were entered for examinations in Commercial subjects, in Music, Singing, Speech and Drama. Outside school hours, these subjects were made available to the wider community and combined choirs and orchestras of adults and students were trained. Skills in self-discipline and co-operation were developed through drills, gymnastics and team sports.

From 1912, as no other local school offered these opportunities, boys and girls of all denominations were welcome to attend Our Lady's College.

In 1912, Mother Ursula Kennedy was elected Major Superior of the Presentation Sisters in Queensland, continuing in that Office, or that of Mother Assistant, until her death. Staying mainly in Longreach, the Mother House, she continued to teach when possible. Requests for sisters to found schools in city and country areas were received from Queensland bishops and priests. While areas in greatest need were preferred, a response also depended on the number of sisters available.

From 1900 until 1953 (when the Novitiate moved to Manly in Queensland), young women wishing to enter the Queensland Presentation Congregation went to Longreach to receive training for and to experience Religious Life and Class Teaching. While their spiritual training took priority, Mother Ursula and other sisters also tutored them to extend their educational qualifications. After their Profession, Mother Ursula encouraged sisters to continue study until, as part-time or external students, university degrees had been gained. Tutors were arranged for those studying towards Teaching Degrees for Music, Singing, or Speech and Drama; and coaches, or attendance at seminars were arranged when changes to a Syllabus were to be introduced.

As Major Superior, Mother Ursula was attentive to the spiritual needs of sisters, arranging priests for annual retreats, urging faithfulness to the recommended spiritual exercises, keeping or copying by hand articles about Nano Nagle for sharing with the sisters. In the schools, days began with prayer and a half hour daily was devoted to religious instruction.

When Mother Ursula was first elected Major Superior, there were two Presentation foundations in Queensland. At the time of her death in 1960, she had been involved in the establishment of twenty more. Most were Primary Schools but three, similar to Our Lady's College, also catered for secondary students and girl boarders. Mother Ursula ensured that each College was registered as a secondary school where Government Scholarships could be awarded. As Major Superior or Mother Assistant, she visited the sisters and schools annually. As in Longreach, outside evaluations, gaining qualifications and outreach to the wider community were arranged by the sisters.

In the *New Year's Honours List* of 1956, Mother Ursula Kennedy pbvm was awarded the MBE in recognition of her outstanding contribution to education in Queensland. Due to failing health, she did not return to Longreach after 1957, but joined the community of sisters at Herston, moving to St Rita's Convent, Clayfield for the school holidays. After a short stay in hospital, she entered Eternal Life on 14 January 1960. A celebration of the life of Mother Ursula Kennedy pbvm was held in St Stephen's Cathedral, Brisbane, before her burial in Nudgee Cemetery.

Select Bibliography

Barbaro, Anna. *Acorn to Oak*. Clayfield: St Rita's College Ltd, 2006.

Fox, Noela. *A Dangerous Dream*. Wagga Wagga: Triple D Books, 2012.

MacGinley, M. R. *A Place of Springs: the story of the Queensland Presentation Sisters 1900-1960*. Clayfield Qld: Congregation of the Presentation of the Blessed Virgin Mary, 1977.

MacGinley, M. R. *Roads to Sion: Presentation Sisters in Australia 1866-1980*. Brisbane: Boolarong Publications, 1983.

Presentation Sisters Archives, Brisbane.

Annals, Presentation Convent, Clayfield, Queensland.

Annals, Presentation Convent, Longreach, Queensland.

Mary Philomena Douglas fcJ (1897–1958)

Scholar, rigorous educator and visionary leader

Carol Rosenhain

Kathleen Douglas, known in religious life as Mother Mary Philomena Douglas, was born at Richmond, Melbourne, on 10 August 1897. She was the youngest of four surviving children of George Douglas and Kathleen Maud Egan. Her father was a Richmond-based jeweller and watchmaker. Although not a Catholic, he agreed to have his children educated at St Ignatius' Primary School before the three girls attended FCJ Vaucluse Convent. Kathleen Douglas lived within walking distance of one of her childhood friends, Kathleen King, and that saw them united in their desire to embrace a vocation with the fcJ sisters. While Kathleen King entered religious life with her parents' blessing, to be known as Mother Euphemia fcJ, George Douglas strongly opposed his gifted daughter's calling to a life of poverty, chastity and obedience.

Mindful of her adored father's opposition, Kathleen delayed her decision to become a religious until after she had undertaken teachers' training at Central Catholic Teacher Training College at Albert Park. She then consolidated her practical skills over seven years at her primary school *alma mater*, before finally entering the fcJ novitiate at Genazzano in September 1922. After receiving the religious habit at Genazzano, as Sr Mary Philomena, she sailed for Europe via Canada. Sr Mary Philomena then joined the novitiate at Upton Hall, Wirral, Merseyside, where she made her vows on 15 August 1925. Three years later, she renewed her vows at Sainte Anne d'Auray in Brittany, the fourth house opened by the Venerable Marie Madeleine d'Hout. Mary Philomena was the last Australian to be professed there. After a further three years, she became Mother Mary Philomena when she made her final vows at Uccle, Belgium.

As a deeply spiritual person, Mary Philomena delighted in all of the beauties of nature. She loved the gentle drift of the seasons she experienced in Europe, although the environment never replaced her enchantment with the Australian bush. She also delighted in animals, especially horses and dogs. Additionally, the calls and plumage of birds held a real fascination for her.

Apart from her spiritual yearning, Mary Philomena was driven by her profound intellectual curiosity. While in Europe, she seized the opportunity to study at the National University of Ireland, where she obtained First Class Honours in English and French. She undertook further courses at the Sorbonne in Paris and joined fcJ communities at Broadstairs and in Belgium. Upon her return to Australia in 1931, Mother Mary Philomena spent time at Benalla, before taking up an appointment in 1932 as Mistress in Charge of Studies and Boarders at Genazzano fcJ Convent. It was during this period that students came to appreciate the breadth of Mother Mary Philomena's scholarship. For example, it was the custom at that time for boarders to have their outward correspondence checked. Naturally, the girls detested this practice as an invasion of their privacy. One student, whose parents were living in Japan, penned her letter in Japanese, no doubt thinking her letter would escape the censor. When her letter was returned after the routine scrutiny, she must have been shocked to see the Japanese spelling and sentence structure appropriately corrected.

Genazzano began a long period of Mother Mary Philomena's most fruitful apostolate as a rigorous educator and visionary leader. Highly educated and passionate about education for women, she was also young and energetic. Under her direction, the school became more disciplined. Her teaching favoured English in the higher classes, and her own love of literature nurtured a similar passion in her students. She had the poise and knowledge to animate the prose and poetry she regularly read to her classes and was prepared to stimulate contrary viewpoints among her students. High standards were expected of the pupils and she was rarely disappointed.

Her own love of literature was evident in her creative writing. She was a regular contributor to a bi-monthly Catholic school paper called *The Children's World*. Despite her heavy workload, Mother Mary Philomena's contributions flowed regularly during the 1940s and 1950s. Her stories were often stimulated by famous quotes from literature and her imagination cleverly wove the quotations into the material she crafted.

Her inspired teaching and formidable administrative skills made Mother Mary Philomena the logical successor to Mother Gerda Prytz. Accordingly, in 1944, she became Superior of the fcJ community and Principal of Genazzano Convent. Undaunted by the responsibility or workload, over the next fourteen years she began to implement change and growth that would bring Genazzano to the fore as an esteemed academic institution. Her friendship with Julia Flynn, who was the government's Chief Inspector of Education, 1936-1943, cemented her academic aspirations for the school. In 1945, she received permission for Genazzano to set its own Intermediate Examination. When the same permission was granted for the Leaving Examination in 1948, Genazzano was classified as an 'A' school. Later, with the establishment of Commonwealth Scholarships, Mother Mary Philomena Douglas encouraged the introduction of Matriculation subjects. Without fanfare, she was opening up the world for intelligent young women, where a rigorous education became a desired rite of passage. As a consequence, enrolments grew. More students required increased space. It was fortuitous that a property adjacent to the school, Grange Hill, came up for sale under her tenure. This property enabled a Junior School to be established as a separate entity.

Amid her hectic schedule, Mother Mary Philomena Douglas never lost sight of her duty to the fcJ Society. After a war time hiatus, it gave her great joy to re-open the novitiate in Australia in 1945, starting with five postulants. Numbers grew over the next decade. She put the highest ideals before these young women and by constant encouragement urged them on to further efforts. 'She was very honest and very fair, had high ideals, didn't like any sort of scheming, she liked you to be straight', said one of her former novices.

In 1948, she accompanied the Mother Vicar, Dorothy Meagher fcJ, as a delegate to the Chapter in the UK. This was followed by residence at Broadstairs for a period of eighteen months, after which, revitalised, she returned to Genazzano in 1952. As Superior of the Society and Principal of Genazzano, Mother Mary Philomena Douglas carried herself with an air of authority. She commanded attention when she spoke. She was thin and erect in addressing the full assembly of girls who sat in expectant and electric silence. A former student recalled that:

> Mother Philomena Douglas was the greatest influence in our school life. She was a purist, a first-class teacher of Language and Literature, a dedicated and very private person, except in classes, where she opened up to us her love of literature and made us love and know it too. Many girls have regretted that though they admired and respected her, they never really knew or talked to her.

When she was terminally ill in the Mercy Hospital in 1958, Mother Mary Philomena Douglas was surrounded with flowers, letters and cards, all expressing loving wishes of concern for her well-being and recovery. Humble to the end, she could not believe that so many people would have expressed such affection for her. Mother Mary Philomena Douglas entered eternal life on 2 August 1958, just a week before her 61st birthday.

Her passing prompted considerable expressions of grief and prayer from both students and religious societies around Melbourne. A Good Shepherd sister wrote that:

> There are many things I recall about Mother, her kindness, justice, patience, her buoyancy. But above all else it was her spirit of prayer, her awareness of God. In those days I could not define it, but in the light of my years of experience in religion, that is what it was.

Mother Mary Philomena's vibrant contribution to the school ensured that one of the houses is fittingly named 'Douglas House'.

Of greater note is that the hallmark of her own rigorous intellect, is stamped in the sustained academic excellence that Genazzano fcJ College inspires in its staff and students.

Select Bibliography

Bell, Maria fcJ (ed.). *And the Spirit Lingers: Genazzano – One Hundred Years 1889-1989*. Melbourne: Genazzano College History Committee, 1988.

King, Mother Euphemia fcJ. *Personal Recollections*. Melbourne: FCJ Archives. Richmond, 1986.

O'Connor, Clare fcJ. *The Sisters, Faithful Companions of Jesus in Australia*. Melbourne: H.H. Stephenson, 1982.

Ryan, Aileen fcJ. (ed.). *Some Stories of Valiant Women. FCJ Sisters Who Lived in Australia Since 1882*. Melbourne: FCJ Archives Richmond, 2018.

Mother Mary Benignus Fitzgerald RSM
(Elizabeth Fitzgerald 1890–1946)

Beloved educationist inspiring generations

Sr Gabrielle Foley RSM

Elizabeth Fitzgerald was born in March 1890. She was the daughter of John and Mary Anne (Connors). She lived at "Huntsgrove", Manilla, a property which is now under the water of Keepit Dam.

In 1902, Elizabeth became a boarder at St Mary's College, Gunnedah, where she completed her secondary education:

> Enshrined in the memory of those associated with her in her schooldays (at St Mary's) is a quiet picture of a most loveable character whose innate honesty and personal charm endeared her to all. It was no surprise to her teachers that she chose to spend her life as a "Bride of Christ."[27]

Elizabeth entered the Gunnedah Congregation of the Sisters of Mercy in 1908 and was professed in 1912, receiving the name Sr M. Benignus. Her connection with St Mary's College spanned a period of forty-four years as a student, teacher, Principal and Mother Superior of the Sisters of Mercy Congregation. She was the first Gunnedah Sister of Mercy to obtain a University Degree, graduating in Arts with Merit from the Queensland University in 1926.

Mother M. Benignus wrote the words of the College Song, "St Mary's of the Plains" in English, French and Latin. The song is still relevant

---

[27] Mother Mary Benignus. A contributed Statement 1 August 1946. St. Joseph's Parish Archives, Gunnedah.

today and at Reunions it is sung with great gusto. She edited the first College Magazine in 1925 and was Principal of the College from 1934 to 1940 and again from 1942 to 1943.

Mother M. Benignus' promotion of the humanities at the College inspired many students with a life-long love of literature and foreign languages. Many were prepared for leadership in civic life by her tuition in public speaking and debating. She was highly regarded in the civic community as a teacher of speech and dramatic art.

The Library of St Mary's College is a memorial to Mother Mary Benignus Fitzgerald, a gentle administrator and brilliant educationist who loved the students and whose noble life and love of learning provided many young people with a role model for their adult lives. Mother Mary Benignus was Mother Superior of the Gunnedah Congregation from 1934 to 1940:

> As Superior of many Convents in the Diocese she was largely responsible for the success of the Institute. Her maternal kindness was strikingly evident, and a tangible proof was the building of an Infirmary for the Sisters during her Term of Office.[28]

Mother M. Benignus was stricken with rheumatoid arthritis for the last few years of her life and she died in July 1946 at the age of 56.

Bishop Coleman presided and preached the Panegyric at the Solemn Requiem Mass celebrated by Monsignor John McDermott. Sixteen priests of the diocese attended the Mass. Burial took place in the Convent Cemetery which has been surrounded by several buildings built at the College since her death.

---

[28] Carney, Judith RSM "That They May Have Life, Life to the Full" (John 10:10) Biographies of Deceased Sisters of Mercy of Gunnedah Congregation 1896–2007.

Select Bibliography

Catholic Weekly, "Obituary". Mother Benignus, 5 September 1946.

Campbell, T. W. "Nuns in the Diocese of Armidale 1890 to 1940". A paper read before the Australian Historical Society Sydney, 8 April 2001.

Campbell, T. W. "The History of the Sisters of Mercy in education in the Diocese of Armidale".

St Mary's College Gunnedah Magazine 1927.

St Mary's College Gunnedah Golden Jubilee Magazine 1879 – 1929.

Carney, J. M. RSM *St Mary's College, Gunnedah: A Profile of the First hundred Years 1879 – 1979*, Gunnedah Congregation of the Sisters of Mercy and St Mary's College 2007, National Library IBSN 9780646473260.

Monsignor John Thomas McMahon OBE (1893-1989)

'Remarkable cleric of all trades'

Damian Gleeson

Eminent historian Patrick O'Farrell aptly described West Australian John McMahon as a 'remarkable cleric of all trades'. In addition to his main role as the first Diocesan Inspector of Catholic Schools and later Director of Catholic Education in Western Australia, McMahon was a prolific writer, highly respected parish priest for nearly half a century and founder of innovative education programs for students living in rural and remote areas such as the Bushies Scheme. This prominent educationalist also took the lead role in enabling Australian women to enter postgraduate studies in social services.

Born on 13 December 1893 at the family home in Jail Street (renamed O'Connell Street in 1911) Ennis, County Clare, John Thomas McMahon was one of eight children of Thomas Joseph (1847-1910) and Kate (nee Costello) McMahon (1857-1940) who had married at the Chapel of the Immaculate Conception, Limerick, in 1883. Both parents came from respectable small business families that also had strong church ties. John's uncle was the highly respected Monsignor John McMahon (1845-1932), Parish Priest of Nenagh and Vicar General of the Diocese of Killaloe; cousins on his mother's side included Archbishop Patrick Clune of Perth and John Aloysius Costello who would become a future *Taoiseach* (prime minister) of Ireland (1948-51; 1954-57).

Young John attended school at Ennis and then, indicative of his family's social class, progressed to the Vincentian-run St Vincent's College, Castleknock in Dublin. A gifted student, he went on to University College Dublin where he completed a Bachelor of Arts (1915), a Higher Education Diploma (1917) and a Master of Arts (1920). Concurrently, McMahon attended All Hallows College, Dublin, and was ordained a priest on 22 June 1919. His first task was pivotal – being Clune's secretary while the Australian archbishop acted as an intermediary during the Irish War of Independence (1920). Before leaving Ireland, family and friends gave the young priest a 'wallet of Treasury Notes'. Upon arrival in February 1921, McMahon was appointed to the cathedral staff, which included chaplaincy of Perth Hospital, and in 1922 he was made diocesan inspector of Catholic schools. The latter position, extensive in policy terms and geographically, transcended into McMahon becoming the first director of Catholic education in 1941, a position he held until 1950.

In the 1920s, Western Australia was fertile territory for this energetic young priest, who with his archbishop's full support, travelled the vast state, visiting families and schools in remote settlements. Conscious of educating young children and the pastoral needs of their parents, he established 'Religion by Post' (1923), which provided catechism and support to children living in isolated communities. In an Australian-first, McMahon founded the Cottesloe Summer School (1925) – *The Bushies Scheme* – which brought children from many parts of the state together for a summer holiday near the sea. The scheme was 'transplanted' across Australia and to the United States, Canada, South Africa and New Zealand. McMahon later wrote:

> My experience is that country children are hungry for the 'good news' and made rapid progress when the summer schools camps were held in every country parish for the religious formation of the 'bushies'.

In 1926, Clune approved McMahon doing further studies. McMahon's undertook doctoral research at Columbia University and the Catholic University of America, and also in Ireland. In Washington, he met the inspirational Agnes Regan, a prominent laywoman associated with the National Catholic School of Social Service (NCSSS). Regan arranged for McMahon to visit facilities providing services for people with disabilities, including the renowned Vineland Training Centre in New Jersey, an institution for intellectually disabled boys. McMahon completed his PhD in religious education through the National

University of Ireland and upon return to Perth in 1928 was appointed editor of *The Record*.

McMahon's American field studies had a profound influence on him. So, too, did Dr Ethel Stoneman, director of the West Australian State Psychology Clinic. Stoneman's visionary ideas for caring for delinquent children – which attracted considerable criticism from an unusual alliance of academics and Catholic religious orders – nevertheless impressed McMahon and Clune, and in 1929 the clerics established Castledare, a large estate with cottage homes for 'mentally deficient' boys. The Christian Brothers operated the home with McMahon as director. The latter envisaged ongoing research into the education and psychological needs of young males. However, the Christian Brothers, never strong advocates of *Castledare*, had other intentions. A senior Christian brother criticised Stoneman's influence over McMahon and Clune:

> What a pity psychology faddists and inexperienced teachers have been allowed to foist such a scheme upon the Archbishop and the Brothers! Miss Stoneham [sic] – the prime mover – was supposed to hold an important government position. His Grace and Dr McMahon placed great confidence in her.

In the broader area of social services, McMahon 'talked enthusiastically about the NCSSS at meetings of the Newman Society' at the University of Western Australia (UWA) and urged students to consider postgraduate studies in social service. Three outstanding graduates – Norma Parker, Constance Moffit and Eileen Davidson – secured, through McMahon's American contacts, scholarships to take masters' degrees in Washington. The women returned to Australia in the 1930s as the country's first professionally trained social workers and successfully convinced a fairly unimaginative church to establish diocesan welfare bureaux – now called CatholicCare – in Melbourne (1935), Sydney (1941), and Adelaide (1942).

At a tertiary education level, McMahon was heavily involved at UWA for many decades. He transformed the fairly low profile of Catholics by founding a Newman Society in 1924. His vision finally was realised with the establishment of St Thomas More residential college in 1955 and two decades later the college named its library after him. McMahon was ecumenical in nature, which attracted many academic supporters and friends. He has the distinction of being the first Australian priest to sit on a University Senate, a position he served with distinction for twenty-seven years.

In 1932, McMahon was appointed parish priest at St Columba's, South Perth, a position he held for forty-seven years before retiring in 1979. In 1946, Pope Pius XII created him a domestic prelate. In 1961, the University of Western Australia conferred on him an honorary D.Litt. McMahon had been a foundation member (1960) of the Australian College of Education and was elected a fellow in 1962. In 1970, he was awarded an OBE.

In addition to being a newspaper editor, he authored more than thirty books. He is remembered for his scholarship, Irish humour and pastoral commitment to parishioners. Monsignor John Thomas McMahon died on 19 January 1989 at Subiaco and was buried in Karrakatta cemetery, Western Australia.

Select Publications

"Religion by Post", *The Australasian Catholic Record*, vol. 1, no 3, 1924.

The 'bushies' scheme in Western Australia: an attempt to face the problem of the isolated Catholic Homestead (Perth, 1927).

The Perth Plan for teaching religion by correspondence, Dublin: Browne & Nolan Limited 1928.

"Castledare: Training for 'Sub-Normals'", *The West Australian*, 16 March 1929.

The child in the Bush: religious holiday schools, Sydney, 1936.

A Little Harvest(Perth, 1944).

One Hundred Years: Five Great Church Leaders, Perth, 1946.

Parish and Pastor: a double diamond jubilee celebration, Perth, 1979.

Select Bibliography

Bourke, D. F. *The History of the Catholic Church in Western Australia*, Perth, 1979.

Freeman's Journal (Dublin), 1921.

Gleeson, D. J. "The Professionalisation of Australian Catholic Social Welfare, 1920-1985", PhD Thesis, November 2006.

Irish Times, 1932.

McMahon collection, Archives of the Roman Catholic Archdiocese of Perth.

Mulcahy, C. "McMahon, John Thomas (1893-1989)", *Australian Dictionary of Biography*, Vol. 18. 2012.

O'Farrell, P. *The Catholic Church and Community: An Australian History*, Fourth Revised Edition, Kensington: NSW University Press, 2000.

Parker Brown, N & Davidson, E. "A Tribute to the memory of Monsignor John McMahon, Some reflections on his influence in the early development of Professional Social Work in Australia", 18 February 1989. Archives of the archdiocese of Perth. Unpublished.

Mona Margaret Griffin
(Mother Mary Xavier osu) (1897–1985)

Gifted educator with a flair for literature and the creative

Maree Byron osu and Mel Williams osu

Mona Margaret Griffin, known by her religious name Mother Xavier, was born in Tenterfield, northern NSW on 4 September 1897. She was the second eldest of seven children of James Griffin, a first generation Australian of Tipperary stock and Phoebe Gertrude (nee McDonald) of Dublin heritage. Mona began her schooling in the small state school of Glencoe before attending Catholic schools in Wee Waa (where her father held a publican's licence), Quirindi and Redfern.

Mona attended St Ursula's College, Armidale, for her secondary education and in February 1929 followed her younger sister, Molly, into the Ursuline Order at Armidale. Mother Xavier made her Final Profession on 21 October 1934 and completed her Certificate of Registration, Catholic Primary Teachers of NSW in June 1935. Mother Xavier specialised in speech and drama as well as primary classes in her early career, but after her return to Armidale from Ashbury in 1953, she taught English and History to St Ursula's High School students and was the school's principal in 1954-1955. She then moved to Toowoomba and served as principal, 1956-1965.

Mother Xavier was not tall and, although quite portly, she moved with a silent, slow grace that conveyed a certain calm. Her greatest significance was in thinking and attitudes. The authors, who were her students, recall that she had no time for the minutiae of rules to do with either religious life or the education of young women. Her entry into the Ursulines at the 'mature' age of 32 may have contributed to an ability to see the larger picture and have a different sense of proportion.

This sense of proportion was invaluable for her students because she not only conveyed a strong and particular belief in who they were but seemed to see who they could become. When they did not always live up to this belief, Mother Xavier expressed her disappointment but was quick to forgive.

Mother Xavier was a gifted formator and educator. She had a vast and interesting knowledge of literature and history and she made it real and alive for her students. There was nothing bookish about this learning. She could draw her pupils into an understanding of the characters and situations of her subjects where opinions could be formed and enlightened discussion take place. Perhaps it was her understanding of human nature that made her historical characters such real people to her students. Again, as former students, the authors recall that she was also most creative in her approach. Who could forget the causes of the Second World War being presented as different clothes strung out on a washing line?

Pageants, written and produced by Mother Xavier, were a feature of education and entertainment wherever she taught. These were usually written in rhyming verse, presented in collaboration with the music teachers and involved as many of the students as possible. They were not only visually and aurally beautiful productions but didactic in nature, deepening both the knowledge and faith of all who participated. Another feature of her teaching was the ongoing speech work she did with individual pupils who excelled under her tutelage, gaining excellent results in yearly *Australian Music Examination Board* (AMEB) exams.

Perhaps one of the secrets of this great educator was the charism of the Ursulines, handed down to them by their Foundress, Angela Merici, with the advice 'the more you respect them, the more you will love them; the more you love them, the more you will care for and watch over them'. This respect for the individual was beautifully exemplified by the fact that, as Principal of the school, Mother Xavier wrote a poem for each girl on her birthday. She did this in the short time between Mass and breakfast. The poems were so accurate and loving that each one knew she was known and valued. These insightful offerings were not confined to her young charges as Mother Xavier also wrote short narratives for each of her Ursuline sisters using a particular flower as a symbol of the character of each. The strengths and weaknesses of the sister were beautifully and respectfully drawn and must have been instrumental in both the growth of the individual and the building up of understanding and respect within the religious community.

Mother Xavier died peacefully in Armidale aged 88 on 2 December 1985 and was buried in the Catholic Cemetery, Armidale.

Select Bibliography

Student recollection by authors: memories of Sisters Mel Williams and Maree Byron, students at St Ursula's College Armidale 1953-1957 and 1953-1958 respectively.

Saint Angela Merici, *Writings Rule, Counsels, Testament,* Counsels addressed to the leaders, Prologue n10. Earliest known Italian Texts and Translation by a team of Ursulines of the Roman Union (Rome 1995).

http://www.australianursulines.org.au/our-community-involvement/latest-news/108-from-the-archives-memories-of-mother-xavier

Loretta Marie Slattery (Sr Clare sgs) (1900–1980)

Visionary Catholic educator

Elizabeth Murray sgs

Loretta Marie Slattery, a visionary Catholic educator, was born on 10 September 1900 at North Carlton, Melbourne, the eldest of seven children of John Thomas Slattery and Ellen Margaret (née Timothee). Educated by the Sisters of the Good Samaritan at St Brigid's, North Fitzroy, and Santa Maria College, South Yarra, Loretta (known as 'Marie') was, according to her family, the first girl from a Catholic school to be granted a University Government Scholarship to Melbourne University. However, this was insufficient for her parents to support her at the University, so Marie joined the Victorian Education Department and taught at the Napier Street State School, Melbourne. A transfer to the country caused her to resign her teaching post and accept a Commonwealth Public Service position as telephonist at Northcote.

In 1922, Marie entered the Good Samaritan Sisters at Randwick and was given the name of Sister Mary Clare. She was professed in 1925 and the same year was appointed to the teaching staff of St Scholastica's College, Glebe, where she showed her dedication to preparing young women to take their place with confidence in the modern world. Combining study with her teaching, she graduated from Sydney University with a B.A. (Honours) in English Literature and the Diploma in Education, then later a Master's Degree (English Literature). While still teaching at the College, in 1936, Clare was appointed Assistant Mistress of Method at St Scholastica's Teachers' College, a training college registered with the Victorian Education Department and responsible for the training of the junior Sisters in primary and sub-primary teaching. Then, from 1947 to 1959, this short, rather stocky, but dynamic, inspirational woman (lovingly nicknamed 'Boots' because of her manner of walking) held the role of Principal of the Teachers' College.

An early supporter of the Catholic Secondary Schools Association, Sr Clare was on the committee for the Annual Conference of Catholic Teachers in the Archdiocese of Sydney, and one of the organisers of the Conference of Catholic Teachers of Religion in 1957. She was also on the Advisory Board of the ABC's School Programme (English section), and a promoter of the development of efficient school libraries. In 1955, at the first Congress of Religious Sisters from Australia, New Zealand and Oceania, Clare delivered a paper entitled 'Catholic Primary Education in Australia,' in which she looked at current problems in education with a deep understanding, and recommended steps to be taken for the future. In 1957, Clare addressed the Second Congress with the paper, 'The Problem of Overwork,' in which she highlighted the developing crisis in education due to a rapid post-war increase in population, with the real threat both to standards of excellence in schools and to the health and well-being of individual religious and hence, community life. That same year was the Congregation's centenary, and Clare, as its official historian, had written the story of the Institute, entitled, *The Wheeling Years: Sisters of the Good Samaritan 1857-1957.*

In 1959, Archbishop Eris O'Brien of Canberra-Goulburn embarked on a unique and daring plan to offset the need for girls' secondary education in Canberra: staff a new school with religious from a number of different religious institutes. At his request Sr Clare was released from her Training College duties to be the school's founding principal. With her outstanding natural leadership and genius for personal relationships, this diverse group of teachers was moulded into a community that worked and faced challenges together. In 1965, a second school was founded along similar lines at Griffith, and Sr Clare was also asked to be its first principal. She continued in this role until ill health necessitated her retirement to Polding Villa, Glebe, in 1976.

Sr Clare's life-long dedication to education did not go unrecognised, however, and in 1960, she became the first religious in Canberra to be invited to become a member of the Australian College of Education;

in 1968, she was awarded an MBE in the Queen's Honours list for her services to education. A further award in 1977 was Her Majesty's Silver Jubilee Medal.

In her later years, Clare was more and more crippled with arthritis, till finally, she was unable even to turn the pages of a book. There, at Glebe, this kindly, compassionate, far-sighted yet ever-practical woman, died peacefully on 18 October 1980.

Writings

Slattery, C. *The Wheeling Years: Sisters of the Good Samaritan 1857-1957*.

Select Bibliography

Archive, Good Samaritan, Glebe, D43, File 623.

Kelleher, M, sgs. *Annals of the Sisters of the Good Samaritan of the Order of St Benedict. Vol II, 1938-1949*, 2010.

Kelleher, M, sgs. *Annals of the Sisters of the Good Samaritan of the Order of St Benedict. Vol III, 1950-1959*, 2010.

McKinlay, Sr M. Peter Damian, SGS. "Sister Mary Clare Slattery SGS." *Tjurunga: An Australian Benedictine Review*, no. 63, December 2002, 47-72.

Walsh, M. *The Good Sams: Sisters of the Good Samaritan 1857-1969*. Mulgrave, Victoria: John Garratt, 2001.

William John Graham msc (Fr 'Bill' Graham) (1912–1966)

Priest, sportsman, teacher and sports master

Seamus O'Grady with James Littleton msc

Known to his confreres as Bill, William John Graham was one of the most vibrant personalities ever involved in MSC Education. His untimely death at the age of 54 from a road accident in 1966 robbed students and past students of Downlands College, Toowoomba, of a priest, father and friend.

Bill Graham was born on 15 October 1912 at Lithgow, NSW. His father was John Patrick Graham. His mother was Annie (possibly short for Hannah) Graham (Morgan). Young William received his early education with the Sisters of St Joseph, Penrith, before winning a bursary to attend St Joseph's College, Hunters Hill, for his secondary studies. At "Joeys", he emerged as an outstanding cricketer and good footballer while not neglecting his studies. Destined for a promising professional and sporting career, he came to know and admire Father Eric Dignam msc. This led to his decision to join the Missionaries of the Sacred Heart.

On 24 January 1931, he entered St Mary's Towers, Douglas Park, to begin his formation as an MSC priest. He was keen to become a foreign missionary and, throughout the years of his theological training, he attended courses at Sydney University's School of Tropical Medicine. Instead of the missions, however, his life as a priest would be spent at Downlands for a career in the education of youth.

Ordained a priest in St Mary's Cathedral, Sydney, on 30 November 1937, he was posted to Downlands as a teacher of mathematics and sports coach. In the next five years there, he earned recognition and acclaim within and beyond the walls of the college.

A year as curate in the parish of Camp Hill, Brisbane, was followed by another in the parish of Randwick in Sydney where he was given care of an area which included the Home for the Aged conducted by the Little Sisters of the Poor. He later confided that it was with these old people he had spent the most consoling year of his ministry. In 1945, Bill returned to Downlands for the remainder of his career in education.

Perhaps typically of maths teachers, he set and demanded an exorbitant amount of homework, the cause of some exasperation to his colleague teachers. He always completed the course twice over and his excellent examination results were over-weighted with A passes.

He was a highly-regarded and much-loved coach. He skilfully guided the destiny of the First XV and First XI teams, besides acting as unofficial coach of any team he happened to meet in transit. A keenly competitive sports master himself, he was the friend and even confidant of opposing sports masters.

For many years, he was the president and life-blood of the Darling Downs Secondary Schools Sporting Association. In 1962, his work in developing Queensland sporting talent was given official recognition when he was presented with a life-membership badge of the Queensland Rugby Union.

Bill's compulsive loud laugh and occasional gaucheries complemented his warm, generous nature. He had the ability to 'break the ice' among guests at formal functions by his outlandish remarks such as 'Where did you get that hat?' In some ways, he seemed like an old-time Australian larrikin.

In 1942, the Australian Army, expecting an influx of war casualties, requisitioned the college for a military hospital. A temporary home was found at Dalby, a town in the western plains, 80 kilometres from Downlands, where two hotels, a boarding house and a maternity hospital were leased. The exodus of students, staff and equipment was a monumental effort, led by Father Bill Graham.

As recorded in the Downlands Archives:

> The driving force, overseer, head ganger, foreman, urger, producer and Director of this change-over was the Rev.

Fr Graham. He will be remembered by many for his fine achievements he has done for Downlands; but surely he excelled himself when he controlled, supervised and so magnificently accomplished this switch.

The town Dalby will always be linked to the name of Bill Graham. It was in late November 1966, when he was driving through Dalby to officiate at the marriage of a past student, that he received fatal head injuries as a result of a collision at an intersection.

In the following year, the Rector of Downlands reported in the Downlands College magazine that in 1967 Toowoomba Grammar School presented Downlands at its Speech Night with the Father Graham Memorial Trophy for Athletics to honour his memory – a rare gesture from one school to another to honour the sportsmaster of a rival college.

The guest of honour, Duncan Thompson, told the audience that the great Australian cricketer, Stan McCabe, a fellow student of Graham at "Joeys," had told him that Bill Graham was one of Australia's outstanding batting hopes. When Duncan first met Fr Graham at Downlands and saw his ability, he felt sure that Father's choice of 'the cloth' over 'the blazer' had been wrong. He concluded:

> After 25 years of association and personal friendship and having witnessed Father's generosity towards thousands of boys at Downlands and elsewhere, I am now convinced that his preference for the humility of 'the cloth' rather than the passing glory of 'the blazer' had been a magnificent choice.

Father William Graham is buried in Toowoomba, Queensland.

Select Bibliography

"Hard Labour for Life", an unpublished autobiography of L. G. Mahony, 147, *Downlands Archives*.

"Rector's Report", College Magazine, 1967.

Fortes, Downlands Past Students Union Quarterly, Sept. 1967, 11.

Johnston, Chilla, "Evan Whitton's long association with college," Chronicle, Toowoomba, 3 August 2018, https://www.pressreader.com/ australia/the-chronicle-8992/ 20180803/283583811202301

Littleton, James msc, *Saints & Scholars, Some Remarkable MSC*, Coogee: MSC Publishing, 2016.

Mooney, J. F. msc, *Downlands. The first Fifty years 1931-1981*, Toowoomba: Downlands College, 1981.

"MSC buried in Toowoomba" MSC Website Published: Thursday, 14 February 2019 https://www.misacor.org.au/index.php/e-magazine/latest-news/2906-msc-buried-in-toowoomba

Lawrence George Carmody
(Br Aloysius Meldan fsc) (1916–1981)

Teacher, Administrator, National and International Leader

Damian Gleeson

It is a salient indicator of a person's future leadership qualities that although they may not succeed at first – often due to a combination of intrinsic and exogenous factors – their resilience shines through and they progress to a successful career. This description might sum up the life of prominent educationalist, Br Aloysius Carmody fsc. Having failed his first attempt at the Leaving Certificate, he subsequently passed, became a teacher and education administrator, and made significant contributions to educational policies within the De La Salle Institute – nationally and internationally – and later at the Federal Catholic Education Office (FCEO) and the National Catholic Education Commission (NCEC).

Lawrence (Larry) George Carmody, born on 1 July 1916 in Malvern, Victoria, was the eldest of five children of Thomas James Carmody (1892-1955) from an Irish-Australian heritage and Elsie Annie Ramsay (1892-1969) from a Warrnambool staunch Methodist family. Elsie's conversion at the marriage, sadly led to both families boycotting the ceremony. Such was the sectarian stain.

The eldest of five siblings, Larry was named after an uncle killed in World War One. When Larry was three months old, his father joined the war effort as a mechanic in the 3rd Squadron Australian Flying Corps. Upon his return in late October 1919, Thomas Carmody was awarded the Meritorious Service Medal and Bar for bravery, although, like many returned soldiers, he shunned the limelight or discussing the war. Larry's siblings included his equally distinguished brother, (Sir) Alan Carmody (1920-1978) whose reformist senior roles in the

Commonwealth Government, including being secretary of the Prime Minister's Department under Malcolm Fraser, and a younger sister, Joan (Sr Loyola osu).

Larry was educated, initially, by the Brigidine Sisters at Malvern, before moving in 1924 to the De La Salle Brothers' school at Stanhope Street, which marked the start of his lifeline association with the Institute. As the eldest in a poor family, Larry's family commitments may have interfered with his otherwise generally-good aptitude. He struggled especially in maths, though he had a singular purpose, that being a religious vocation. When Larry sought to join the Institute at the tender age of 14, his father, who deeply valued Catholic education for all his children, disallowed this, mindful that a man should be 21 before making such a decision. An accompanying factor was his mother's reluctance, influenced to a large extent by her family. Larry sat for the Leaving Certificate in 1932 but failed. His 'unhappiness' and persistence wore down his father and in March 1933, at the age of 16, he was allowed to join the De La Salle Institute at Cootamundra (NSW), where he received the name Br Aloysius Meldan.

It was a momentous decision as the family was losing an eligible bread-winner at the depths of the Great Depression when Thomas Carmody had intermittent employment and it also reignited religious differences with his mother's relatives who were deeply unhappy that Larry had chosen this path. It took three decades, and Aloysius' public relations' skills, before some reconciliation occurred. Also, in 1933, employment attracted the Carmody family to Canberra: when the gifted Alan won a bursary to the (then) St Patrick's College, Goulburn, Thomas took out more loans so that the other two male siblings – Thomas junior and Frank – could attend likewise on an equal footing.

In 1934, Larry moved to the De La Salle Scholasticate at Castle Hill (NSW), where he passed the Leaving Certificate and matriculated for the University of Sydney. Aloysius was appointed a teacher at De La Salle College, Armidale, in 1935. When the University College of New England (now the University of New England), then affiliated with Sydney University, opened in 1939, Aloysius was amongst the first intake of students. He graduated with a Bachelor of Arts (1942) and was the first non-government employee to obtain a Diploma in Education from Armidale Teachers' College (1943). Back in Sydney, he was appointed Director of Scholastics at the De La Salle Training College (1943-1944), before being appointed a science teacher and vice-president of St Bernard's College, Katoomba in 1945. Concurrently, Aloysius continued studying and was awarded a Master of Arts Degree in Education from the University of Sydney (1945) for a thesis on 'Lasallian Pedagogy' – a study of the contribution of the founder of the Brothers of the Christians Schools, St John Baptist De La Salle, to educational theory and practice.

In 1946, still at a relatively young age, Aloysius was appointed Principal of De La Salle College, Marrickville, then the Institute's largest Sydney school with 700 students. In 1951, he was appointed to the principal's position at Ashfield. In addition to these large operational responsibilities, he engaged widely in the educational sphere being a foundation member (1959) and then Fellow (1964) of the Australian College of Education, and President of both the Catholic Secondary Schools' Association (1947-1949) and the Catholic Science Teachers' Association (1950-1952). Aloysius, a gifted poet and writer, also produced the Institute's history for the 1956 Golden Jubilee celebrations of the Brothers' arrival in Australia.

The ongoing development of the Castle Hill Scholasticate under Aloysius' directorship (1953-1964) paved the way for this campus becoming part of the Catholic College of Education, Castle Hill Campus in 1982.

In 1964, Aloysius was appointed to Rome as sub-director of the International Spirituality Centre of the De La Salle Brothers. Aloysius attended the De La Salle Institute's general chapter in 1966 as an invited specialist in education and catechists. The chapter elected him as Assistant to the Superior-General and Secretary-General of the Institute, positions he held until 1976. Aloysius transformed the previously low-scale secretary-general role and established an Education Bureau – the De La Salle Central Education Office – and became a board member of the International Catholic Education Office, Brussels. He travelled widely and frequently and was the charismatic public face of the Institute in many countries. Before his appointment ended, he did a 'debriefing tour'. Perhaps no other De La Salle brother had built up the extensive networks within and outside his own order.

Sr Loyola and the Australian brothers, however, were worried about how Aloysius might settle back into Australia. Aloysius, in his PR style, told them not to worry, but it was an issue for someone with such extensive networks. An appointment in Sydney was fraught with internal politics. Aloysius received an offer from Melbourne after the quietly-spoken but clever Archbishop James Carroll took up the matter:

> I have devised a plan which after consultation with our mutual friend [Br Ambrose Payne fsc] at Castle Hill, seemed to provide just the situation in which your rich experience could have been the ideal remedy for certain deficiencies in the local scene.

Carroll's plan involved Aloysius being appointed to the fledgling Victorian Catholic Education Commission working with Fr Frank Martin (also profiled in this publication). However, after less than a year, Aloysius felt his Melbourne role as an 'animator and facilitator' had not extended him. With Monsignor James Bourke, the FCEO foundation Director and NCEC executive secretary intending to return to his native Perth, Archbishop Carroll and Bishop Frank Carroll (NCEC Chair) negotiated for Aloysius to succeed him. Aloysius' enthusiasm and organising ability were again pivotal, and he was at ease mixing with government and challenging negative attitudes towards the Catholic sector. Aloysius publicly articulated the need for appropriate funding for Catholic schools. In one contribution to the Canberra Times, he concluded:

> As for people waxing 'lyrical and sanctimonious' about parents sacrificing to send their children to private schools, "he jests at scars that never felt a wound" (*Romeo and Juliet*, Act II, scene 2). The depth to which parents are prepared to reach into their pockets voluntarily is at least some indication of their convictions.

Cardiac disease had led to the early deaths of his three brothers. Aloysius enjoyed good health until 1977 when he experienced a mild heart attack. This did not dent his resilience. However, in 1981 Aloysius suffered two serious heart attacks. He was hospitalised only for a short time, and at the age of 65, he died at Canberra's Calvary Hospital on 23 August 1981.

A very large funeral befitted this significant educationalist at the Castle Hill parish church. Archbishop James Carroll, Bishops Bede Heather and William Murray, a former Marrickville student of Br Aloysius, were among the many officiating clerics. Accolades and condolences came from teachers, numerous religious orders across Australia and virtually all international districts of the De La Salle Institute. Archbishop James Gleeson of Adelaide remarked on the 'wonderful contribution Aloysius was able to make to the educational apostolate of the Church in Australia and beyond'. In his condolence to the *Brother Visitor*, the noted Christian Brother educationalist, Br Athanasius McGlade cfc wrote that Aloysius had 'a distinguished and illustrious career in your congregation and in Catholic education'. Aloysius' last remaining sibling, Sr Loyola reflected:

> I am glad I was not in Canberra [when he died]. If I had been there he would have been concerned for me, whereas as it was he seems to have had that last day as a time of preparation. To me he was always a loving big brother, but there was always a certain detachment. Although I have realised that his life had a great deal to do with my own vocation, his death has been the means of a deep renewal.

Aloysius Carmody – teacher, administrator, leader – a truly stellar career.

Publications by Br Aloysius

Our Apostolate (editor), 1953-1964.

The De La Salle Brothers in Australia 1906-1956 (Sydney, 1956).

Second National Catholic Education Conference, John 23 College, ANU, May 4-8, 1980 (National Catholic Education Conference, Canberra, 1980).

Aboriginal or Torres Strait Islander enrolments in Catholic schools (National Catholic Education Commission, Canberra, 1981).

Select Bibliography

Canberra Times, 5 October 1977; 25 February 1981, 26 August 1981.

Catholic Weekly, 16 August 1945.

Hyslop, R. 'Carmody, Sir Alan Thomas (1920-1978)', *Australian Dictionary of Biography*, Vol 13, 1993.

Moe, C. *Br Aloysius F.S.C. Brother Aloysius Carmody, 1916-1981: secretary general of the Brothers of the Christian Schools*, Kensington, NSW, April 1982.

Br Aloysius Carmody personal papers, De La Salle Provincial Office, Bankstown:

- Archbishop James Carroll letter to Br Aloysius, 26 November 1976.

- Br Aloysius correspondence to the *Brother Visitor*, 1940s-1981.

- Br Aloysius correspondence with Fr Frank Martin, 1976.

- Br Baptist 'Observations on the Carmody family and of Larry in particular', n.d.

- Clare Staples (nee Carmody) recollections, 1981.

- Joan (Sr Loyola) Carmody correspondence to Br Baptist, 1981-1982.

- Tom Carmody (jun.) recollections, 1981.

REFLECTION

Sister Said!
Catholic schools staffed by religious sisters, brothers and priests 1880 to 1960

Graham English

The Catholic Church in Australia began, as many things non-indigenous on this wide continent did, as a group of migrants looking for a safe place.

These migrants were mostly from Ireland. After the failed attempt to make the Catholics here an English Benedictine church, the Irish provided the bishops, many of the clergy and especially many of the sisters and brothers who built on the efforts of the first century of immigrants to more firmly establish Catholic schools and the Catholic community.

The late Cyril Hally, Columban missionary priest and scholar, used to say of the Irish Catholic community spreading out and establishing itself here that first they built a school and a tennis court. The tennis court was to have the young Catholics socialising with each other lest they get to know Protestants and marry out. The school was used for lessons on the weekdays, for working bees on some Saturdays, and, with the desks shifted back, it became the place for Mass on Sundays. Only later did actual churches appear.

The Irish clergy were afraid of proselytism, the attempt by some Protestants to lure Catholic children away from their faith, to the extent that while children in the new Catholic schools read Bible stories as if they were literally true (Bible History it was called), they were kept away from the Bible, the King James Bible, particularly, one of the foundations of modern English language.

Almost all the teachers in Catholic schools from the 1880s until the 1960s were religious sisters, brothers and a few priests. Catholic schools were possible because they had a voluntary, hard working, usually overworked taskforce who were obedient and poor and, because they had no partners, children or possessions, were relatively easy to move to wherever their superiors wanted them.

The religious orders that came here were mostly Irish, the Mercy, Presentation, and Brigidine Sisters, the Christian Brothers and the Patrician Brothers for example or French like the Marist and De La Salle Brothers, the Marist Sisters, the Sacré Coeur Sisters, and the Vincentian and Sacred Heart Fathers. A small number like the Loreto Sisters were English. Even the orders that came here that were not Irish (the Jesuits, Dominicans and the Ursuline Sisters for example) were made up of Irish folk as were the orders begun here such as the Good Samaritan Sisters and the Josephites. For many years, lots of the priests here were men who'd grown up and trained for the priesthood in Ireland.

When I was in kindergarten at the Presentation Sisters' convent school in Young in 1949, there were several small Catholic schools round about as well as the Christian Brothers and the Presentation Sisters in town. At Wombat, fifteen kilometres away, there was a small school run by the Black Josephites, the diocesan version of the Brown Josephites founded by Sister Mary MacKillop. They took a few boarders as well as the local day children who walked or rode to school each day.

There was a slightly bigger boarding school a further fifteen kilometres away at Galong to which my Aunty Mena threatened to send us if we did not behave ourselves. Aunty Mena used look after us when Mum was in the Mercy Sisters' Hospital maternity wing yet again and as Mena was not married she took charge of us for the time being.

In those days, there were many small villages mostly about thirty kilometres apart as that was what the average adult could walk in a day. These villages usually had a shop or two, a blacksmith, a small public school, an Anglican and a Catholic church and a few houses. People walked or rode horses or travelled in sulkies or drays, horse drawn vehicles that carried a few people. Eventually, nearly every one of the villages had a Catholic school with a few sisters. Often the Catholic school was established after the state school and Catholic children left it to go to the sisters, making both schools less viable but that's the way it was. 'The faith' came first.

There was a small convent at Murringo where my father and his siblings went to school. There was another convent school at Koorawatha. My father's six siblings rode to Murringo convent school from the farm in a sulky, the oldest child in charge. As each older child left school, the next eldest took the reins. There were stories told to us much later of horses bolting and sulkies overturning but usually no one seemed to be seriously hurt. We who lived only a few hundred metres from the schools in town and walked unaccompanied each day back and forth thought that our father's family had really lived on the frontier.

Our cousin Sister Declan, then the accountant at the Mercy Hospital at Cootamundra, had gone to Murringo convent school and later taught at the convent school at Boorowa. Murringo convent had about twenty children spread over as many classes as were needed. The sisters lived in the tiny village convent without transport, electricity or running water and relied on the small amounts of money the children brought as 'school money', and the support of the local Catholics. Children left school at various ages, few of them with any certificates and none of them completing matriculation.

Some of the wealthier parents sent their daughters or sons to board at the Goulburn boarding schools or even to the Loreto or Sacré Coeur Sisters in Sydney or the Jesuits at Riverview but all that was well beyond us. Most of the adults I knew had left school at the end of primary and some at the Intermediate Certificate when they were fourteen or fifteen. New South Wales had only one university then and none of us knew anyone who had attended it.

There were fifty-three children in my second-grade first communion class photo. At the end of the year, we boys moved over to CBC, the Christian Brothers' school which they insisted on calling a college though it was hardly that. The girls stayed at the convent school. CBC had boys from year three to the Leaving Certificate; the convent school did the same for the girls. Both schools had double classes, third and fourth class in one room, fifth and sixth in another and so on. We boys were good at rugby league, 'punching well above our weight' as they say now, but not always a shining example of scholarship. We seldom saw girls from the convent school except in the church at Benediction on

Fridays. Pope Pius XI had forbidden coeducation for Catholic children and in our parish the ban was strictly enforced once we turned seven, the 'age of reason,' as the catechism assured us.

Catholic schools, especially after the Second World War, often had big classes, occasionally as many as a hundred students with the sister or brother a page ahead of the students (and sometimes a page behind). Parents were threatened with excommunication if they sent their children to public or other schools even though some of these schools were educationally better than their Catholic equivalents.

Five brothers ran our school, boys came from the town and many came in each day by bus from the orchards and farms round about, and we and the Brothers did our best mostly, though in unguarded moments visitors were heard to comment that there was not an enthusiasm for learning among some of the students.

At the brothers, the main form of discipline was corporal punishment, though their rule said 'corporal punishment is on no account to be the main form of discipline'. Some brothers used it sparingly and some did not. One wag later said he'd learned maths by 'the hit and say method'.

The American poet Mary Oliver wrote that most youngsters 'are directed toward the acquisition of knowledge', meaning not so much ideas but demonstrated facts. Education as I knew it was made up of such a pre-established collection of certainties.[29] In Catholic schools in all classes, including religion, this was almost universally the case. 'Education' as we knew it was a pre-established collection of certainties, much of it learned off by heart. We were part of an Ultramontane church where the pope was always right. Thinking for oneself was not encouraged and where for many Catholic children and some of their parents the final word on all sorts of subjects was, 'Sister said!'

In spite of all this, there was no doubt we were being brought up to be good Australians. We said lots of prayers and school days revolved around Catholic practices like 'the five first Fridays', school retreats, and devotion to the Virgin Mary. We spent quite a lot of our childhoods praying for a happy death!

---

[29] Mary Oliver. *Upstream: Selected Essays*, (New York: Penguin Press, 2016), 153.

Catholics had slightly different school holidays from public schools; we had no school on the 'holy days of obligation' or St Patrick's Day. We did not get a half holiday on Guy Fawkes Day like 'the publics'. I suspect some of the Irish clergy thought Fawkes and his plot were 'a good idea'. But there was no hint of being anti-English and when the Queen came to Australia in 1954, many Catholic school students spent hours travelling to stand in the February sun much of the day; as the then Prime Minister said, we 'did but see her passing by' before we set off for the return trip home.

We also took Anzac Day seriously. Catholic men from our town had died in both wars, and we were proud of our cadet unit. We heard not a word of Irish history, except stories about the beginnings of the Christian Brothers and the Presentation Sisters. We saw almost no Irish literature. The few songs and poems we heard were sentimental stuff like 'The Dear Little Shamrock'. We heard no Irish folk music. Like the rest of Australians, we were British citizens and we stood for *God Save the King* then *God Save the Queen* just as everyone else did and thought of it as normal.

On Anzac Day, we had a ceremonial requiem Mass: 'we Catholics pray for the dead unlike the Protestants'; then we went down town for the march after which the boys from CBC played football against the boys from the De La Salle School at Cootamundra fifty kilometres south of us. We beat them as often as they beat us and we thought that the De La Salle Brothers were pretty much like our Brothers only they wore wider collars with their black suits. Sometimes we played against the boys from the Brigidine Convent at Cowra and noticed that one of the sisters there knew a lot about rugby league. Cowra Convent School was famous for turning out top footballers coached by Sister Scholastica.

My father used say of the Murringo convent school, 'Everything I know I learned from Sister Bonaventure'. He'd left school early but was an avid reader who might have made a good teacher in different times. He was determined that we would go right through school and do as well as we could. Though I never met Sister Bonaventure, I feel I owe her something.

Mum's mother grew up on a farm with her twelve siblings at Crowther. They had an Irishman living there who taught all the children to read and write and do basic maths. Each of the girls was sent to the convent school at Carcoar on the other side of Cowra for a while, as their father said, 'So the nuns could teach them to be ladylike'. Grandma was ladylike so I presume the sisters were successful.

The sisters taught Catholics more than how to be ladylike. Sir Bernard Heinze (1894 –1982) was an Australian conductor, academic, and Director of the New South Wales State Conservatorium of Music. His entry in the Australian Dictionary of Biography says of him: 'Without doubt the dominant musical figure of twentieth-century Australia, Heinze raised and maintained national musical standards, providing an unparalleled example of leadership to the profession'.[30] Heinze had gone to school at St Patrick's College, Ballarat.

One of the ways the sisters supported themselves was to teach piano before and after school for a small charge. Children, not all of them Catholic, came to the convent and one of the sisters gave them piano lessons. Late in his life, Heinze declared that these piano lessons made a significant contribution to music, particularly classical music in Australia.

Another result of the religious orders conducting schools was that some orders and their former pupils became tribal. Adult Catholics came to regard themselves as Josephite girls, or Brigidine girls, or Mercy or Loreto girls. Men thought of themselves as Marist old boys, or Christies' or De La Salle boys. The rivalries between orders were quite fierce and some bishops played orders off against each other. One bishop told the Christian Brothers when they turned down his first request, 'If you don't open an agricultural school in my diocese, I will ask the Marist Brothers'. The CBs opened the school.

There was also Catholic networking. Sisters and brothers moved around the country. Catholics felt united by the religious orders

---

[30] Thérèse Radic, "Heinze, Sir Bernard Thomas (1894–1982)" in *Australian Dictionary of Biography*. (First published in hardcopy 2007). Accessed online 31 March 2020 http://adb.anu.edu.au/biography/heinze-sir-bernard-thomas-12617

who'd taught them or their children. Individual teachers, particularly good teachers, become known by many ex-students. As they moved around, their ex-students could form links saying, 'You know Caesar Healey?' 'What, you knew Brother Eulogius?' 'You went to the Good Sams. Did you know Sister Clare?' 'Ah, Mother Leonard, a brilliant English and French teacher!'

There were drawbacks to all this. Some religious orders spread themselves too thinly. A school with classes from year three to Leaving Certificate and five religious with no ancillary staff could not hope to teach all the subjects well. Too many of the teachers were not qualified in the secondary schools subjects, particularly sciences and maths. Some young women and men wanted to be nuns or brothers more than they wanted to be or were suited to be teachers. There were children and teenagers at Catholic schools who did not receive an adequate education because some of the sisters and brothers were inadequate teachers.

On the other hand, some schools with one or two outstanding teachers could do very well by their students if the teachers knew their limits and picked the right subjects.

The American philosopher John Dewey believed that 'we are participants in an unfinished universe not observers of a finished universe'.[31] Young people are inclined to think that the world they are living in has always been as it is and some presume it will always be as it is now. Some clergy and religious encouraged this belief or suggested that there was once a Golden Age and we should all try to re-establish that wonderful time. The period in Australian Catholic education from about 1800 until sometime in the 1960s was a First Vatican Council church inclined to this view.

In 1960, the sisters, brothers and priests had many young people in their novitiates and teacher training colleges. The years after World War Two in Australia saw a flourishing in religions. Catholic and Protestant training colleges were full as were churches on Sundays. These numbers increased over the next six or seven years. Despite this, the orders

---

[31] J. W. Garrison, "Realism, Deweyan pragmatism and educational research", *Educational Researcher* 23:1, (1994), 8.

sought to encourage more young people to enter; the schools were still increasing and the numbers of children attending them had ballooned in the 'baby boom' after the Second World War. One might have been forgiven for thinking this state of affairs would go on forever.

1800 to 1960 was before the Second Vatican Council. It was – in the words of John W O'Malley, the Jesuit historian of the church's councils – an 'Ultramontane Church'.[32] It was a church of certainties in reaction to the uncertainties of Europe since the French Revolution and the other revolutions since 1789 and the loss of the Papal States in the Italian unification. It was a church strongly committed to the belief in the infallibility of the pope. In Australia, it was a church in which Catholics were underprivileged and defended themselves and strengthened their community by having an enemy. The until-then unsuccessful project to obtain government aid for Catholic schools was also one of the things that united Catholics.

St Cassian of Imola was martyred in 363 AD in the reign of Julian the Apostate. He'd been a teacher, a fairly tough one it seems, and when his time for martyrdom came, the authorities handed him over to his pupils. They stabbed him to death, slowly. None of the sisters, brothers or priests in Catholic schools here died at the hands of their students. Some died or suffered, though, in the name of Catholic education: in outback hot, dry and isolated towns, women, Irish and native born alike, wore heavy serge habits, summer and winter. They wore clothes perhaps suited to wet, cold Ireland but quite unsuited to any Australian climate. They had limited diets in a time when many illnesses we can now cure were fatal or debilitating. The Catholic plots in remote cemeteries tell their stories: *Sister Mary Joan, Aged thirty two, May She Rest in Peace. Sister Mary Dolores, Aged Thirty six. Requiescat in Pace.* Brothers, too, wore inappropriate clothing, serge habits again, and lived lives designed for Europe but not for here.

Then, Australia – like much of the western world – changed.

---

[32] John. W. O'Malley, *Vatican I: The Council and the making of the Ultramontane Church*, Harvard University Cambridge: Belnap Press,(2018).

In 1963, I was in a brothers' teacher training college. We'd had no contact with the media for four years. After one visiting Sunday, Brother Jerome told us of this group in England his brother had told him about, 'They come from Liverpool and they have long hair. And all the girls scream right through their concerts. They call themselves *The Beatles*'. In the mid 1960s, after the Goulburn Catholic school strikes, the government began making grants to Catholic schools to build science laboratories. In Rome, the Second Vatican Council, recently finished, was beginning to take effect. In Asia, the USA was losing the Vietnam War.

One of the major outcomes of Catholic schooling, the large number of young Catholics with university educations, had people beginning to question and to ask for change. The Ultramontane church was collapsing. Government aid meant that Catholic schools could hire more teachers who were not religious sisters, brothers or priests and the overall quality of Catholic education improved even in country towns. Modern transport meant the closure of many small village schools. Coeducation was renamed co-institutional education to get around Pius XI's rule and this made some schools more efficient. The number of young people entering convents and monasteries declined quickly to the point where the average age of sisters and brothers now is somewhere in the seventies. The age of 'Sister said' was over.

The movie *Jojo Rabbit* is a black comedy lampooning ideology that ignores reality. In it, Jojo, aged ten, sees some people who have been murdered by the Nazis and asks his mother, a resister to Nazi propaganda and violence, 'Mother, what did they do?' She answers, 'They did what they could'.

When the religious sisters, brothers and priests were almost the only teachers in Catholic schools from 1800 to about 1960, nothing was perfect. But they managed to build a Catholic community and bequeath a Catholic school system to the nation. They did what they could. Perhaps one cannot ask for more.

Select Bibliography

Oliver, Mary. *Upstream: Selected Essays*, New York: Penguin Press, 2016.

O'Malley, John. W. *Vatican I: The Council and the making of the Ultramontane Church*. Harvard University, Cambridge: Belnap Press, 2018.

Garrison, J. W. "Realism, Deweyan pragmatism and educational research" in *Educational Researcher 23:1*, 1994.

Radic, Therese. "Heinze, Sir Bernard Thomas (1894–1982)" in *Australian Dictionary of Biography*. First published in hard copy 2007. http://adb.anu.edu.au/biography/heinze-sir-bernard-thomas-12617

Chapter Five
Developments in Catholic Education in Australia 1960-2000

Context

System Development

Kelvin Canavan fms

Introduction

The earlier eras in this book provided the contexts for the establishment of Catholic schools in Australia. The 1960s and 1970s witnessed the formation of diocesan school systems across the country. What follows is essentially a case study of how Catholic schools fared in NSW which mirrored similar developments across the nation. While there were variations across the dioceses, Catholic school systems emerged in each.

The 1960s

In the 1960s, Catholic schools, parish primary and regional secondary, were stand alone, relatively independent, with zero government funding. In Sydney, WWII immigration resulted in large (and some very large) classes. Demand for places exceeded supply and between 1965 and 1971 there was a significant decline in the proportion of students attending Catholic schools. Accelerating retention rates in secondary schools exacerbated the problem, but increased school fees and parish assessments helped a little.

These were precarious times with the Wyndham scheme in NSW extended in secondary schooling from five to six years and questions being canvassed included:

- are Catholic schools justifying themselves?
- should we focus on primary or secondary schools?
- should we think more about Catholic children in State schools?

The Principals of all Catholic schools were Religious. Payment of lay teachers' salaries was a continuing struggle as principals and parish priests negotiated salaries or in-kind payments with individual teachers. A $1 million overdraft with the Commonwealth Bank was another concern.

My own career illustrates the prevailing situation. After completing a one-year teacher training program at the Marist Scholasticate, I was appointed in 1960 to Parramatta Marist to teach sixty boys in fourth class. The training program was recognised by the Council of Public Instruction of Victoria. In my second year, I began a BA degree as an evening student at the University of Sydney. At Parramatta, I was also responsible for the school canteen (staffed by the mothers of the students) the profits from which helped pay salaries for three lay teachers. The annual fete and various concerts were also important fund raisers as were the raffles and bottle drives. With the help of parents, the 18 classrooms were repainted during Saturday working bees. Each year, many students were turned away as class sizes at Parramatta were limited to sixty. Subsequently, I also taught at Marist Brothers Dundas and Eastwood and then came a very different kind of involvement.

In 1968, Cardinal Gilroy approved my appointment as Inspector of Schools at the age of 31 and I was to spend the next forty years in the management and leadership of Catholic schools in the Archdiocese of Sydney.

1965-1975

During this decade in the Sydney Catholic Education Office (CEO), I witnessed four developments that permanently changed the structure, organisation and face of Catholic schooling, but not the mission:

1. Financial control of schools by the Archdiocese.

2. Employment of lay principals by the Archdiocese.

3. Government financial assistance for Catholic Schools.

4. Establishment of administrative and accountability structures to utilise government funding for systemic schools.

Each, in turn, contributed to the emerging central administration of the Greater Sydney Catholic school system, which as early as 1975 was beginning to exhibit characteristics of a school system. I will address each of these developments.

1. Financial control of schools by the Archdiocese

In response to a desperate situation and serious questioning about the survival of Catholic schools in the Archdiocese of Sydney, Cardinal Gilroy established the *Catholic Building and Finance Commission* (CBFC) early in 1965. This body took immediate financial control of income and expenditure of all Parish primary and Regional secondary schools in the Archdiocese. The Cardinal chaired the meetings which lasted only one hour. At the fifth meeting, he is reported as saying:

> It is my intention that all decisions on matters relating to education which result in financial demands on parishes, and/or in the construction of new buildings, shall be made by the Commission, and recommended to me, so that I may give the required authority.[33]

---

[33] Minutes of CBFC meeting, 26 May 1965.

Parishes, schools and Religious Congregations were informed of this decision to centralise income and expenditure. There was no consultation.[34]

Another early decision of the CBFC was to establish a scale of tuition fees for Parish and Regional schools from the start of 1966. Fees collected by schools were to be remitted to the CBFC where they were banked in a common account from which salaries for lay teachers and stipends for Religious were paid. Principals were pleased to be relieved of the responsibility of ensuring sufficient cash was available for the weekly pay envelopes for teachers. Procedures for Capital Works and Building Loan repayments were put in place. Expenditure was tightly controlled and proposals for additional buildings were submitted to the CBFC. Parish priests and principals could not proceed without formal authorisation from the CBFC.

Geoffrey Davey, a retired engineer, was Executive Commissioner until June 1967 when he stepped down to begin studies for the priesthood. He was replaced by Bernie McBride who served as Executive Secretary of the CBFC from 1967 until 1986. An annual budget for the school system was approved by the CBFC and the Diocesan Director of Schools, Fr John Slowey, would be informed as to the number of teachers to be employed. Subsequently, the Sydney CEO began establishing staffing levels for each school.

The new authority, the CBFC, was separate from the CEO and eventually located on a different site. Cardinal Gilroy and his advisors could not have foreseen the inevitable consequences of the implementation of this policy decision to centralise the finances of the System. Their immediate priority was the very survival of the schools. The first seeds for the development of a System of schools in Greater Sydney had been sown.

---

[34] John Luttrell, *You've Taken Our Schools: The Role and Development of the Catholic Education Office*, Sydney, (M.Ed. Hons Thesis, Sydney: University of Sydney, 1992).

2. Employment of lay principals by the Archdiocese

Traditionally, principals were appointed to Catholic schools by the relevant Religious Congregation which would also notify the Archbishop of Sydney. For many decades, all principals were Religious Sisters, Brothers and Priests. In 1972, the Provincial of the De La Salle Brothers informed the parish priest at St Vincent's, Ashfield, that the Congregation was no longer in a position to appoint a Brother as principal. This took both parish and Archdiocese by surprise. There were no established procedures to engage a lay principal. In 1973, a similar situation arose at St Bernadette's primary, Dundas Valley and more were to follow. Two obvious questions were 'Where will we find a lay principal?' and 'Who will be the employer?'

While some preliminary discussions considered School Boards, the Sydney CEO soon emerged as the employer of lay principals and subsequently of teachers and support staff. Salary scales and conditions of employment were progressively developed for lay principals and teachers.

The first Award for male teachers in Catholic schools in NSW (effective 1 January 1970) set salaries at 80% of that for NSW government school teachers, with full parity to be phased in over four years. The Award for female teachers was 70% of that paid to government school teachers. Equal pay for female teachers was to be phased in over the same four-year period. From 1 January 1974, male and female salary differences ceased and salaries for Catholic school teachers were similar to those paid to government school teachers.[35]

A superannuation scheme was established a decade later. Concurrently, stipends for religious were regularised, with significant increases phased in over three years, including the equalisation of stipends for female and male religious. Cost of living was the underlying principle. Gerry Gleeson, as member of the NSW Public Service Board, played the key role in the systemisation of stipends.

---

[35] "Teachers (Assistant Masters and Mistresses in Non-Governmental Schools) (State) Award from 1970," *NSW Industrial Gazette*, Vol. 178, (30 September 1970).

For the 1976 school year, 22 new lay primary principals had to be found. At this stage, the demand for lay principals was clearly ahead of supply. Within the decade, 102 lay principals had been appointed. Leadership development programs were quickly implemented, assisted by an innovations program grant from the new Australian Schools Commission.

Communication to parents that a lay principal was to be appointed to replace Sister was challenging. Initially, parents were slow to accept the concept of lay leadership in their schools. 'This is unthinkable... it will never work!' History, however, shows that the transition to lay leadership was quickly accepted by parents and had nil impact on school enrolments. A new employment authority had evolved and the seeds for a future school System continued to be sown.

3. Government financial assistance for Catholic Schools

The NSW Budget 1967-1968 contained a modest allocation1 for a direct payment to non-government primary schools based on enrolments.[36] The initial per capita grants of $6 per primary student were made in the first half of 1968.[37] This was the first financial support Catholic schools had received from a NSW Government since 1882 (excluding the *Free milk scheme*, access to Government Stores and modest assistance with interest payments on approved building projects). After decades of waiting, a little State Aid had arrived and suddenly the future looked brighter.

Primary student grants for 1968-1969 were $24, for 1969-1970 $30, for 1970-1971 $36 rising to $75 for 1973-1974. Further grants for primary students in non-government schools had been foreshadowed in 1968 by Premier Askin:

> Reasonable aid to independent schools is now a generally accepted principle... The burden on the taxpayer as children leave the independent schools and enrol at State

---

[36] $900,000 for financial year 1967-68.
[37] *NSW Budget Papers 1967-1968*, 144.

schools is immeasurably heavier than if they had been assisted to stay at the independent schools... Our view on State Aid, briefly, is that parents who elect to send their children to independent schools must be prepared to pay a reasonable share of the cost, but under today's conditions it is too much to expect them to pay all the costs.[38]

At the secondary school level, initial grants (scholarships/allowances) were paid to parents of eligible students in non-government schools in 1963-1964. These were means-tested and restricted to those in the third and subsequent years. The program was extended in 1964-1965 to include eligible students in all secondary classes. In 1968, these allowances were increased from $18 to $28 a year.[39] The means-test for secondary school allowances to parents was progressively phased out as a prelude to paying allowances direct to the schools.

The gradual increase in per capita grants could be seen, in part, as a response of the major political parties to the relentless campaign conducted by Catholic parents. In Sydney, the Federation of Parents and Friends' Associations employed a variety of strategies culminating in a series of public meetings.

The meeting in the Odeon Theatre, Rowe Street, Eastwood, on Sunday evening, 20 April 1969, was particularly memorable. Some 2,000 packed the venue and those unable to get in were asked to remain on the footpath until all ten Members of Parliament had arrived. The function was brilliantly stage-managed, and the State and Federal MPs faced a passionate and well-informed audience calling for specific commitments to future funding: 'How much and when?' MPs had nowhere to hide. Preselected parents were given prepared questions and sat in designated seats. When the MC invited questions, they immediately queued at the two microphones effectively excluding all others. After the function, most MPs accepted the invitation to join

---

[38] R. W. Askin, Policy speech, (9 February 1968), 10.
[39] J. B. Renshaw. NSW Hansard, (25 September 1963), 5300; R.W.Askin, Financial Statement, (25 September 1968), 11.

the organisers for supper in the Catholic Presbytery in Hillview Avenue. More politicking occurred until midnight.

Gough Whitlam, Leader of the Federal Opposition, spoke at 7 of the 8 public meetings. His message was always the same: If a Labor Government is elected, we will establish immediately an Interim Australian Schools Commission to examine the need of all Australian schools and, if elected, a Labor Government will fund all schools 'according to need'.

The eighth and final Sydney meeting was held 1 June 1969, a wet Sunday evening, when 5,000 crowded into the Sydney Town Hall and the lower hall (days before Health and Safety Regulations for public buildings). Proceedings were broadcast live on Radio 2SM. There was extensive coverage on television and in the press, including some scuffles with anti-State Aid protestors. The meeting concluded with a motion asking Commonwealth and State governments to each provide $50 to every student in a non-government primary and secondary school and that this amount be increased progressively. While these amounts were modest, they certainly consolidated recent gains and were not likely to be opposed. Central to the motion was 'that this amount be increased progressively'. There was an increasing confidence among Catholic parents that their demands for financial assistance were being heard.

At the Federal level, the secondary Science facilities program began in 1964 to be followed in 1969 by secondary school Library grants. Direct per capita grants commenced in 1970.[40]

---

[40] "Commonwealth payments to or for the States 1970-1971", (Canberra 1970), 36.
"Commonwealth payments to or for the States 1972-1973", (Canberra 1972), 53.
"Commonwealth payments to or for the States 1973-1974", (Canberra 1973), 44.

Table 1. *Commonwealth Government Student Grants to Non-Government Schools*
1970-1973

	Primary	Secondary
1970	$35	$50
1971	35	50
1972	50	68
1973	62	104

The campaign for school funding had had a long history. In 1962, for example, parents in Goulburn had drawn attention to their needs, when protesting against the financial impossibility of the upgrading of toilets demanded by Inspectors, they sought to enrol their children in local government schools. Catholic bishops, various parent organisations, clergy and parishioners, with the support of Religious Congregations, kept the needs of their schools before politicians. It was a long struggle, with countless magnificent campaigners.[41]

By 1970, major political parties had agreed in principle to financial assistance to non-government schools. There was disagreement, however, as to the method of distribution: either *per capita* or *according to need*. The Liberal/Country Party policy was to fund schools on a *per capita* basis with all students attracting the same level of support. For the electorate, these two terms differentiated the policies of the major parties.

Following the election of a Labor government on 2 December 1972, an Interim Committee of the Australian Schools Commission was established and immediately asked to 'examine the position of government and non-government primary and secondary schools

---

[41] For a more detailed account of this historic strike, see John Luttrell, "Recalling the Goulburn Strike: An Interview with Brian Keating, *The Australasian Catholic Record* 89:3 (2012), 349-359.

throughout Australia, to make recommendations on the immediate financial needs of these schools' and report by end of May 1973.

The Whitlam government lost no time implementing the directions of the *Schools in Australia* report (*Karmel Report*)[42] and immediately National, State and Diocesan structures needed to be established as a prerequisite for Catholic systemic schools to access forthcoming grants. Catholic authorities were well placed to establish the required administrative and accountability structures in order to access the new *Schools in Australia* programs.

Following the historic Conference on the Administration of Catholic Education, held in Armidale in August 1972, an expert committee was convened and reported in August 1973. In essence, the committee recommended the establishment of a National Catholic Education Commission (NCEC), State Commissions and appropriate Diocesan Catholic Education Offices. That these recommendations closely paralleled the *Schools in Australia* report could be explained by common membership – Fr Frank Martin, Director CEO Melbourne and Dr Peter Tannock, Dean, Faculty of Education, University of Western Australia, who served on both bodies.

While recommending increased funding, the Report was explicit that 'the (Schools) Commission should not be involved in the detailed operation of schools or school systems' (14.9). The Catholic Education Commissions in each State readily accepted a request to distribute Federal recurrent grants to Catholic systemic schools *according to need*. This was a game changer, the equivalent of delegating key responsibilities from a government department in Canberra to Catholic education authorities across Australia.[43]

The Federal budget allocation for Catholic systemic schools for 1973-1974 was $63m. The allocation for 1974-1975 remained at $63m. For 1975-1976, supplementation was introduced to assist with wage

---

[42] Peter Karmel, *Schools in Australia: report of the Interim Committee for the Australian Schools Commission*, (Canberra: May 1973).

[43] Karmel, *Schools in Australia*, 141.

Catholic Education 1960-2000

and other cost increases.[44] These new arrangements, while restricting the direct involvement of the Commonwealth government in Catholic schools, increased significantly in a permanent manner, the responsibilities and spheres of influence of the NCEC, NSW Catholic Education Commission (CEC), the Sydney CEO and CBFC, and the parallel bodies in the other states and territories.

In some ways, the early 1970s marked the end of the State Aid campaign, apart from the failed Defence of Government Schools (D.O.G.S) challenge in the High Court. Perhaps it would be more correct to say, phase one of the campaign. In the decades ahead, the campaign across Australia had to continue. An ongoing challenge was the education and support of the electorate on the justice issue of financial assistance to non-government schools and the rights of parents to choose the schools for their children.

In NSW, there was a need to nullify the continuing campaigns of the NSW Teachers' Federation, the NSW Parents and Citizens' Association and from the early 1990s, the Greens political party. In some ways, these three organisations gave the NSW Catholic Education Commission and the Catholic Education Office a ready platform to explain the 'true facts' of government financial assistance. Messages were clear and concise, professionally printed and widely distributed. Effective use was made of the print and electronic media and, prior to Federal and State elections, the distribution of a statement comparing policies of the major parties was an essential strategy.

Much use was made of school functions, in particular at the blessing and opening of new facilities, to explain to parents and MPs some particular aspects of government financial assistance to Catholic schools. The continuing contribution of parents including

---

[44] "Payments to or for the States on the occasion of the Budget 1973-1974",(Canberra:1973), 44; "Payments to or for the States and Local Government Authorities on the occasion of the Budget 1974-1975". *Budget Paper 7*,(Canberra: 1974), 50; "Payments to or for the States and Local Government Authorities on the occasion of the Budget 1975-1976" *Budget Paper 7*, (Canberra:1975), 44.

responsibility for loan repayments would be detailed along with Commonwealth and State contributions.

It was important that government financial assistance not be taken for granted. Seeds for the development of a school System continued to be sown and for the decades ahead annual grants from governments kept pace with rising costs.

Table 2. *Combined Commonwealth and State Government Grants for Students in Catholic Systemic Schools in NSW 1979–2017*[45]

1970-1973

	Primary	Secondary
1979	$479	$745
1989	1,568	2,390
1999	3,358	4,631
2005	5,261	7,056
2006	5,580	7,312
2007	6,212	7,947
2017	10,689	12,280

4. *Establishment of administrative and accountability structures to utilise government funding for systemic schools*

Let us consider again how this embryonic but now flourishing system had begun. Prior to 1965, Catholic schools in Sydney were relatively independent. Each raised its own funds and any lay teachers were paid by the principal or parish priest. The demands for administrative structures at an Archdiocesan level were minimal. Periodically, a Priest Inspector would make a visit generally for a half day.

As mentioned earlier, when I was appointed to the Sydney Catholic Education Office in 1968 as an Inspector of Schools, the staff occupied

---

[45] Source: *Sydney Archives/Catholic Schools NSW*, (Sydney: Catholic Education Office).

four small rooms at the end of the Housie Hall, Cusa House, 175 Elizabeth Street, Sydney. From memory, the CEO and CBFC had a total staff of about 12-15, mostly priests, religious and semi-retired laymen, two secretaries and an office manager. Most worked part-time and on a voluntary basis. Housie regulars would begin taking up 'their' seats during the afternoon and were happy to assist stuffing envelopes for the occasional mailing to schools.

At this time, the CEO had a limited mandate. Survival was the key and reporting and accountability minimal. There was little System administrative experience or culture at diocesan level. The major asset was good will and a commitment to support the schools.

The development of the Sydney CEO/CBFC quickened with the election of the Whitlam Government and establishment of the Australian Schools Commission. Overnight, fledgling CEOs and CECs were engaging staff to manage and deliver a plethora of new well-funded programs. Staff were also employed for Curriculum support, Teacher Development and Education Centres, Human Resources, Industrial Relations, Capital Works and the Leadership Development of Principals. Payroll Clerks, Accountants and Auditors were also appointed.

The introduction of new national catechetical texts and related pedagogical developments required the employment of Religious Education specialists and the provision of major professional development programs. Catholic schools were now part of a developing network or System characterised by increasing government financial support with a sense of confidence and excitement – particularly in staff rooms. A rapidly expanding organisation of this size was a new phenomenon for the Archdiocese and staff were on a steep learning curve. Providing leadership programs for principals resulted in senior CEO staff becoming familiar with leadership theory and management best practice.

More appropriate accommodation had to be found and in 1973 the CEO/CBFC moved to St Benedict's Broadway into spaces formerly occupied by the Marist Brothers school and now by the University of Notre Dame. This location provided 20-30 rooms across three floors of the building. The parish primary school and the parish occupied the rest of the building. A staff of perhaps 40-50 lay, religious and clergy received Award wages or stipends.

The growth in the staffing level at the CEO and the corresponding expansion of centralised activities was facilitated by the availability of Commonwealth funds for use by diocesan education authorities to administer their school Systems according to government program guidelines. The early 1970s were hectic times as we scrambled to develop sufficient infrastructure to start accessing available funds and providing new programs as well as satisfying the accountability requirements of the Commonwealth. The bureaucratic seeds were germinating fast. There was no turning back.

1980-1985

By the early 1980s, there was much excitement and growing confidence among Catholic School System Leadership personnel but also a developing awareness that our major goal as Catholic educators was not primarily the effective implementation of Commonwealth programs. In a prophetic talk to the CEO staff in 1982, Fr Cyril Hally SSC, an eminent anthropologist, reminded us that 'as an evangeliser, the CEO must begin by being evangelised itself'.[46] Hally continued 'in these days, a bureaucracy is needed to support and conduct a large organisation. When that organisation is directed to the spreading of the Kingdom of God, that must also be the goal of the bureaucracy. If the school has a vocation, so does the CEO. If there is a vocation, then there must be a distinctive spirituality. And for those who work in this bureaucracy, the spirituality must be worked out and lived within that ministry. We should not seek a ministry' he said, 'that ignores the workplace'. 'The evangelisation of the CEO bureaucracy' became part of the CEO's lexicon for decades.

The role and function of the CEO continued to expand and in April 1983 more suitable accommodation was found in the St Martha's complex, Renwick Street, Leichhardt, which the Archdiocese had

---

[46] *Evangelii Nuntiandi* (EN) *Apostolic Exhortation of Pope Paul VI*, (December 1975), #15.

purchased earlier from the Sisters of St Joseph. With extended responsibilities, the school system required a different leadership structure and in 1983 Archbishop Clancy established the Sydney Archdiocesan Catholic Schools (SACS) Board, with Archbishop James Carroll as the first Chairman. This was a more representative body than the CBFC.

By 1985, the staff employed in the CEO and CBFC had grown to about 200 women and men, most of whom were full-time professionals and moved over time from Cusa House to St Benedict's Broadway to St Martha's Leichhardt and into five regional offices. The CEO was now influencing most aspects of Catholic schooling in Greater Sydney ranging from the establishment of new schools to the distribution of resources, to the employment and appraisal of principals and teachers: finally, to the development of curriculum and religious education materials and the implementation of programs to meet particular student needs.

1985 to the turn of the century

The movement to coordinate Parish and Regional schools begun in 1965, was to continue inexorably and by 1985 the Archdiocese of Sydney had a highly centralised System of 264 Parish and Regional schools, educating 110,688 students. Archdiocesan authorities were responsible in 1985 for the distribution to these schools of student grants from governments, exceeding $A152 million, up from zero dollars in 1967.[47] The rapid growth of the CEO and CBFC bureaucracy was a response to the four developments described in this paper. The growth had been accompanied by some System discontinuity and role conflict as the new bureaucracy struggled to clarify responsibilities and mutual expectations.

After all, the System had grown up like topsy. To this end, the Archdiocese supported a doctoral study that surveyed 256 systemic

---

[47] Kelvin Canavan, *Perceptions and Expectations of Roles, Services, Structures and Goals of the Sydney Catholic Education Office held by Principals and CEO Staff*, (Ed.D. Dissertation, San Francisco: University of San Francisco, UMI 86-14594, 1986), 28.

school principals and all 124 CEO professional staff.[48] The doctoral study in 1985 reported:

> Across the 161 survey items the Sydney Catholic Education Office was perceived positively by principals and CEO staff. The importance of the 40 services provided to schools by the CEO in 1985 was accepted unequivocally by principals and CEO staff. There were clear indications that both groups favoured some increased emphasis on these services. There was nil support for discontinuing any services.[49]

In 1986, Archbishop Clancy responded to the role conflict and ambiguity problem when he accepted the recommendation from the SACS Board for a restructured administration that saw the amalgamation of the CEO and the CBFC. Press advertisements appeared for a new position, the Executive Director of Schools. In December 1986, Brother Kelvin Canavan was appointed to this position with a five-year contract. This appointment in Sydney coincided with the formation of the new dioceses of Parramatta and Broken Bay and the subsequent establishment of separate administrative arrangements and CEOs. The three offices operated independently from December 1986.

Looking back... looking forward

The development of the Sydney CEO, and its acceptance by its major clients, within twenty years, would indicate that this complex organisation now exhibited the characteristics of a rational bureaucracy including the structures and mechanisms to provide for its own survival and regeneration.[50]

---

[48] Canavan, *Perceptions and Expectations*, 252.
[49] Canavan, *Perceptions and Expectations*, 260.
[50] Canavan, *Perceptions and Expectations*, 45, 260.

What had generally been a large number of struggling poor schools isolated from each other, existing mainly on heroism and good will, slowly became a recognisable, cohesive and integrated System of schools. Another chapter in the history of Catholic schooling in Greater Sydney had begun.

Select Bibliography

_____"Payments to or for the States on the occasion of the Budget 1973-1974." Canberra, 1973.

_____"Payments to or for the States and Local Government Authorities on the occasion of the Budget 1974-1975". *Budget Paper 7*. Canberra, 1974.

_____"Payments to or for the States and Local Government Authorities on the occasion of the Budget 1975-1976". *Budget Paper 7*. Canberra:1975.

_____"Commonwealth payments to or for the States 1972-1973". Canberra 1972.

_____"Commonwealth payments to or for the States 1973-1974". Canberra 1973.

_____ "Commonwealth payments to or for the States 1970-1971". Canberra 1970.

_____ "Teachers (Assistant Masters and Mistresses in Non-Governmental Schools) (State) Award from 1970". *NSW Industrial Gazette*, Vol. 178, 30 September 1970.

Askin, Hon. R. W. "Policy Speech," 9 February 1968.

Askin, Hon. R. W. *Financial Statement*, 25 September 1968.

Canavan, Kelvin. *Perceptions and Expectations of Roles, Services, Structures and Goals of the Sydney Catholic Education Office held by Principals* and *CEO Staff*, Ed. D. Dissertation, University of San Francisco, UMI 86-14594, 1986.

Evangelii Nuntiandi (EN) *Apostolic Exhortation of Pope Paul VI*, December 1975.

Karmel, Peter. *Schools in Australia: report of the Interim Committee for the Australian Schools Commission*. Canberra, May 1973.

Luttrell, John *You've Taken Our Schools: The Role and Development of the Catholic Education Office*, Sydney, M.Ed Hons Thesis. Sydney: University of Sydney, 1992.

Minutes of CBFC meeting, 26 May 1965.

NSW Budget Papers 1967-1968.

Renshaw, Hon. J. B. *NSW Hansard*, 25 September 1963.

Sydney Archives/Catholic Schools NSW, Sydney: Catholic Education Office.

BIOGRAPHIES

Brother Ronald Edwin Fogarty fms
(Thomas Fogarty, 1913–2009)

Religious, researcher and teacher-educator

Br Julian Casey fms

Thomas Fogarty, the son of Elsie Jane Adams and Patrick Joseph Fogarty, was born in Broken Hill, NSW on 15 October 1913. He completed his schooling at Marist Brothers' College, Broken Hill and the Marist Brothers' Juniorate, Mittagong. As well as matriculating, he sat and passed the Australian Music Examination Board exams for Piano, Violin, and Singing at Grade VI level. He entered the Novitiate, where he received his religious name, Brother Ronald Edwin, a name he was known as for the rest of his life. He took his first vows in 1935 and undertook teacher training before he began his first teaching appointment at Marist Brothers' College, Maitland, NSW in 1936.

In 1939, Br Ronald was appointed to St Joseph's East Brunswick, Victoria, where he attended Melbourne University on a part-time basis. He graduated with a Bachelor of Arts in 1942. He was moved to St John's Hawthorn in 1943 and continued studying, completing a Bachelor of Education (1944) and a Bachelor of Science (1948).

In 1950, Br Ronald received a research fellowship from the University of Melbourne to undertake research into the History of Catholic Education 1806–1950. As a backdrop to this work, Br Ronald undertook significant responsibilities on behalf the Marist Brothers, including being a Provincial Councillor of the newly formed Southern Province 1948–1956. At the same time, he accepted the role of Master of Scholastics at Camberwell Victoria, where he personally undertook the teacher training of between 10-16 younger Brothers each year, for both the Southern and Northern Provinces. He supervised practice lessons, lectured in educational practice and philosophy as well as introducing younger Brothers to the early development of Catechetics. In 1952, the Scholasticate was shifted from Camberwell to Drummoyne, NSW, where Br Ronald continued his research, whilst still managing his responsibilities as Master of Scholastics and Provincial Councillor.

His research took him to state archives across Australia and to the archives of most dioceses and religious orders. In his foreword to Br Ronald's book, *Catholic Education in Australia 1806-1950* Volume I, Archbishop Eris O'Brien mentions the author's extensive network of contacts and resources, which 'had been in hitherto unexploited fields as well as a wide bibliography, and copious reference notes'.

In his seminal work, Br Ronald traced the development of a separate system of Catholic Education against the background of Australian society and in the context of an overall emerging Australian educational philosophy and practice. His scholarship was scrupulous, his analysis was insightful, and his historical investigation was seminal.

He was awarded a PhD in 1957 and, in 1959, Melbourne University Press published the thesis in two volumes. These volumes were most favourably reviewed at the time and continue to be a reliable reference in Australian Education.

Because of his experience in researching education, Br Ronald was convinced of the need to ensure that future Marist teachers were scholars and teachers as well as apostolic religious and he exerted significant but gentle pressure on Religious Superiors to plan for a four-year University Programme for secondary teachers and at least an accredited programme for primary teachers who were not proceeding to University. It was a courageous act to spell out a coherent and compelling vision of formation at a time when there was a large and somewhat desperate demand for Brothers to be in the classroom. However, Superiors, to their credit, began responding positively to his recommendations and began planning for a large scholasticate in Sydney. His dream was finally realised in 1957 when Champagnat College, Dundas with accommodation for 80 scholastics was opened.

At Dundas from 1958–1965, Br Ronald was responsible for a large cohort of Brothers, and introduced these young men, not yet in their 20s to religious life in an apostolic congregation. He believed that they would be spiritual leaders of the future and as such required a substantial formation. As well as their university studies, he insisted on course work in Philosophy and Theology. For those not attending university, he established a rigorous programme of study and course work covering a wide range of Education, Special Methods, Catechetics, practice lessons and cultural subjects. He took a personal interest in all the young men, met with them regularly, supervised their studies, played the piano at musical soirees and encouraged them in their developing religious life. As Master of Scholastics, he guided more than 60 young Marist Brothers until they graduated and 111 Brothers in their teacher-training. He himself had a deep attachment to scholarship and was forever studying. He studied theology at the Aquinas Academy under Dr Woodbury and later at the Holy Spirit Institute of Theology. In 1961, he gained his Diploma of Education Administration at the University of New England. He was in much demand and as well as his Marist commitments, lectured in other tertiary Institutes and universities.

In 1955, he was elected a Fellow of the Australian College of Education and was recipient of the Britannica Award in 1966 for distinguished contribution to scholarship in Australia.

In 1966-1969, he began a new phase of his life. Going to the United States on a Fulbright scholarship, he pursued a Masters' program in Psychology at Loyola University, Chicago and then engaged in post-doctoral studies at the Research Centre on Psychotherapy and Counselling at the University of Chicago. He studied Clinical Psychology with Dr Carl Rogers and with his encouragement undertook an internship in clinical psychology for an additional two years.

He returned to Australia in 1970, was appointed Master of Marist College Monash and became a member of the Australian Psychologists Association. He undertook lecturing to Fourth Year honours students in Psychology and Psychotherapy at Monash University. He maintained this lecturing commitment until 1992.

Br Ronald had a long and distinguished service to the Marist Brothers both as individuals seeking counselling and as a community needing its Chapter facilitated. But by 1970, formation was in someone else's hands and, although still Master of Marist College Monash, Br Ronald turned his attention to other needs in the Church.

Following Vatican II, there was a significant demand on Religious Congregations for renewal. Conscious of the stress that this caused individual and groups in the Church, Br Ronald began work with other apostolic and contemplative religious orders who were in the process of making the transition and grappling with change in the way they administered their monasteries, convents, schools, hospitals and other works. As Joan Chittister says of him in *The Way We Were*:

> He lectured for hours every day, yes, but then listened between conferences, during meals, through half the night working with one individual after another. He got to know them. He listened to their fears, their anger, their frustration their desires to be a community again. The community loved him. Most of all they trusted him.[51]

His peaceful presence was widely appreciated, and he found himself being invited to work with many Congregations in Australia, the South Pacific, in Ireland, United Kingdom, South Korea, South East Asia, United States, and Canada. He spent over 35 years in this work, developing complicated schedules and itineraries to fulfil commitments to each order as well as to Monash University.

In 2003, he finally stepped back from his work, continued his correspondence and *Lectio Divina*, read philosophy, fed the magpies, played the piano and attended to chores. He had chosen 'Contemplata aliis tradere' as the motto for the Scholasticate at Dundas. In some ways, this motto was also a statement about his own life and aspirations, namely 'to hand on to others the fruits of his contemplation'. He died at the age of 96 on the 13 December 2009. His funeral was held at Marcellin College, Bulleen.

---

[51] Joan Chittister, *The Way We Were*, Orbis Books, Maryknoll, N.Y. 1982, pp. 154–155

Writing

Fogarty, Br Ronald fms. *Catholic Education in Australia*, Vol. 1 & 2, Melbourne: Melbourne University Press, 1959.

Select Bibliography

Chittister, Joan. *The Way We Were*, Maryknoll, New York: Orbis Books, 2005.

Family details, Curriculum Vitae, Speeches, Academic awards and scholarships, Marist Brothers Australian Archives.

Annual Reports from Champagnat College Dundas by Br Ronald, Marist Brothers Australian Archives.

Casey, Julian fms. *Eulogy: Br Ronald Fogarty, 1913-2009.*

Fr Charles Fraser sj (1913–2004)

Disciplined scholarship graced by Christian humanity

Damian Gleeson

In the centenary year (1980) of St Ignatius' College (familiarly known as "Riverview"), the president of the Old Boys Union, Charles Fraser sj, himself a teacher at the school for nearly three decades, injected an even greater than usual effort in creating a superb red rose garden of more than 500 plants. The garden, the joy of Fraser's hobbies, coupled with his intense loyalty to Riverview, meant that with few exceptions, the garden was for admiration only. Indeed, in 1955 when two cows again strayed onto his beloved rose bed – and the brother in charge would not do anything – Fraser acted and shot the cows with a .303 rifle. Such was the unorthodox character of this otherwise-conservative priest who was a brilliant educator of the classics at Riverview spanning nearly fifty years. (For the record, the surviving cows wandered around till 1957, but untroubled by Charles Fraser who was in New Zealand in 1957.)

Born in his mother's home town of Gundagai on 14 March 1913, Charles was the second son of Walter John Fraser, a solicitor of Tumut and Eva Bibo Mackenzie, possibly a non-Catholic. Both families were widely respected in the Gundagai and Tumut areas and had high expectations for Charles. Walter, though, despite being a gifted sportsman when he too attended St Ignatius', did not want his generally unhappy school experiences repeated by Charles and so he determined that Charles' secondary schooling be elsewhere. In 1926, however, Walter's premature death left the decision for Charles' mother, who reinstated St Ignatius' College and thus began Charles' lifetime association with Riverview.

Charles's early grades at Riverview confirmed his natural bent towards literature and the humanities, though he also was a good sportsman, such as long-distance running. In the 1931 Public Examinations, Fraser matriculated with As in English, Latin, French and Modern History. He continued his previous academic focus during 1934-1936, graduating with an Arts Degree from the University of Melbourne, majoring in Latin, Greek, and English, whilst concurrently studying to be a Jesuit, the order he had joined in February 1932 after completing high school.

Fraser's first appointment to Riverview was in 1940-42, where he taught English and classics. Further studies took place at Loyola, Watsonia. When Charles Fraser was ordained with seven other Jesuits by Cardinal Gilroy on 5 January 1946, the event was notable, as all the *ordinandi* had done their training in Australian houses of study and universities and all belonged to the Australian vice-province of the Jesuits.

From 1947-1952, Fraser worked at the Holy Name Seminary, Christchurch, New Zealand, a position that filled him with great satisfaction as he was involved in training future priests. He seemed to relish parish life, too, but loyalty to his superiors meant that when he returned to Australia, he quickly adjusted again to life at Riverview, where he remained for nearly fifty years, most of his working life.

Generations of students nicknamed him "Chisel" as a result of a dry, rasping voice. He prepared his classes meticulously and controlled them effectively from his seated position. He was strong on method and precision, though possibly a little less engaging than a 21st century teacher. Nevertheless, his style and dry wit attracted many a student. Robert Hughes, the historian and art critic, noted in his memoir that he

> liked this controlled, scholarly man. He [Fraser] had an elegantly ironic sense of humour, and a dry way of praising your work if you did it well, that left you, not self-satisfied, but keen to do more.

Fraser regarded Socrates second only to St Paul as the greatest human who had ever lived. He had a bust of Socrates in his bedroom. His favourite books were the *Apology*, the Bible and the *Imitation of Christ*.

Fraser particularly made an impression on the boys while he was in charge of Riverview's boarding facilities ('minister'), 1962-67. While firm and strict, he was also fair, with a soft spot for the scallywag and sinner. He was particularly attentive to individual students who had special needs. He roamed the grounds after school, setting rabbit traps, digging flowerbeds or playing squash with tennis racquets in the handball courts with the boys.

For over four decades, Fraser was the driving force behind the Old Ignatians Union, moulding it into a large and cohesive force. He travelled to numerous country reunions and knew alumni by name. He wrote comprehensive notes on Old Ignatians for publication in *Our Alma Mater*, of which he was the editor from 1967 to 1984. Old Ignatian and playwright Justin Fleming described him as combining 'disciplined scholarship graced by Christian humanity'.

Charles Fraser came from a generation that understood policies and clear boundaries and expected them to be upheld. Despite his outreach to many students and their families, Fraser was an intensely private man, sharing little about his personal life. Traditional by nature, he may also have been scrupulous. His faith remained strong despite being uncomfortable with many changes in the Church after the Second Vatican Council (1962-1965). He went to Manila for a renewal course in the early 1970s, but he returned unimpressed with what he had heard. He reputedly ceased hearing the confessions of the boys because he said that they did not know the Act of Contrition.

In his limited free time, he enjoyed the company of men and entertained them with stories and dry wit. In the company of women, he was always the epitome of courtesy and charm, but he never sought out their friendship, except to play bridge.

After his retirement from full-time teaching in 1987, Fr Charles Fraser stayed on at Riverview as spiritual father to the old boys' association, a school chaplain and also helped out when the need arose.

In 2002, the Riverview community were unable to continue to care for him and he was moved to the community at Arrupe House, Pymble, and fairly soon after, to McQuoin, the Mercy Aged Care, Nursing Home at Waitara.

Fr Charles Fraser sj died in Sydney on 12 February 2004, aged 90 years.

Riverview College named one of its houses, Charles Fraser House, after this man who gave so much and cared so much for the College. Fittingly, also, the rose garden continues to this day.

Select Bibliography

Catholic Weekly, 5 January 1946.

Freeman's Journal, 3 June 1926.

Gundagai Independent and Pastoral, Agricultural and Mining Advocate, 7 June 1926.

Hughes, R. *Things I didn't know: a memoir* (New York, 2006).

Strong, David sj, Charles Fraser in *The Australian Dictionary of Jesuit Biography 1848-2015*.

Sydney Morning Herald, 30 April 1980.

Windsor, G. 'Obituary: Charles Fraser, Jesuit, classicist, larrikan', *Sydney Morning Herald*, 23 February 2004.

Mother Loyola Fraser csb (1918–2008)

In her, the love of God and of literature were beautifully blended

Sr Clare Keady csb

Joyce Eva Fraser was born in Gundagai, NSW, on 23 December 1918 to Walter John Fraser and Eva Bibo Fraser (nee Mackenzie, also spelt McKenzie). She was the youngest of four children, sister to Walter (also known as David), Charles (later Fr Charles Fraser sj, legendary Classics Master at St Ignatius' College, Riverview), and Marie. Their father was a highly respected solicitor in Gundagai and Tumut and their mother a gifted singer and pianist. In her memoirs, *The Last Leaf Left*, Joyce speaks of her father's 'clarity of mind and penetrating judgment' recognised locally in the citation presented on his premature retirement. His early death profoundly affected the family.

Joyce was educated at Brigidine College, Randwick (1930-1934) and Our Lady of Mercy College, Goulburn, where her love of music and literature was nourished. She taught music before entering the Brigidine novitiate at Randwick in 1939. Upon profession of vows as Sister Loyola, her first appointment was to Coonamble, NSW, for four years. Her Leaving Certificate literature classes are still remembered there, the impact of a young and spirited intellect.

At Sydney University (1945-51), Mother Loyola's BA (Hons.) was followed by an MA in English Language and Literature (1951). She was awarded the Sydney University Women's Graduates Association Award for the best English essay of 1946. A chance encounter with the poem, 'Carrion Comfort' kindled a lifelong passion and her thesis on Gerard Manley Hopkins, examining his journals, letters, prose and poetry, and exploring their impact on the faith of the 'star of Balliol'. 'Understanding with great clarity his most difficult poems', she wrote in her 1998 *Memoirs*, enabled the poems to be unlocked for countless students.

Returning to teach at Brigidine College, Randwick, in 1951, she was appointed principal of the College in 1954 where she remained for fifteen years. During that time, the Wyndham Scheme in NSW in 1962 created new challenges, with the addition of Sixth Form, the need for greater resources and broader subject options. Sr Loyola responded to the Catholic Education Office's request that Brigidine College become a regional school. This was a highly divisive move, driven by her eagerness to educate the widest possible range of students. As principal, she had written, 'we shall not condemn ourselves to a sterile learning that does not teach us how to live and wondered if the old have failed the young as transmitters of truth'.

As principal, Mother Loyola was keenly aware of 'two incipient dangers – larger numbers, mass groupings and the collateral submerging of the individual with advanced equipment, objective techniques and the diminution of the personal influence of the teacher... machine teachers, cipher-children'. She critiqued the new system while embracing the opportunities for wider and deeper education and enriched learning.

She was an exacting teacher: her ex-students can still quote from her quixotic French grammar rules. She was merciless, too, towards floating participles and 'purple' prose. Her influence was enormous, awakening for many of her students 'a lifelong love of poetry'.

More complex programs, increased pupil enrolments (the College had over 700 students in 1968) and new facilities all added greatly to 'the adventure of Catholic Education'. College examination results were encouraging at this pivotal time – Commonwealth Scholarships show the College adapting to radical change under her leadership.

At Brigidine College, Indooroopilly, Queensland, Mother Loyola brought a new emphasis to the Arts in education. As Principal (1969-1973), Head of the English Department and later, as an innovative librarian (1973-1980), she relished the emerging technological developments in learning and new facilities that funding from Commonwealth grants offered. The Radford Scheme imposed new demands in secondary education: moderation meetings, an expanding curriculum and the implementation of internal assessment. Under the Radford Scheme, music, drama and art gained momentum at Brigidine College. Appropriately, in 1995, the college recognised her through the establishment of the annual *Sister Loyola Fraser Prize for Appreciation of the Arts, Poetry, Painting and Music*.

In 1982, while in Scarborough, Queensland, Loyola spent some months doing extensive research on Brigidine Spirituality and the influence of St Francis de Sales on the life of Bishop Daniel Delany, founder of the Brigidine Congregation. Returning to Indooroopilly in 1985, she moved into adult religious education. A course at The Cenacle in Brisbane led her to begin home retreats: 'Spirituality drenched with literature', as one eager participant wrote. The groups flourished for more than a decade from 1986.

Between 1991 and 1998, Mother Loyola wrote three books for private circulation. In *How Right It Is* (1991), the literature that had shaped so many minds found new expression. Drawing on Annie Dillard, Yeats, Hopkins, Hildegard of Bingen and others, she explored their struggle towards faith in the midst of suffering and doubt, a recurring theme in her classroom and later, in adult groups. She quoted James McAuley harvesting his apples:

> 'Something is gathered in,
> Worth the lifting and stacking'.

For Mother Loyola, that 'something' was faith illuminating life. The book is a treatise on the love of God, given and received.

Not Love Them the Less (1994) examines Simone Weil's life and works, particularly her essay "The love of God and Affliction". She explores the mystery of human suffering, reflected in life and literature, in 20 chapters from Sophocles to Patrick White, cameos of poignant moments in world literature. She sees Weil's 'real gift to the world' as perhaps 'the contagion of the divine'. In schools and in adult groups, she had never shrunk from addressing that mystery.

In *The Last Leaf Left* (1998), personal memoirs and reflections probe the theme of diminishment: insights harvested from theology, literature and the mystics, coupled with a frank autobiography. She may have left the classroom but still had much to contribute to eager learners in their later years.

Sister Loyola's final years at Randwick brought her the challenges of age and impaired sight, yet she remained in contact with many of the ex-students who held her in high regard. Her final years were reflective and prayerful, and she died on 3 March 2008.

'Wisdom shared unstintingly', one ex-student wrote, on learning of her death. Another expressed it thus: 'She made words dance'. After her Mass of Christian burial at St Brigid's, Coogee, Sr Loyola was buried at Eastern Suburbs Memorial Park Cemetery.

Writings

'Gerard Manley Hopkins as a Religious Writer', BA Hons. Thesis, University of Sydney, 1948.

'Principal's Report 1963', *Brigidine Convent Randwick Annual*, 11.

Acts of the General Chapter of the Brigidine Congregation, Philosophy of Christian Education, Brigidine Archives NSW, 1971.

How Right It Is, 1991.

Not Love Them the Less, 1994.

The Last Leaf Left, 1998.

Select Bibliography

Brigidine College Ex-Students Association, *Newsletter*. Brigidine College Randwick, 2008.

Fortiter et Suaviter: Annuals of Brigidine College, Randwick 1954-1967.

Garaty, J, *Providence Provides. Brigidine Sisters in the NSW Province*. Sydney: UNSW Press, 2013.

Keady, Sr C., 'Sister Loyola Fraser CSB 1918-2008', *Focus Magazine*, April 2008, 25.

Sherington, G. E. 'Wyndham, Sir Harold Stanley (1903-1988)', *Australian Dictionary of Biography*. Melbourne: Melbourne University Press, Volume 18, 2012. adb.anu.edu.au/biography/wyndham-sir-harold-stanley-15880.

Sydney Morning Herald, 5 March 2008.

University of Sydney Records, Faculty of Arts, 1945-1951, University of Sydney Archives.

Windsor, G. 'Obituary: Charles Fraser, Jesuit, classicist, larrikan', *Sydney Morning Herald*, 23 February 2004.

Francis (Frank) Irenaeus McCarthy cfc oam face (1920-2010)

Long-serving teacher and lover of art

Bill Wilding cfc

At the time of his death in late December 2010, Dr Frank McCarthy cfc, aged nearly 90 years, was reputedly the oldest registered working teacher in Australia. Throughout his long teaching career – spanning seventy years – he had been an inspiring and dynamic educator. who fired the imagination of his pupils in Melbourne, Queensland, Adelaide and Canberra.

Francis Irenaeus McCarthy, the son of Justin McCarthy and Hilma Lundmark, was born in Melbourne on 31 December 1930. Justin had played first grade VFL including kicking the winning goal for Essendon in the 1923 Grand Final. Frank's parents encouraged their children to attain success through education.

Frank, as he was known, attended primary school at St John's, West Footscray. His secondary education was at Parade College, East Melbourne and then at Saint Enda's Juniorate, Strathfield, Sydney, where he made his vows to be a Christian Brother in 1939.

His tertiary education included a BA, MA, DipEd and BEd from the University of Melbourne and a PhD from Cambridge University. His early teaching appointments were at Bundaberg, Toowoomba, St Kevin's in Melbourne and Rostrevor in Adelaide. Frank dedicated his life to the Christian Brothers. With his capability and qualifications, he could have successfully achieved fame in other fields of endeavour.

His students at Parade College from 1951-1960 and 1964-1965, St Kevin's College 1949, 1977-2009 and elsewhere held him in the highest regard. They sensed that their interests were his interests and their future his concern. There was more to this man than his classroom instruction. The tributes following his death came from many parts of the world for a man who spent most of his life teaching in the one Australian city. They told of one who was way beyond the ordinary.

Many of his students ventured into significant areas of life and contributed greatly to the public good. From his past students came the frequent statement: 'I would not be here in this position today if it were not for Br Frank'.

Art became a great love of his life, and rather than being limited by his chosen profession, he went beyond the conventional path to open the eyes of so many young and old to its beauty and inspiration. He was widely appreciated in this field and frequently invited to deliver addresses and open exhibitions. Francis Haskell, the Professor of Art History at Oxford University and world-renowned authority, claimed Francis McCarthy as a dear friend.

His guidance and teaching were not just about the present, or just about the past, but also about the future. Career teachers were still half a century away but some were at it anyway. Frank had an ability to assess a boy's abilities and interests and gently suggest the best way forward.

His biographer noted that:

> Students seek from their teachers the spark to ignite processes of thought, ever widening imagination, and especially confidence and curiosity. Most teachers produce some sparks for their students. But in the case of Francis Irenaeus McCarthy this happened for so many, at such an intensity and for so long that he can be described as a veritable flaming torch; a flaming torch that was not confined to the students in his classes but extended generously to students at other schools, to fellow teachers, to parent groups, to members of this family and to anyone he met.

From 1961 to 1963, he accepted the opportunity to study at Cambridge University where he was awarded a PhD on 14 December 1963 for his thesis on *Mountain scenery in British Art 1750-1815*. His scholarship, sense of excellence and great rapport with Fellows and students led the Council of Pembroke College to offer him a much-sought Fellowship. Frank declined this impressive honour and honoured his commitment to his Congregation to return to education in Australia.

He was Headmaster of CBC St Kilda, 1966-1971, and Parade College from 1974-1976, and led both schools to pursue excellence in all fields. At St Kilda, he is remembered for enhancing academic results and a new commitment to style and tradition. Masters were instructed to wear academic gowns, Assembly was held for the whole school on each morning except Wednesday, and an increased emphasis was placed on ceremony and formality.

The staff gave their full support to these changes, agreeing that both tone and spirit in the school needed attention. Br McCarthy, in fact preserved the traditions of the school during his term as Headmaster; under his leadership, CBC expanded its curriculum offerings, increased involvement in sports, and flourished. He placed particular emphasis on academic achievement and maintained high standards.

His unbounded energy also flowed into very active membership of many educational committees and as a visiting lecturer in Art History at Melbourne University. Francis brought an equal passion to his extra-curricular activities. In Rugby he sought out the overlooked and gave them self-belief and opportunity. In debating his teams soared to the top of the competition.

Br Francis was honoured as a Fellow of the Australian College of Educators. In 2006, he was awarded an OAM for 'service to education through the Christian Brothers particularly at St Kevin's College, Toorak'.

His funeral occurred in the midst of the holiday season in early January 2010 when large numbers of Melburnians have departed the city for the summer break. Despite this, St Ignatius' Church in Richmond was crowded to overflowing, with nearly 1,000 assembled to honour a man held in great repute. The mourners were mainly men whom he had taught, with a high proportion of them being still in their 20s. Their grief was heartfelt.

Select Bibliography

Wilding, Bill, cfc., *Flaming Torch, a biography of Br Francis McCarthy cfc*, St Mary's, South Australia: Mirrabooka Press.

Sr Mary St Bernard fdnsc (1925-2016)

No device will take the living, loving teacher's place

Sr Helen Simpson fdnsc

Edna Ellen Dent was born on 18 May 1925 in Mildura, Victoria, the eldest of the three children of Clyde Dent and his wife Ellen (nee O'Donoghue). Her father served in the Light Horse Brigade during World War I and later joined the police force which caused many moves for the family and so disruption to the children's education. When she was almost 14 years old, Edna continued her secondary education at a one-teacher school in Elmore, near Bendigo, Victoria. There, she was blessed with a teacher, who, with practically no library or reference books, had a staggering breadth of knowledge, who taught with competence and authority, preparing her pupils right through to university entrance.

Edna entered the novitiate of the Congregation of the Daughters of Our Lady of the Sacred Heart at Hartzer Park, Burradoo, New South Wales, on 21 November 1949 and entered her novitiate on 1 July 1950.

Edna modelled her own teaching on that of her last teacher as she became a brilliant, creative educator who was in many ways ahead of her time. She gained her secondary teacher's certificate through the Victorian Department of Education and with one year of a Bachelor of Arts degree embarked on her teaching career which spanned more than 30 years, 1951 to 1989. In her personal writings, Enda wrote about teachers as follows:

> A teacher is the best audio-visual aid. Our aim is to be something like a catalyst: to bring the encounter of each individual child with Christ... It is imperative to remember that only a person can introduce us to reality, normally

speaking, even to Divine reality. No electronic device will take the living, loving teacher's place.

This motivated her teaching ministry. Her former students have described her variously as 'brilliant, inspiring, amazing, unforgettable'. One of her former pupils said:

> Final year students of Religious Education at Kensington in the early nineteen-sixties recall with amazement that she broke open the Gospel of John for them under the symbolism of blood and water, light and darkness, and the like. This biblical exposition was just becoming available in the works of scholars and Sr M. St Bernard was able to absorb it and make it attractive to sixteen-year-olds!

When Edna, as Sr Mary St Bernard, was teaching Middle Eastern Studies in Bentleigh in the 1970s, the class sizes increased dramatically because the girls encouraged others to come to such wonderful lessons. One of these students of forty years ago marvelled at the fact that at different stages in the course, a Buddhist, a Moslem, and a Rabbi were invited to address the class.

Vatican Council II (1962-1965) ushered in an era of great change for the Church and consequently for religious life. The Constitutions, the Rule of Life, of the Daughters of Our Lady of the Sacred Heart had remained virtually unchanged since 1928. As the second Vatican Council required all Religious to revise their Constitutions so they would be more suitable for the following of Christ in a rapidly-changing world, Bernie, as she was called by many, was asked by the Superior General to come to Rome in 1969 to make a complete revision of the Constitutions. To do this work well, Edna enrolled in the Pontifical Institute, *Regina Mundi*, where she studied the documents of Vatican II and the history and theology of Religious life. This revision was fundamental for the future of the Congregation. On completion of this work, she returned to Australia before she could complete the degree. Later, 1976-1978, she studied at the Catholic Theological College, Melbourne, and gained a Bachelor of Theology. She now changed from being an excellent teacher of English and French to teach other subjects such as the Middle Eastern Studies mentioned above.

Edna's contribution was not only confined to the school scene. In the years 1962 to 1965, she was the novice director. She always strove for the highest ideal herself and expected the same of her novices, something which was not always achievable although they are still grateful that they were well instructed in the charism, spirituality and mission of the Congregation and about the three vows and the spiritual life. Her formation was characterised by her acute intellect, her energy and her striking blue eyes, which missed little.

In 2001, at the age of 75, Bernie accepted an appointment to the mining city of Mt Isa. There she conducted Parish Retreats, offered programs of Adult Education in the Faith, worked at the Christian radio station, with the parish Liturgy and discussion groups, Centacare, the St Vincent de Paul society and did many other things as well.

She returned to Kensington in 2006 when her health was failing and as she lived out the words of a prayer she had written: 'Let me grow old wisely and graciously. Let me smile peacefully as change leads to change'. She died on 29 May 2016.

Selected Writings

Personal reminiscences in *Faith Memories, Our Lady of the Sacred Heart Parish Elmore*, a Project for the Year of the Great Jubilee, 2000.

Unpublished personal writings written for the Congregation.

Dent, M. St Bernard, 1979, "Charles Gavan Duffy in Victoria: 1856-1880", *Catholic Theological Review*, 1979 Vol II, 88-109.

Select Bibliography

Congregational Archives of the Daughters of Our Lady of the Sacred Heart, Kensington NSW.

Eulogy, from Congregational Archives.

Memories of her former pupils and of some OLSH sisters, Congregational Archives.

Francis (Frank) Michael Martin (1928–2015)

Astute negotiator and visionary architect of a Catholic education system

Anne O'Brien

Frank Martin, son of Katherine Hoare and Joseph Martin, was initially deemed unsuitable for entrance to the seminary: the vicar-general opined he was of illegitimate birth. Catholic Katherine had married Walter Kenworthy in the Anglican church at Bendigo; on his death, she married Joseph Martin in the Methodist manse at Kalgoorlie. But, unbeknown to her family, she and Joseph had long since had their marriage 'rectified'. Thus, Frank was in fact qualified for entrance to Werribee, where he began his studies in 1949.

Born on 17 August 1928 in Coburg, Martin was educated at the local parish school and later at Christian Brothers College, East Melbourne. One of his post-school public service jobs (1945-48) – as personal assistant to the secretary of the War Cabinet to report on conditions of service for the armed forces – enabled Martin to gain insight into how processes could be used to formulate policies. This experience was later to be deployed and further developed to great effect in navigating the complexities of implementing system-wide funding for Catholic schools.

Archbishop Justin Simonds ordained Frank Martin for the Archdiocese of Melbourne in July 1956. After a short stint at North Brunswick parish, Martin was appointed as an inspector of schools at Melbourne's Catholic Education Office (CEO) in 1958. This would be the start of an impressive contribution to the transformation of Catholic education in Victoria – with national reverberations – over the next twenty years. In the post-war period of increased immigration, Catholic education was in severely straitened circumstances, even 'floundering', as Professor

Dick Selleck had observed. Staff were carrying intolerable burdens and some religious orders considered phasing out commitment to parish schools. Moreover, between 1963 and 1979, profound educational, political, theological and ecclesiastical developments were propelling what had been a 'collection of schools and children' towards a fully articulated system. As Hedley Beare affirmed:

> '... the current powerful presence of Catholic education was made possible by the consistent, sustained, creative and brilliant work of just a few visionaries, chief among whom was Father Frank Martin. He was both the architect and the first Director of the Catholic Education Office of Victoria, a confidant of people in high places, a representative of the Catholic sector on the Schools Commission, an extraordinarily adept negotiator, and an astute political tactician'.[52]

Frank's first efforts in Catholic education were directed towards improving religious instruction in government schools. In 1961, he appealed to all parishes for lay people to give religious instruction in government schools and at the same time organised teams of priests, religious and lay educators to prepare them. By the end of 1962, 810 catechists had graduated, and Frank was appointed Director of Religious Education in Government schools. Under his guidance, the publication *Let's Go Together* was produced fortnightly for use in government schools.

When it came to address the all-pervasive financing, staffing and training problems of the schools in a comprehensive way, Frank's more prominent qualities – or set of qualities – became apparent. His *modus operandi* reflected Vatican II teaching that the church's structures and processes should be characterised by collegiality, co-operation, co-responsibility and subsidiarity. This was evident in Frank's ability

---

[52] Hedley Beare, "Foreword", *Anne O'Brien, Blazing a Trail. Catholic Education in Victoria 1963-1980*, (Melbourne: David Lovell Publications, 1999) viii.

to work productively with stakeholders who had never met together before – archdiocesan representatives, parish priests, superiors and representatives of teaching orders and laity. To prepare for a successful first meeting with these key partners, to be chaired by Archbishop Simonds on 9 July 1963, Frank, together with Fr John Keaney, ensured that religious order participants would be adequately briefed on the meeting's purpose by visiting them beforehand. His respectful and collegial style was evident, too, in the way he later related with religious orders and managed the sensitive politics of emerging regional schools vis-à-vis the order-owned independent colleges.

In 1970, following the dismissal of the previous Director and at a time of church turmoil after Vatican II, Fr Martin was appointed Director of the Catholic Education Office in Melbourne. On the national scene, the question of government funding for Catholic schools was becoming more critical. When Labor won government in December 1972, the scene was set for Martin's transformative work in Catholic education to expand in scope and depth. Prime Minister Gough Whitlam immediately set up an Interim Committee of the Schools Commission, with Professor Peter Karmel as chair, to investigate the needs of all schools throughout Australia. When Martin accepted nomination to this Commission to represent the Catholic sector, he was told that he would be pilloried throughout Australia and that he was unlikely to survive B. A. Santamaria's (The Movement, Democratic Labour Party, DLP), undermining of him. Nevertheless, at the initial meeting of the Interim Committee, Martin achieved a major coup whereby a block fund would be allocated to each state Catholic authority which in turn was required to allocate the fund according to need.

The block grant saved Catholic schools; but it led to open warfare among Catholic authorities. A public rift involving bishops, Catholic Education Offices, laity, Santamaria independent school protagonists and the Australian Parents Council was so vociferous that the government Bill to approve release of money was delayed. The Bishops' Central Commission made an extraordinary dissenting response to the Karmel Report – at the behest of Santamaria – leaving Martin and the Karmel Committee out on a limb. Looking back, Frank Rogan (a former

Melbourne CEO staffer), was dismayed: 'I marvelled at the fact...[you were humiliated] and seemingly abandoned by those very people who should have been your greatest support'.

By this time, however, Martin had a supportive body behind him. As far back as the 1960s, he had moved to set up state structures. A representative of diocesan bishops, diocesan directors of Catholic education, plus Melbourne CEO staff formed the initial group. By 1973, the Catholic Education Commission of Victoria (CECV), serviced by the Catholic Education Office of Victoria (CEOV), with Martin as Director, was firmly established. This provided a forum for Frank to test proposals and 'cover... his back' in the face of warring factions. Beyond state borders, Martin, believing it crucial for New South Wales and Victoria to collaborate, worked closely with Archbishop James Carroll of Sydney for years, informing him of Schools Commission deliberations so that both men operated in tandem.

It was a long road, but by 1980, after years of painstaking negotiations, an identifiable and viable Catholic system, with re-aligned power exercised through sophisticated structures, and with a balance of centralised and decentralised services, had been firmly established. In 1981, the Commonwealth Government awarded Fr Martin an MBE. Later, Eminent Professor Hedley Beare would say:

> Frank Martin landed in the office from which he could exercise such profoundly insightful leadership, carried through with such unwavering, uncompromising integrity, and I must add imagination.

Fr Martin resigned his education portfolio at the end of 1979 to take up the challenge of establishing the parish of St Paul Apostle at Endeavour Hills, followed by a lengthy ministry at Our Lady of the Assumption Parish, Cheltenham, from 1987 to 2007.

Fr Frank Martin MBE, pastor and educator, died in Melbourne on 2 September 2015.

Select Bibliography

Bowden, M & Bowden, F. "Obituary: Father Frank, the Catholic priest who had his own cheer squad", *Sydney Morning Herald*, 1 December 2015 (online edition).

Melbourne News: Vale Father Frank Martin, 4 September 2015.

O'Brien, A. *Blazing a Trail: Catholic Education in Victoria, 1963-1980*, Melbourne: David Lovell Publishing, 1999.

Personal Tributes.

Rogan F., Letter to Frank Martin, 18 May 2005.

Margaret Toohey rscj (1930–2014)

An educator ahead of her time

Sr Cecilie Amiet rscj

Margaret Mary Toohey rscj, was born on 12 November 1930 in Malvern, Melbourne, Victoria, Australia, the second daughter of John William Toohey and Dorothy Agnes Denehy, and the youngest of their five children. She was sister to John, Leo, Philip and Patricia who also entered the Society of the Sacred Heart. Her parents chose a Sacred Heart education for her primary and secondary years at Sacré Coeur, Glen Iris, Victoria, where her sister, Patricia, preceded her.

Before she entered religious life, Margaret spent some time living and teaching at the Convent of the Sacred Heart School, Rose Bay, Sydney. She entered the Society there in 1952 and made her first vows in 1954. Her teaching began in primary classes at Rose Bay and Sacré Coeur before she completed an Arts degree in German, Latin and History from Sydney University, with two years at Sancta Sophia College at the University of Sydney. After final profession in Rome in 1960, Margaret obtained a Diploma of Education in England and for several years, taught secondary classes at Rose Bay and Sacré Coeur.

In 1966, she took up a new role, responsible for the formation of several young religious sisters at Rose Bay. With another sister of the Society and three young professed, she travelled by ship to England for further formation. Margaret gained a Diploma in Theology and Scripture at Corpus Christi College, London. This equipped her – once back in Sydney – to become involved in programs of religious education and catechetics with another member of the congregation. This was followed by a period when she lectured in English and Religious Education at Loreto Hall Teacher Training College in Auckland.

A new chapter began for Margaret in 1971 when she was appointed Principal at Stuartholme School in Brisbane, a position she held till 1983. In the year of the centenary of the death of Janet Erskine Stuart (2014), a former Superior-General of the Society of the Sacred Heart, the educational vision of Janet and Margaret were compared. In awakening young minds and hearts, both Janet and Margaret saw intellectual values developing cognitive growth, as well as imagination and creativity. An associate remembered Margaret's great sensitivity for families of boarders from outback Queensland and Papua New Guinea, and the trust and respect she won from staff who enjoyed her sense of humour and foibles.

As Principal, Margaret was confronted by the challenges and cultural changes following the Second Vatican Council – a time of significant transition for both the Church and for Catholic education. The "living tradition" of the community demanded changes as well improved finances for the school. Margaret responded by increasing academic standards and school enrolments and appointing lay teachers as the educators of the students within the Sacré Coeur charism.

She fostered a learning community steeped in the goals of Sacred Heart education and grounded in the charism of Madeleine Sophie Barat, foundress of the Society of the Sacred Heart. She personally described three significant features of Sacred Heart education as family spirit, strong studies with a broad cultural perspective, and the valuing of the individual child, making room for differences. This resonates with millennium educators, who recognise the importance of relationships, critical thinking, global awareness, and individual differences, social and intellectual. She believed strongly in the contribution made by women.

The demands of the role of Principal took their toll on her health. She moved from Stuartholme in 1983 and, after a rest period, resumed some teaching at Sacré Coeur.

In 1991, she embarked on a new ministry, training in Pastoral Care and joining teams in several hospitals in Melbourne and in Sydney. Always an educator at heart, Margaret made a very significant contribution to Sacred Heart Education in the Australia-New Zealand

(ANZ) Province when, in 1994, she edited a book, *Heart of our God, Documentary Sources of the Goals* [of Sacred Heart Education]. Working with fourteen other members of the Society, she developed what she called in her introduction 'a gathering together of source material which may help present and future interpreters of the tradition find their way'.

In 2001, Margaret entered Karlaminda, Kensington, (in Sydney) the community's aged care facility, and when it closed in 2009, was transferred to Lewisham Retirement Hostel. With increasing dementia, she moved to Lewisham Nursing Home where she died peacefully on 6 April 2014. After the Requiem Mass at Kensington on 10 April 2014, Margaret Toohey was buried in the Society's cemetery at Rose Bay.

In life, Margaret was a tall, slim, person with a beautiful face, often pensive and at times difficult to read, but with a characteristic bright smile.

Writing

Toohey, Margaret, rscj. Editor. *Sacred Heart Education. Heart of our God, Documentary Sources of the Goals.* 1994.

Select Bibliography

Archives: Society of the Sacred Heart, Rose Bay, Sydney.

McGrath, Anne, rscj. Eulogy. 10 April 2014.

Ann Dennis Clark (1935–1997)

Visionary, Charismatic, Elegant and Innovative Leader

Anne Benjamin

Ann Dennis Clark was a nationally-respected educator, described on her death by historian Edmund Campion, 'as a symbol of the new lay leadership emerging in Australian Catholicism'. At the time she assumed the role in the Diocese of Parramatta (1987-1997), she was the first female Director of Catholic Education in New South Wales.

Ann Clark was born at Randwick, New South Wales, on 26 March 1935, one of eight children of George Dennis Clark (1902-1986) and Roberta Hunter (1899-1974). She completed her early schooling at the local Catholic parish school and then at St Vincent's College, Potts Point. The relationship with the Sisters of Charity, begun in her school years, matured as Ann herself entered the Congregation assuming the name Sister Christopher, and completed her teaching training. Ann taught in primary and secondary schools associated with the Congregation between 1961 and 1972, holding positions of teacher, Head of Department, Deputy Principal and Principal. She also completed a Bachelor of Arts, a Bachelor of Science and a Master's Degree in Educational Administration, all from the University of New England.

After leaving the Sisters of Charity, Ann spent a year in New Zealand as Head of a Science department before returning to Australia to teach at Santa Sabina College in Strathfield. Between 1976-1978, she held the position of Deputy Director of Education in the Diocese of Bathurst, NSW, and of Acting Director of Education there from January to June 1979. In June 1979, she was appointed Secondary Consultant in the Archdiocese of Sydney Catholic Education Office. In 1981, when Sydney

She intuitively grasped the potential of big ideas, borrowing, adapting or creating her own. Her close associates said of her that 'Ann didn't dream in detail', but having sketched a bold dream, left it to others to flesh out and implement. In this she was well served because of her ability to recognise and attract highly competent and motivated staff. One such dream was the establishment in 1990 of a Spiritual Formation Team who worked with teachers and school and office staff. Another dream was the creation of *Elim*, a residential professional and spiritual enrichment experience for senior Catholic educators, which since 1995 has attracted principals and other educational leaders from around Australia. In similar ways, Ann initiated bold programs in professional development for teachers of Religious Education and school leaders. Under Ann's leadership, Parramatta Catholic schools became a Diocesan system to emulate.

Ann enjoyed looking good, and always dressed with panache. Her role as Executive Director and the public functions that came with it provided Ann with many opportunities to exercise her flair for sophistication and verve in her costumes. Even through her long illness she retained her fascination with style and elegance.

Brian Croke, then Executive Director of Catholic Education Commission NSW, summed up Ann as a person who was a gifted communicator, a lady of elegance and style, a person of passion, commitment and engagement, committed to her own learning as well as to the quality of education for all Australians and who advocated constantly that education was about 'making a difference' in the life of each student. (Adapted from speech at the Launch of Ann D. Clark Trust).

She became ill in January 1994 and battled ovarian cancer with extraordinary determination for the next three years. She surrendered her role as Executive Director only on her death bed, on 27 January 1997. On her death, the NSW Minister for Education, Mr John Aquilina, observed that the 'education community, especially the students, has lost a great friend and a devoted servant'. St Mary's Cathedral, Sydney, overflowed for her funeral Mass as bishops, clergy, religious principals, teachers, staff and students paid their respect. Ann is buried at Northern Suburbs Lawn Cemetery.

Selected Writing

The Changing Principalship of The Catholic Secondary School in the Archdiocese of Sydney (Major work for Master of Educational Administration, University of New England, 1981.

"School leadership Development for the Twenty First Century", Paper presented to Seventh International Inter-visitation Program in Educational Administration *Towards 2000 Preparing Educational Managers School for leadership*, Manchester: England, 1990.

"The Less Travelled Road – Nation & State & Education Institutions walk together. Do we, can we have a Common Agenda?" *A.C.E. News*, The Journal of The Australian College of Education, 1992.

"The School of the 1992 Future," *A.C.E. News*, The Journal of The Australian College of Education, 1995.

"Civics and Citizenship and the Teaching of Values," *Unicorn*, 1996.

Selected Bibliography

Campion, Edmund. "Educator led by example", *The Australian*, 31 January 1997.

Canavan, Kelvin fms. Eulogy, St Mary's Cathedral Sydney, 31 January 1997.

Citation, UWS, Award of Doctor of Letters, *honoris causa*, 1996.

Croke, Brian. "Ann Clark and her Memorial," Launch of the Ann D. Clark Trust, University of Western Sydney, 24th February 1998.

Croke, Brian. "Ann Clark, A Personal Reflection," 4th February 1997.

"Ann Clark" *Sydney Morning Herald*, 30 January 1997

Armstrong, Mary. "Tribute to Ann Clark," *ACEA*, 1997

Deirdre Rofe (Sr Mary Anne ibvm) (1943-2002)

"A quester by nature, and a commander at need"

Robin Scott, Archivist, Loreto Australia & South East Asia

Deirdre Ann Rofe was born in Sale, Victoria, on 6 October 1943. Deirdre was the eldest daughter of five; her father, Bryan Rofe MBE, an eminent nuclear scientist, and her mother, Pat Rofe (nee Whitford).

Bryan Rofe, a member of the RAAF at the time of Deirdre's birth, was stationed in Sale, recovering from malaria contracted in Timor, from where he had been rescued by an American submarine along with his fellow Australian prisoners-of-war. The family returned to Beaumont, Adelaide, after Bryan's discharge.

Deirdre began primary school at Loreto Marryatville. A keen student, she particularly enjoyed literature, drama and sport and, in secondary school, drama and debating. She was elected Head Prefect, Sports' Captain and Captain of Barry House in 1959/1960. Deirdre completed her schooling, with English, French, Latin, Greek & Roman History, Maths I, Physics, Chemistry and Physiology in the Leaving Certificate and received prizes for Honours English, History and French.

In 1961, Deirdre began reading Law at the University of Adelaide and embraced challenges and opportunities for debating.

Mid-year 1962, the draw of religious life became overwhelming and she entered the novitiate of the Institute of the Blessed Virgin Mary (more commonly known as the Loreto Sisters) at Normanhurst, Sydney, on 24 May 1962. Deirdre made her first Profession in the Normanhurst Chapel on 9 January 1965.

She studied at the University of Melbourne and completed a BA (Hons) majoring in English and History but also studied Fine Art which contributed towards a life-long love of art, which along with poetry, was like a thread of beauty and joy running through her life. She took final profession on 2 February 1970, receiving the religious name of Sister Mary Anne and taking the appropriate motto, *Fiat Alleluia*.

Deirdre began her teaching career at Loreto Convent, Normanhurst, where she taught English Literature and History and cared for the boarders. In 1971, aged 27, she was appointed Principal at Normanhurst, a huge challenge that she met with the support of her parents; her father, in particular, telephoned her every day. Normanhurst students of that time remember her with great affection, talking, playing tennis and passing on a love of literature and the arts. She revived debating and public speaking which she encouraged with endless enthusiasm.

From 1979-1988, Sr Deirdre was Principal of Loreto College, Mandeville Hall Toorak. Celebrating Australia's Bicentennial in 1988, the whole school went on a Pilgrimage to Uluru, a pilgrimage to the heart of the country.

During her leadership in Loreto schools, many innovations were made across religious education, relating religious education to life experience, programs of social responsibility and involvement in welfare and student leadership programs with the introduction of student-led Performing Arts Festivals. Sr Deirdre co-authored the *Mission Statement for Australian Loreto Schools* in 1986.

Her contribution to education beyond Loreto and beyond Catholic education was very significant. With her natural charm and gifts for friendship, her presence on committees of the Heads of Independent Schools of Australia helped break down traditional religious barriers.

In 1990, Deirdre was appointed the 11th Province Leader of the Australian Province of the IBVM, a position held until 1995. In this role, she supported Sisters working in education, parishes, pastoral and social work in Australia and overseas in the refugee camps in Asia. During her leadership, the Loreto schools developed school councils and a central school governance structure with the Loreto Education Board and established an administrative and advisory office, the Loreto Education Office.

In 1993, she completed a Bachelor of Theology degree after studying in London, Toronto and Melbourne. Between 1996 and 2000, Sr Deirdre held the new role of Assistant to the Provincial in Matters of Education.

From 1997 to 2000, Deirdre was Principal of St Mary's College, University of Melbourne. Here she contributed to tertiary education as a member of the Heads of Colleges and Council for Chaplains in Tertiary Institutions. A new learning centre shared with Newman College was designed and built.

In recognition of her achievements, she was made a Fellow of the Australian College of Education in 2000. In 2002, she was awarded an Honorary Doctorate from Australian Catholic University.

Sr Deirdre was diagnosed with cancer in 2000. She died on 16 August 2002 at St Mary's College. At her funeral, Father Peter Steele SJ said:

> One of the things which made Deirdre so deeply attractive was her evident sense that there was more to common events and circumstances than their ordinary face: and that that "more" was good, and promising, and fertile... Deirdre was a quester by nature, and a commander at need.

Selected Bibliography

Browne, Sr Frances. *Fiat Alleluia, Sr Deirdre Rofe – a biography*, unpublished, 2011.

Clark, Mary Ryllis. *Loreto in Australia*, Sydney: University of New South Wales Press, 2009.

Comments by Sr Margaret C. Honner ibvm, a Loreto Sister who has worked in education, formation and spiritual direction in Australia, Vietnam and Timor Leste. Sr Margaret entered religious life at the same time as Sr Deirdre Rofe and was a lifelong friend.

Encyclopaedia of Australian Science, Bryan Rofe (1918-1971). http://www.eoas.info/biogs/P000754b.htm

Loreto Province Archives.

Sr Winifred Agnes Ryan mss (1915–2011)

Founding Congregational member and pioneer educator

Sr Corrie van den Bosch mss

Agnes Ryan's obituary in the *Courier Mail* noted that to 'give adequate coverage of her story as a Missionary Sister of Service would require a book of no mean proportions'. This biography, therefore, is a challenge to overview a life filled with many achievements and "firsts", as Sr Agnes (who went by her middle name), stands out as a founding member of the Missionary Sisters of Service, a pioneer in Australian catechetics and, if not the first, then one of the first women to teach in an Australian Catholic seminary.

Agnes' parents, Roger James Ryan and Lillian Ethyl (nee Lynam), married in an impressive Nuptial Mass at St Brigid's Catholic Church, Bridgetown, 270kms south of Perth, on 10 January 1910. Agnes was the fourth of eleven children and religion was a central element of the family. Another influence may have been a community service tradition inherited from her father, who in 1914 was the Labour Party's candidate for the State seat of Nelson. Although unsuccessful, Roger Ryan continued his public profile and demonstrated a strong, if unpopular, conviction when he opposed conscription during World War One.

Agnes was educated by the Sisters of Mercy at Bridgetown until the age of 10, matriculated from Sacred Heart College, Highgate Hill, WA, and trained as a teacher.

In 1944, Agnes saw a paragraph in Perth's *Catholic Record* announcing that Tasmanian priest, Father John Corcoran Wallis (1910-2001) was gathering a group of women for missionary work in rural Australia. Agnes wrote to Fr Wallis, expressing her interest. Her letter arrived on 8 July, the founding day of what became the Missionary Sisters of

Service. On 1 December 1944, Agnes arrived in Launceston to join this new community.

Together, the early members gave form to the vision of Father Wallis: they went 'into the highways and byways'(their motto) to isolated communities, visited people in their homes, provided religious instruction for children and developed correspondence courses to help parents educate their children in faith. Realising that the parents themselves needed education in faith, in time this became a further focus of their mission.

In 1965, Agnes was asked to develop a catechist scheme for the Hobart archdiocese. The Confraternity of Christian Doctrine (CCD) had been in place on the mainland in the Archdiocese of Sydney, New South Wales, since 1938, but not in the island state of Tasmania. Agnes set about establishing the CCD in Tasmania. Encouraged by the teachings of Vatican Council II and the Missionary Sisters of Service, Agnes became a strong advocate for education beyond the Catholic school to become an integral dimension of the Church's education system; it was to be many years before it gained that status.

In 1970, when Fr Bill O'Shea, Director of Catholic Education in Brisbane, approached the Missionary Sisters of Service for a sister to head the CCD in Brisbane, Agnes was assigned to this mission from January 1971. While Fr John Egan had already instigated catechist training to meet the needs of children in government schools, Agnes' task was to develop a co-ordinated diocesan approach and a standardised training program for catechists.

Agnes was convinced that the formation of an informed and competent laity was crucial if the Church was to fulfil its mission in the 20th and 21st centuries. In 1971, she requested that a steering committee be formed to investigate a cohesive approach to three areas of Catholic Education beyond Catholic schools: training catechists for government school students, parish-based faith education for adults and education for youth beyond school age; she asked for these to become integral to the mission of Archdiocesan Catholic Education. Fr Frank Lourigan, whom Agnes recruited to assist in the work, wrote of her at the time of her death:

She was a remarkable woman who made a big impact on the Brisbane Archdiocese ... she was a vibrant breath of fresh air in the exciting '70s ... when Archbishop Rush arrived in May 1973, the Archdiocese exploded with activity, and Sr Agnes was a key figure.

Furthermore, from 1971, at the request of the Queensland Bishops, Agnes taught pastoral catechetics at Banyo Seminary, reputed as being the first woman to teach in an Australian seminary. Her experience of life in rural and remote parishes had made her acutely aware of the needs of priests and their parishioners. She developed a program covering the six years of the seminary course. A former student wrote that she not only taught them, she changed the ethos of the seminary to one of mission.

In 1979, Agnes moved to the Toowoomba Diocese where she set up a training program for religious educators, similar to the one she had established in Brisbane. From the mid-1980s, she worked in various parishes from Miles and Goondiwindi to Howard and Hervey Bay.

Agnes was a deep and broad reader, always keeping abreast of developments in theology and spirituality. When the discoveries of modern science were brought into dialogue with the Christian faith tradition, she embraced the emerging cosmology. In her senior years, as a pastoral presence in various parishes, she gathered groups of people to explore with them her learnings from such reading. In her eighties, she moved to Currimundi retirement village, where she formed a spirituality support group and developed with them a wide-ranging program of faith and spirituality courses in the Caloundra (Queensland) region. Aged 90, Agnes moved to St Catherine's Aged Care in Balwyn, Victoria, where six years later she died on 25 August 2011.

Agnes was inspired throughout her life by a deep abiding love for Jesus who had captured her heart as a young woman and her ever deepening appreciation of the Mystery of Christ. Her greatest joy was to share that love with people wherever she was. In the last period of her life, she radiated that love to all who came in contact with her.

Selected Bibliography

Agnes Ryan Personal File, Autobiographical statement 1978, Reports written by Agnes Ryan, Diaries, and other papers, Archives, Missionary Sisters of Service.

Blackwood Times, Bunbury, Western Australia, 21 January 1910, 3.

Blackwood Times, Bunbury, Western Australia, 6 October 1916, 3.

"Obituary: Sister Agnes Ryan", Courier Mail, 27 October 2011. https://www.couriermail.com.au/ipad/obituary-sister-agnes-ryan/news-story/b28e71155ca114850be5913fa2095de9

Edman, P. A. *Around the Kitchen Table with the Missionary Sisters of Service: a portrait of the spirit and the heart of this Tasmanian-bred, Australian-grown congregation of religious women*. Rangeview, Victoria: Missionary Sisters of Service, 2008.

Spirituality In–Form, newsletter for members of the spirituality groups, Caloundra parish, 1995 – 2005.

"Sister taught and radiated God's love", *The Record*, Perth, 30 November 2011. https://therecord.com.au/news/local/sister-taught-and-radiated-gods-love/ van den Bosch, C. Eulogy at Sr Agnes's funeral, 2011. MSS.

Wallis, B. T. *Dear Mother, Dear Father, Letters Home from John Corcoran Wallis 1927-1949*. Bayswater, Vic: Coventry Press, 2019.

Woodhouse, F. *John Corcoran Wallis (1910 to 2001): A Man of Vision*. 17 September 2014. https://mecomcomau.files.wordpress.com/2018/08/obituary-fr-john-corcoran-wallis-17-09-14-photo-edit-2018.pdf

REFLECTION

Looking ahead

Brian Croke

If anyone encapsulates the story and the spirit of Catholic schooling in its transformative phase, from the 1960s to the 1990s, it is Ann D. Clark (1935-1997). From being a student at St Vincent's Potts Point, Australia's oldest Catholic girls school, she joined the religious congregation who owned and operated the school, the Sisters of Charity. In the 1950s, all Catholic schools were staffed and generally managed by the religious congregations, even if they were established and owned by individual parishes. Known as Sr Christopher, Ann prepared herself for a lifetime of education by acquiring, through study in her own spare time, university degrees in both science and arts.

On top of that, she added a Masters degree in Educational Administration at a time when the future administration of the diverse Catholic school community was becoming an issue, in fact *the* issue. She was fully prepared to teach any part of the curriculum, from primary years right through to the end of school. And she did. She also learnt administration on the job, especially as a young principal, although she knew that models and theories of good practice were the pathway to self-improvement.

Leaving behind the sisters, Ann continued her life and career in Catholic education. She was part of a generation that was formed in the discipline of religious life and deeply knowledgeable about their faith. Often too, at a young age, they had held positions of responsibility such as Principal. Ann was one of the many who exchanged the structure of their congregational life for the lay state in the 1960s and 1970s, especially under the impulse of the Second Vatican Council (1962-1965). She became an educational administrator in the diocese of Bathurst, then a Regional Director in Sydney and then the first Diocesan Director in Parramatta (1987-1997). Nevertheless, like Ann, most of the former vowed religious were not lost to Catholic education. Instead, they proved to be an enormous asset, in fact a sort of leaven to help raise up the commitment and purpose required of Catholic educators. They were a vital example to younger lay teachers and principals, not to mention the students they taught.

Meanwhile, by the early 1960s, many religious who had received only minimal tertiary education themselves, especially those teaching secondary school classes, were behind their government school counterparts who mainly all had university degrees in the subject they were teaching. Accordingly, a minor industry for religious sprang up which involved being part-time evening students at metropolitan universities or external students at the University of New England. While for most, it meant acquiring a basic qualification, others flourished in the university environment.

Like Ann Clark later, Brother Ronald Fogarty (1913-2009) completed both an Arts degree (1942) and a Science degree (1948), before going on to a doctorate in history (1957). Already a distinguished historian for his 2-volume history of Australian Catholic schooling to 1950, he later spent four years studying in Chicago (1966-69) to turn himself into a qualified psychologist. No less distinguished, but in a different field, was Brother Francis (Frank) Irenaeus McCarthy, cfc (1920-2010). Frank was an earnest student at the University of Melbourne while teaching his students at St Kevin's (1949) and Parade (1951-1960), acquiring degrees in Arts and Education as well as Master of Arts and Diploma in Education. He then went to Cambridge (England) where he completed a doctorate on 'Mountain Scenery in British Art 1750-1815'. Subsequently, he was offered a Cambridge fellowship, which he declined and returned to teaching boys at St Kevin's in Melbourne. The rest of his career was in Melbourne, as Headmaster (1966-76) where he was remembered for his emphasis on high academic standards and old-world formalities, as well as an art adviser to the University of Melbourne.

It was only the introduction of easier and faster international travel in the 1950s that enabled religious in Australian schools to spend time abroad studying, thereby bringing new ideas and fresh energy to be shared across their order, and with others. Sr Margaret Toohey rscj (1930-2014), for example, had made her vows in Rome in 1960, as many of her Sacred Heart sisters had already done. However, she went on to study in England for her Diploma in Education. She returned to London some years later to undertake a Diploma in Theology and Scripture.

Sr Mary St Bernard fdnsc (1925-2016) had already established herself as an inspiring teacher and director of novices (1962-65) when she went to Rome in 1969 to work on revising the constitutions of her order in the light of Vatican II, but later (1976-8) she completed a Bachelor of Theology at Catholic Theological College, Melbourne.

Sr Deirdre Rofe, ibvm (1943-2002) was actually a younger member of a generation of religious sisters and brothers who had grasped the opportunity to widen their horizons and subsequently those of their Australian fellow-religious through their overseas experience. She spent three years on her religious formation as a Loreto sister before undertaking her Arts (and Fine Art) degree as a full-time student at Melbourne. She became a young principal in Sydney and Melbourne and only later went on to complete a degree in Theology, having studied in London, Toronto and Melbourne in the 1970s.

By contrast, the Fraser siblings were much older and spent most of their lives (and all of their education) in Australia. Charles (1913-2004) was educated by the Jesuits at Riverview in Sydney and his sister Joyce, later Mother Loyola (1918-2008) attended Brigidine Randwick. They were both born in Gundagai and spent their early years in Tumut. She joined the Brigidine sisters and went to Sydney University, graduating with the honours BA degree in English followed by a Master of Arts degree, at a time when there were very few women students at university. Charles, meanwhile, had become a Jesuit and, other than a stint lecturing in Christchurch to seminarians (1947-52), spent all of his life at Riverview until 1992 as teacher and mentor. Thereafter he took special responsibility for building relations with the Old Ignatians. Mother Loyola was the principal of Brigidine Randwick (1954-68) who saw through the transition to the Wyndham scheme with its extra year of secondary schooling in 1967. Later, she was principal of Brigidine Brisbane (1969-1973) where she brought a new emphasis on the Arts in Education.

In the working lives of all these exemplary, but different, religious of the 1950s to 1970s, we see the seeds of change that bore fruit in the 1980s and 1990s. Many were attracted to their lifestyle by the idea of teaching as a 'calling' or 'vocation' which they had and could articulate. Then they were educated by their congregation as teachers in the first place, were able to be deployed across states and were freed to study at university, including overseas, when most teachers in government schools, for example, were married with their employment confined to their local department of education. As for university study, if they had not completed it prior to teaching, they had to make their own arrangements. Many did of course and some of those later became lay teachers in Catholic schools.

More broadly, the lives and careers of those profiled here illustrate that world in which each religious congregation was an organisation unto itself. Each congregation, in its own way, recruited, trained, educated, appointed, employed, developed and cared for each of its members. The certainty of this world for each congregation was destabilised in the 1960s as their numbers shrank and they had to look to each other and/or replace religious with lay teachers in various places. Then they found that control over appointments required discussion with a new diocesan authority, if not approval.

Some congregations withdrew to concentrate their energies on certain schools or regions, others chose to diversify beyond schooling altogether. Sooner or later, some faced the question of merging some or all of their own provinces. A few congregations chose to open up their teacher education program to other congregations in the 1950s and 1960s, for example the Dominican sisters at Signadou, Canberra, in 1963, to maximise expertise, then to lay teachers in their own schools, then more generally to anyone for any schools. These were band-aid measures at best, however. Before long, almost all the new teachers employed in Catholic schools were lay, and trained outside the immediate supervision of the traditional training of an order.

It was a series of quick steps from the original congregational teacher education programs still operative around 1970, to the colleges admitting mainly lay students in Sydney, Melbourne, Canberra and

Ballarat, to the formation of a single Catholic university (ACU) in 1990. By now, for the most part, the 'vocation' based Catholic school teacher had given way to the industry-based employee of a Catholic education office. In many places, the quest to establish who a teacher's employer was dragged on for years. In others, it was clearly the bishop and in some states the parish priest. Only now, in the wake of the Royal Commission, is the matter of employer finally being standardised. Perhaps the time has come too, to reintroduce the language of 'vocation' into teaching.

The escalating demand for teachers in Catholic schools and the progressive employment, school by school, of lay teachers more or less coincided with the Second Vatican Council which itself led to a re-examination of religious life and sudden demise in recruits to the religious life. The rich resources of the Council involved two seminal documents to guide the work of the Catholic educator, the council decree on Christian Education (1965), followed by *The Catholic School* (1977) which proved an inspiring document for school use, and was reinforced twenty years later by *The Catholic School on the Threshold of the Third Millennium* (1997). The Council also tapped into various sources of unease within the church and the Catholic education world. This lead to two subsequent statements on lay teachers (by then the majority in Australia) and on Religious Education: *Lay Catholics in schools: Witnesses to faith* (1982), and *Religious Dimension of Education in a Catholic School* (1988). Each of these documents was heavily utilised in Australian Catholic schools in the 1980s and 1990s and played a role in shaping their culture and purposes.[53]

By the late 1960s, if a young Catholic wanted to be a teacher in a Catholic school it was no longer essential to commit to a religious life. A funded teacher training place at a College of Advanced Education or University was now the prerequisite to employment in a Catholic school. Even so, by 1969/1970, staffing of Catholic schools had become a crucial conundrum, but as salaries approached parity with salaries

---

[53] B. Croke, 'Australian Catholic Schools in a Changing Political and Religious Landscape' in G. Grace and J. O'Keefe (eds.), *International Handbook of Catholic Education* (Dordrecht 2007), 811-833.

in government schools many experienced an influx of young Catholic teachers from Government schools.

Something similar happened with principals. That is, as principal positions became vacant in Catholic schools, they were filled with a new generation of experienced lay Catholic principals, experienced that is, as principals or deputy principals of government schools where they had established their seniority. This first generation of lay principals, and those who accompanied them as directors of education at diocesan and state level, provided a sudden injection of expertise and bureaucratic method into the fledgling Catholic school system at the time. In return, they had to be fully enmeshed in the spiritual and religious education dimensions of the school. By now too, new university graduates were able to be recruited directly into Catholic schools which had never been an option previously. Some of these new teachers spent their whole career in Catholic schooling and are only now retiring. They too will form an important part of this project and will be profiled in future publications.

Certainly, the most publicised aspect of Catholic schooling from the 1960s to the 1980s was the call for secure government funding for Catholic schooling. It regularly involved bishops, politicians, parents, parish priests, and others, all fed by a media generally adverse to the interests of Catholic schools.[54] The most celebrated incident in this process occurred in Goulburn on a cold July day in 1962 when Catholic school parents turned up at the local government schools to enrol their children there. It was a spectacular statement of protest. While the impact of this incident is much exaggerated, it is worth noting in passing certain aspects of it. Goulburn was a disproportionately Catholic town with a long established Catholic schooling tradition involving several congregations. The issues in Goulburn were essentially capital and most concern was felt by the boys and girls high schools which were required to provide sufficient

---

[54] Details in M. Hogan, *The Catholic Campaign for State Aid* (Sydney: Catholic Theological Faculty 1978) and Ian R. Wilkinson et al, *A History of State Aid to Non-government schools in Australia* (Canberra: Commonwealth 2006).

science laboratories for the new mandatory science curriculum in Year 7 from 1963, and then to provide space for an additional year of secondary schooling. This was a major issue with Catholic schools all over NSW at the time. In Goulburn too, all the teachers were religious. Unlike other parts of the country and most of the metropolitan area of Sydney, there was not a single lay teacher to be paid in Goulburn in 1962.

With the rapid growth in the number of students and schools in the 1960s and 1970s, combined with the advent of various forms of government financial aid for Catholic schools from 1964 and the establishment and staffing of new schools by dioceses, an urgent question became the organisation and management of the Catholic school enterprise. A seminal conference, held at the University of New England in September 1972, where Ann Clark had been studying for her Master's degree in Educational Administration, laid out a model with individual/state Catholic Education Commissions, established by and responsible to bishops, and a National Catholic Education Commission.[55] Before long, these structures were in place everywhere, but with responsibilities and relationship varying according to state need.

Certainly, in the large metropolitan dioceses, there had long been an awareness and plan of action to deal with the resourcing, staffing and religious curriculum issues identified for Sydney by Br Kelvin Canavan. In the case of the archdiocese of Melbourne, for instance, many of the same issues had surfaced in the 1940s and were actively engaged, especially by the bookish Fr John F. Kelly as diocesan inspector of Schools and later Director of Catholic Education,[56] followed by Fr. Frank Martin as Director from 1970 to 1980, then Monsignor Tom Doyle (1980 to 2002). Crucial, but unfortunately short-lived, was the period when Justin Simonds was archbishop because he took

---

[55] P. D. Tannock (ed.), *The Organization and Administration of Catholic Education in Australia* (Brisbane: UQ Press 1975).
[56] R. Pascoe, *The Feasts and Seasons of John F Kelly* (Sydney: Allen and Unwin 2006), 121-98.

decisive steps in involving lay people in the governance of education.[57] The Melbourne experience paralleled that for Sydney except that the Sydney system developed a more centralised financial operation than Melbourne.[58] Moreover, whereas in NSW some sixty established schools were resolved by their congregational owners to remain outside the new diocesan systems, only two schools (representing two congregations) stood outside the Melbourne diocesan school system.

The advent of substantial funding under the first *Schools Assistance Act* (1974), following the election of the Whitlam government in 1972, required all school owners to decide how they wanted their school, or schools, to be treated for Commonwealth grant purposes: they could opt to be part of the newly formed state Catholic system, under the new *Act*, or be treated directly by the Commonwealth as an independent 'non-systemic' school. The decision on which schools a congregation would retain control over was decided fairly quickly in 1974, and has hardly varied since. These schools were known by the language of the *Act* as 'non systemic schools' which meant that they lay outside the responsibility and the purview of the local CEO, but not the bishop, at least after 1993. By 2000, these schools, and the congregations sponsoring them, came to discover and highlight the particular charism of the founder (however long ago), as well as to create for its schools many of the administrative functions of the diocesan system for its schools.

With the formation of the Catholic diocesan systems and the increasing disconnection of the Catholic school from the life of the parish, the important distinction between Catholic education (the lifelong quest to grow closer to Christ in knowledge and spirit) and Catholic schooling was slowly diminished. Catholic education, strictly speaking, embraced the education of Catholic students in government schools which always represented about 50% of all Catholics of school age. It too was the responsibility of every bishop.

---

[57] M. Vodola, *Simonds. A Rewarding Life* (Melbourne: CEO Melbourne 1997), 89-95.
[58] H. Praetz, *Building a School System. A Sociological Study of Catholic Education* (Melbourne: Melbourne UP: 1980).

Enter Sr Winifred Ryan mss (1915-2011). She realised that although Catholic schools were full of Catholics in the early 1960s, there were other Catholic students in need of a Catholic education. She became a true pioneer in Australian catechetics. From Western Australia, she responded to a calling to come to Tasmania in 1965 and make catechetics in government schools her religious life. Having established an independent *Confraternity of Christian Doctrine* in Tasmania, she was invited to do the same in Brisbane in 1971. Sr Winifred always had a clear vision of what was required, namely strong episcopal and parish support. Her pioneering work climaxed in 1971 when she became one of the first women to teach in an Australian seminary: pastoral catechetics at Banyo, Brisbane.

Sr Winifred's place in the BDACE is a reminder that there are other areas of Catholic education which have been actively pursued in Australia and need to be considered: teacher education, nurse education, adult education, sacramental education, theological education (including Seminaries) and, most recently, higher education generally, especially in Australia's two Catholic universities, both founded in 1990: *Australian Catholic University* and *Notre Dame Australia*. Therein lies another story for another time.

Chapter Six
Developments in Catholic Education in Australia 2000-2020

Context

Dr Lee-Anne Perry AM

Social context

The new century began in Australia with great hope, excitement and buoyancy reflected in the celebrations to mark the start of a new millennium, followed by the Sydney Olympics later in the year and then the centenary of Federation on 1 January 2001. This mood was shattered in Australia and in much of the rest of the world with the cataclysmic terrorist attacks on the World Trade Centre and the Pentagon in the United States on 11 September 2001, marking the beginning of what has been called the 'War on Terror' which was to shape the decades since.

The Bali bombings in 2002 in which eighty-eight Australians died and a later series of terrorist related attacks in Australia heightened civil anxiety. The Tampa incident and a series of other actions by successive Australian Governments presaged an increasingly reactive, exclusionary and defensive attitude towards people seeking asylum in Australia. Public discourse and political activity came increasingly to be shaped by nationalistic and polarised narratives while, concurrently, the rapid development of the world wide web and social media facilitated global engagement on an unprecedented scale. As data proliferated, notions of privacy and security became heavily contested.

Sharing, being liked and followed, 'going viral', became markers of popularity and success at the same time citizens became increasingly concerned about governmental and commercial surveillance and access to personal data.

The Global Financial Crisis[59] in 2008 caused not only severe economic distress to many, it also prompted what has become an ongoing and escalating crisis of confidence in institutions including major financial institutions, governments and churches. Australians were not only buffeted by these global events but by a series of natural disasters in every state and territory with unprecedented human and economic impacts including the 2009 Black Saturday bushfires in Victoria with 173 killed, the 2011 Queensland floods, and widespread and prolonged drought. The existence of global climate change was substantiated by extensive scientific evidence but also became a lightning rod for political disputation. Understandings of what constituted fact and truth became increasingly blurred and polarised on ideological grounds.

Schools were expected to manage the impact of these major social upheavals on young people while simultaneously responding to expectations that they foster 21st century skills, maintain the basics (the 3Rs), and navigate the tensions of respecting traditions of Western Civilisation while fostering deeper understanding and engagement with indigenous history, knowledge and culture. In Catholic schools, these competing demands were to take place in a context of significant changes in the Catholic Church, most particularly the impact of the Royal Commission into Institutional Responses to Child Sexual Abuse.

School policy

The period since 2000 has seen considerable interplay between the Federal and State/Territory governments to determine school policy. While constitutionally, State governments have responsibility for

---

[59] Also known as the Great Recession in the US and other countries.

schools, the Federal Government has increasingly used its considerable funding power to gain greater policy influence.

A new national education infrastructure,[60] together with the growing importance of decisions by Education Council,[61] has underpinned an increasingly national approach to school education. The introduction of a national standardised assessment program in 2008, and the Australian Curriculum and My School website in 2010, heralded a new national paradigm in school curriculum, assessment and public reporting.

Publication of data from NAPLAN[62] and other national and international standardised tests, was welcomed by all governments as important measures of school transparency and accountability. To the dismay of many educators, mainstream media quickly realised the commercial benefits of creating and publishing annual school performance leagues tables and have continued to publish ever more extensive comparative lists using data published on *My School*. Schools perceived that these league tables had an increasingly significant impact on parental choice of school. While the results for Catholic school students over the first decade of NAPLAN testing (2008-2018) were generally above the results for government school students, the gap has been closing and has added to the pressure (real or perceived) on enrolments for Catholic schools.

Federal Governments have increasingly made funding for all schools contingent on commitment to a national reform agenda. While this agenda has been used to drive greater national alignment, particularly of the school curriculum, and eased the dislocations for more mobile students and families, it has been used also to drive a range of individual reforms. Schools have been asked to respond to initiatives as divergent as installing functioning flag poles to programs on countering violent

---

[60] The national infrastructure established in the period 2008-2010 comprised the Australian Curriculum and Assessment Authority (ACARA), the Australian Institute for Teaching and School Leadership (AITSL), and Education Services Australia (ESA).
[61] Education Council comprises all Federal and State/Territory Education Ministers and operates by consensus.
[62] National Assessment Program Literacy and Numeracy.

extremism, driver education, healthy eating, and cyber bullying and safety. Unsurprisingly, and almost at the same time, there are frequent calls to 'de-clutter' the curriculum.

Funding and education policy were also increasingly linked to Federal economic policy, most clearly in the Rudd Federal Government responses to the Global Financial Crisis. In 2009, then Federal Education Minister Gillard, announced the *Building the Education Revolution* (BER) program providing capital funds for primary school halls and libraries and secondary school science and language learning centres. The program intention was to provide an immediate infrastructure stimulus in every school, and thus almost every town, city and suburb, in Australia.

In 2008, the *Digital Education Revolution* (DER) program was launched. The primary objective was to achieve a computer to student ratio of 1:1 for all Australian students in Years 9 to 12 by the end of 2011. This was a watershed moment in the embedding of computer technology in schools, initially in secondary schools but, quite rapidly, across most primary schools. By 2019, personal computing devices and digital education had become ubiquitous in almost every school.

Another significant policy shift occurred in November 2008 with the Australian and state and territory governments committing to universal access to an early childhood education (ECE) program for all children in the year before school. While strongly supported by educators, the various models of ECE provision would gradually cause increasing enrolment-pipeline-pressure on Catholic schools as Catholic agencies struggled to match the provision of ECE on government school sites.

Royal Commission into Institutional Responses to Child Sexual Abuse

This Royal Commission was announced by Prime Minister Gillard on 12 November 2012 and ran from 13 January 2013 until 15 December 2017. The nature and scale of abuse disclosed to the Commission was staggering and devastating. The Commission received over 4500 allegations of sexual abuse against Catholic Church authorities. A total of 1,880 alleged perpetrators were identified; 46% of the alleged incidents occurred in schools and 29% in orphanages and residential care facilities. The Commission findings and recommendations pertaining to the Catholic Church reflected what it identified as a catastrophic and systemic failure of care.

The Commission made 409 recommendations, directed at both governments and institutions, aimed at shaping a much safer future for young people. Governments moved quickly to introduce much more comprehensive child protection legislation, incorporating child safe standards, expanded screening of those working with children, and more extensive reporting and training requirements. Catholic schools, as with all institutions working with children, responded with concerted and sustained attention to the rigorous compliance requirements but, more importantly, to implementing proactive programs to help ensure students felt safe. In a 2019 survey, parent feedback indicated these efforts were having a constructive impact, but that ongoing attention will be required.[63] Notwithstanding the positive regard of current parents for Catholic schools, the reputational damage to all Catholic institutions was keenly felt by school leaders and staff.

School funding

Another quite different issue which re-emerged during this period also had consequences for public perceptions of Catholic education. Several significant changes to funding arrangements commencing in the early part of the 21st century once again fanned the flames of the state aid debate. A new socio-economic status (SES) funding model for non-government schools was introduced in 2001 by Minister Kemp. Then, in 2011, the Gonski review of school funding[64] proposed a radical re-think of school funding arrangements, replacing the SES model with the Schooling Resource Standard (SRS). As with the SES model, the Federal Government insisted that in the implementation of the SRS

---

[63] National Catholic Education Commission, *Australian Perceptions of Catholic Education*, *Quantitative Report* prepared by Utting Research (May 2019).
[64] D. Gonski, et al, *Review of Funding for Schooling*, Department of Education, Employment and Workplace Relations, Final Report, (December 2011.

model no non-government school would lose a dollar. Consequent protracted negotiations with all sectors and jurisdictions resulted in 27 individual agreements rather than the intended needs based, sector-blind, universally applied funding model.

A critical component of the Catholic sector agreements was the continuation of system funding including the so-called system weighted average (SWA) mechanism. This was quickly branded a 'special deal'. Rather than settling the school funding debate, a new even more intense battle began, dominated by the government school lobby "I give a Gonski" campaign.

The next substantive funding policy shift was announced on 1 May 2017 by Prime Minister Turnbull and Education Minister Birmingham. The new model required all schools to transition to their SRS determined funding arrangement in no more than ten years meaning, for the first time, there would be cuts to some non-government schools. Critically for Catholic schools, the system weighted average was to be abolished. This decision was strongly opposed by the Catholic sector which argued that it would have a devastating impact on its schools, particularly low-fee parish primary schools.

A tentative resolution was achieved in late August 2018 when new Education Minister Tehan offered additional funding through a 'Choice and Affordability Fund' and a commitment to review certain still contentious elements of the funding model, particularly those impacting on low-fee systemic schools. The Fund was quickly labelled a 'slush fund'[65] and has become the latest focus of the ongoing simmering tensions characterising any discussions of school funding.

Throughout this time, the ongoing educational developments and mission of service to students and their learning in Catholic schools were frequently overshadowed by the public contestations over school funding.

---

[65] Hon. Tanya Plibersek, MP, "Malcolm Turnbull's secret special deals for elite private schools."Media Release, (13 April 2018).

Catholic school demographics

The impact of the Royal Commission, changes to school funding methodology, and the closing gap in NAPLAN results were not the only factors placing growing pressure on the core mission and ongoing viability of Catholic schools.

At the beginning of the new century, total national Catholic school enrolments were just over 640,000; by 2018, they had reached 765,512, a total growth of 18.3% with an average annual growth of 1.0%. Concerningly, the average national growth figures mask some significant variation between states. Queensland and Western Australian Catholic schools benefitted from strong population growth, particularly in the early part of the first decade, and experienced a total growth of 46.2% and 28.2% respectively in the period 2000-2018; in this same period, total growth in the Northern Territory was -5.8%. Average annual growth rates for all states and territories, other than Queensland and Western Australia, were less than 1.0%. South Australian enrolment trends were particularly concerning with consecutive negative growth from 2014-2018.

Enrolment growth reached its peak in 2007 (1.7% nationally), just prior to the Global Financial Crisis. In the years since 2008, enrolment growth in both the Catholic and independent school sectors has slowed while growth in the state sector has steadily increased. In 2014, enrolment growth in the state sector exceeded Catholic school enrolment growth for the first time this century. Fluctuations in growth rate have impacted on market share between the three schooling sectors. Catholic schools reached a peak of 20.61% in 2014 and have since been slowly losing market share to both the Government and Independent sectors.

Meanwhile, proportionately more Federal education funding came to be directed to non-government schools and State/Territory government funding increases to government schools failed to keep pace with the Federal funding increases. This eventually resulted in differential rates of funding growth.

From 2000-2017, total (Federal and State) government funding per student increases in each sector were: Government schools 4.2%, Catholic schools 5.0% and Independent schools 5.0%. During this same period, private income per student growth rates were: Government schools 2.9%, Catholic schools 5.5% and Independent schools 3.9%. Consequently, funding increases per student (combined government grants and private income) were higher for Catholic schools (5.1%) than for Independent (4.4%) or Government schools (4.1%). These differential funding increases fuelled much of the debate regarding the fairness of the various school funding models that operated from 2000-2018.

Private income is largely derived from school fees and Catholic school increases during this period were significantly above the increases in the other two sectors, despite the quite marked increases in government funding. Unsurprisingly, there was growing concern about the affordability and accessibility of Catholic schools to lower income families. In the 2019 survey of families with children attending school conducted by the National Catholic Education Commission, affordability was identified as the biggest weakness of Catholic schools.

The impact of increasing cost (due to rising fees) and lack of affordability can be seen in the changing socio-educational (SEA) profile of Catholic school families. Families in Catholic schools have increasingly been drawn from the higher (most advantaged) socio-educational quartiles. In 2018, almost 60% of students in Catholic schools were from families in the top two SEA quartiles.[66]

Catholicity of students, families and staff

Another significant shift has been in the proportion of Catholic students in Catholic schools. In 2006, 76% of student enrolments in Catholic schools nationally were Catholic; by 2016, this had declined to 69%, ranging from 44% in Tasmania to 74% in New South Wales. In part, these changes reflected broader changes in the Australian population.

---

[66] The figures for government schools and independent schools were 43.4% and 71.0% respectively.

In the period 1996-2016, the proportion of the Australian population identifying as Catholic declined from 27.0% to 22.6%. That this trend is likely to continue is revealed when other ABS Census data is also examined. In the same period, the median age of Catholics increased from 33 years to 40 years, the proportion aged over 65 increased from 10.9% to 16.6%, while those aged 0-14 years declined from 23.0% to 19.8%.[67] Migrants have long been the source of Catholic school enrolments, but this too is changing. While Australia has experienced a net overseas migration of more than two million people in the ten years covered by the last two census collections, analysis of the most recent census data (2016) reveals that children of recently arrived migrants are most likely to attend a government school (77% in 2016). Conversely, fewer are attending Catholic schools with enrolments among migrant groups decreasing from 12% in 2011 to 9% in 2016.

Catholic schools are now almost entirely staffed by lay people. The proportion of Catholic teachers stabilised by 2018 at around 72% nationally but with a significant range across States/Territories from 44% in the Northern Territory to 81% in New South Wales (2018 data). While most teachers still identified as Catholic, Catholic system and school leaders were noting that the proportion regularly involved in parish life and/or demonstrating any strong knowledge or understanding of Catholicism, or commitment to the Institutional Church, was diminishing rapidly.

The days of Australian Catholic families almost by default sending their children to a Catholic school have long since passed. School choice has become a defining feature of the school landscape in Australia. Families, irrespective of the schooling sector their children currently attend, identify choice as a high priority. In the 2019 survey conducted by the National Catholic Education Commission, 90% of respondents indicated that it was extremely or very important that parents can choose between different types of schools for their children; parents are seeking what they see as the 'best fit' for their children.

---

[67] Australian Bureau of Statistics Census data.

This same survey also examined the factors underpinning choice of school. The top factors for parents (with a weighting of over 88%), irrespective of the type of school attended by their children, were: number and quality of teachers; emphasis on respect, manners and discipline; academic standards; and the quality of facilities for teaching. Parents of children at Catholic schools rated religious values more highly (59% versus 34%) than parents of children attending government or independent schools; important, but clearly not one of their top factors.

Religious education and formation

Australian Catholic educators have responded to the challenges of the changing demographics, attitudes and expectations within their school communities, by concerted efforts to review and renew their religious education and formation programs. Greater academic rigour has been brought to Religious Education programs and more formal accreditation programs for both teachers and leaders in Catholic schools, including requirements for academic studies in religious education and theology, have been introduced. By 2008, programs had begun to reflect an understanding of the distinct but complementary nature of different dimensions of religious education. Programs included strands such as Sacred Texts, Beliefs, Church and Christian Life.[68]

These concerted efforts to renew Catholic schools were underpinned by a number of seminal Vatican documents. On 28 December 1997, *The Catholic School on the Threshold of the Third Millennium*, was published. Its influence was to be radical and long-lasting. The document reaffirmed the Catholic School as a vital place at "the heart of the Church". It acknowledged that the world was experiencing a time of rapid change and a growing marginalisation of the Christian faith and set out the fundamental goal of Catholic schools as 'the promotion of the human

---

[68] This example drawn from the Brisbane Catholic Education Religious Education Curriculum.

person' (# 9). Another important Vatican document, published in 2007, was *Educating Together in Catholic Schools: A Shared Mission between Consecrated Persons and the Lay Faithful*. It too emphasised the critical importance of formation.

Catholic educators responded to these imperatives and began to undertake a clearer, more systematic approach to formation for all members of the community. One of the most influential developments in formation and Catholic identity, was the Enhancing Catholic School Identity Project (ECSIP). This began in 2008 as a collaboration between the Catholic Education Commission of Victoria and the Catholic University in Leuven, Belgium. It has since spread throughout Australia. During this same period, as the number of Catholic Religious continued to decline, many Religious Institutes invested thought and resources into taking their charism into the future. Many established ministerial Public Juridic Persons[69] (PJPs), including Edmund Rice Education Australia (2007), Mary Aikenhead Ministries (2008), Mercy Partners (2008), and Good Samaritan Education (2011). The ministerial PJPs developed formation plans to support school boards, staff and students with understanding and reflecting the founding charism.

Pope Francis

The papacy of Pope Francis which commenced on 13 March 2013 has had a profound impact on the Catholic Church including Catholic education. Soon after his papacy started, in an address to students and teachers from Jesuit schools in Rome, Pope Francis stated: 'Do not be discouraged by the difficulties that the educational challenge presents. Educating is not a job but an attitude. It is a way of being... Most importantly, be witnesses with your lives'. This message was developed further in *Educating Today and Tomorrow: A Renewing Passion* which was

---

[69] Canon law defines a PJP as 'an aggregate of persons or things constituted by the competent ecclesiastical authority to fulfil a proper function given them in view of the common good'(*Can.* 114 §1). In simpler terms, a PJP has its own identity within the Church. It is a group of persons entrusted with overseeing the mission of the particular ministry.

published in 2014. It celebrated fifty years since the seminal document on education from Vatican II, *Gravissimum Educationis*, and identified the key challenges facing contemporary Catholic schools. In his closing address to the World Congress celebrating these two documents, Pope Francis highlighted that:

> The greatest failure that an educator can have is to educate "within the walls" ... walls of a selective culture, the walls of a culture of security, the walls of a social category that is affluent and no longer goes forward.[70]

As all Catholic schools sought to respond to Pope Francis' imperatives while also grappling with the changing demographic, experiences and attitudes of members of their school communities, efforts began to develop a more nationally consistent approach to religious education and formation and to issues of funding, accountability and sustainability. Increasingly, there has been a more unified national response to the quite profound challenges facing Catholic schools as they enter the third decade of the new millennium.

Looking ahead

In August 2016, Archbishop Coleridge announced the decision of the Catholic Church of Australia to hold a Plenary Council in 2020 (later postponed to 2021). In announcing the Council, Archbishop Coleridge stated: 'We are going through a time of profound cultural changes not only in society but also in the Church... How do we respond...?'[71] Catholic education will undoubtedly be one of the focus areas during the Plenary Council process for reflection, discernment and response.

Catholic schools in Australia are clearly facing many pressures but, as at previous times of great challenge, they are responding with optimism, vision and energy. It is hoped that, guided by Pope Francis,

---

[70] Pope Francis, Address to Participants, World Congress: *Educating Today and Tomorrow. A Renewing Passion*, Congregation for Catholic Education, (21 November 2015).

[71] *Catholic Leader*, (17 August 2016).

Catholic schools of the future will 'open up to new horizons, create new models and draw on all three languages – the language of the head, the language of the heart, and the language of the hands – in harmony'.[72]

Select Bibliography

Australian Bureau of Statistics, *Census*, 2016.

Coleridge, Mark. "Brisbane Archbishop calls for first synod for entire Catholic Church in Australia since 1937", *Catholic Leader*, August 17, 2016.

Congregation for Catholic Education. "Final Communique", World Congress, *Educating Today and Tomorrow: A Renewing Passion*, Rome-Castel Gandolfo, 2016.

Congregation for Catholic Education. *Educating Today and Tomorrow: A Renewing Passion*, Instrumentum Laboris, 2014.

Congregation for Catholic Education. *Educating Together in Catholic Schools: A Shared Mission between Consecrated Persons and the Lay Faithful*, 2007.

Congregation for Catholic Education. *The Catholic School on the Threshold of the Third Millennium*, 28 December 1997.

Gonski, D. et al, *Review of Funding for Schooling*, Department of Education, Employment and Workplace Relations, Final Report, December 2011.

Holy See, *Code of Canon Law*, 1983. http://www.vatican.va/archive/cod-iuris-canonici/eng/documents/cic_lib1-cann96-123_en.html

My School website (https://www.myschool.edu.au/)

---

[72] Pope Francis quoted in "Final Communique,"*Educating Today and Tomorrow: A Renewing Passion, Congregation for Catholic Education*, World Congress, Rome-Castel Gandolfo 18-21 November 2015, (February 2016).

National Catholic Education Commission, *Australian Perceptions of Catholic Education*, Quantitative Report prepared by Utting Research, May 2019.

Plibersek, Hon. Tanya. "Malcolm Turnbull's secret special deals for elite private schools," Media Release, April 13, 2018.

Pope Francis, Address to Participants, World Congress: *Educating Today and Tomorrow. A Renewing Passion*, Congregation for Catholic Education, November 21, 2015.

Pope Paul VI. *Gravissimum Educationis*, Declaration on Christian Education, October 28, 1965.

BIOGRAPHIES

Br Bernard Noel Bulfin fsp (1936–2018)

Humble service and commitment

Br Aengus Kavanagh fsp

Only a few months before his death, Br Bernard Bulfin fsp was asked what inspired him to become a Patrician Brother. He responded: 'It was so as to work my way to Heaven and to help others to get to Heaven as well'. Br Bernard's long religious life provided a sturdy foundation for many young men and their families, as he made an indelible mark on Catholic education in rapidly-growing western Sydney in the second half of the twentieth century, and in 'retirement' he was a pivotal prison chaplain for more than 15 years.

Edmund (or Edmond) Noel Bulfin was born in the small village of Ballinure, near Thurles, Co Tipperary, Ireland on 27 December 1936. His parents, Edmund and Margaret Bulfin (nee Curran) had married at Rosegreen, Cashel, Tipperary on 3 October 1935. Edmund senior was a small farmer. Edmund Noel, the eldest child of Edmund and Margaret, was named after his paternal grandfather in keeping with Irish naming practice. Next in age was Austin who spent most of his adult life as a diocesan priest in Manchester, England. Other siblings were Thomas, Jack (Br Gerard fsp) Patrick (for a period of time, Br Cathal fsp), Helen (Quinlan), and Josephine. Edmond received his primary school education at Ballinure National School. In September 1950, he went to the Patrician Juniorate in Tullow, Co Carlow, to commence studies and training to become a Patrician Brother.

In August 1954, he was admitted to First Profession of vows as a Patrician Brother, taking the name Bernard as his religious name.

Br Bernard was assigned to the Australian Province of the Patrician Brothers in 1955, and upon arrival, aged 19, he joined the staff at Patrician Brothers' Blacktown, a boys' school that had opened just three years' earlier in the newly-developing western suburbs of Sydney. During his early years of teaching, Br Bernard was "in at the deep end", barely beyond survival mode as he adapted to a new culture and multiple demands. On top of classroom duties, he actively engaged with the boys in extra-curricular activities, including coaching sports in some codes he had never heard tell of before his migration, such as rugby league and cricket.

Apart from some family visits to Ireland and well-earned sabbatical breaks, Bernard spent the next forty-five years actively involved in Catholic school education, spending almost all of those years at schools staffed by Patrician Brothers in Western Sydney.

Bernard was an energetic "on the job" educator, undertaking many courses in tandem with his roles as a full-time teacher and teaching principal. In 1970, Bernard completed a Diploma in Theory and Practice of NSW Curriculum from the Catholic Teachers' College, Sydney. Later he graduated with a Diploma in School Administration from Armidale College of Advanced Education (1977). In the next decade, he completed a Graduate Diploma in Religious Education (1981) and a Bachelor of Education (1984) both from Catholic College of Education Sydney, a Graduate Diploma in Educational Studies – Career Education from MacArthur Institute (1986). Br Bernard's respected leadership and senior positions positioned him well to undertake successfully two Masters' degrees: Master of Education from the (then) Catholic College of Education Sydney (1988) and Master of Arts in Pastoral Studies from Loyola University, Chicago (1990).

While Br Bernard's competence and confidence would have been boosted by his ongoing formal studies, the real source of his effectiveness as an educator and as a leader was anchored in the humanity he brought to his interactions with staff, students, and parents.

Br Bernard's journey starkly reflects a professionalising of staff in Catholic schools that became a bedrock in the emergence of Catholic schools as a highly respected sector of the Australian education landscape. Aided by the post-war migration waves from Europe, demand for Catholic school education was so great that many religious sisters and brothers were hastily rushed into service, often with minimal formal qualifications other than possible summer school and week-end courses and training. Such was the case for Br Bernard. While not overly academic by nature, he realised his teaching and leadership would be considerably enhanced by a good grasp of foundational theories, principles, and practices, as well as emerging trends in education.

Br Bernard lived through, and participated actively in, a number of significant transitions in the history of Catholic school education. His up-front role in the transitions is reflected in lengthy tenure as Principal of two large boys' schools characterised as "multi-cultural melting pots" – Patrician Brothers' College, Blacktown (1966-1988), Patrician Brothers' College, Fairfield (1991-2001). Class sizes were huge, facilities and resources were below basic, and qualified teachers were hard to come by.

On the occasion of Br Bernard's twenty-five years' service at Blacktown, the foundation bishop of Parramatta, Bishop Bede Heather remarked on Bernard's religious qualities:

> I would like to underline especially his qualities as a religious. These qualities help us to understand the man. The religious by very definition surrenders all such aspirations for the love of God. It is not for religious then to seek rewards or scholastic laurels, but to serve humbly like Jesus...I venture to say that the most notable achievement of Bro Bernard over 25 years in Blacktown has been to have exemplified those qualities so admirably.

Hansard records a tribute to Bernard from former NSW Education Minister, John Aquilina, that referred to Bernard's time as principal when John Aquilina was mayor of Blacktown and later State Member for Blacktown:

> Even then he was a legend in his time. He is one of those fantastic teachers who can walk through the

playground and instantly be admired by students and be highly respected by fellow teachers and members of the community.

It was only in the late 1960s that the first trickle of government funding was directed to Catholic and other non-government schools. Up until then, Catholic schools relied on modest school fees, local parish support, and enterprising school fund-raising. Bernard was to the fore as an enterprising fund-raiser. The annual fete at Blacktown was a two nights' mega-affair and a monster raffle was a major source of revenue coming from the fete. The drawing usually featured a sporting celebrity grasping into a mass of tickets in the container of a large ready-mix concrete truck!

In 1965, Catholic schools in NSW were staffed almost exclusively by an unsalaried workforce of religious sisters and brothers. Lay teachers were a tiny minority and there were no lay principals in Catholic schools. Fast forward to 2001 when Br Bernard "retired", and one gets a sense of the magnitude of the seamless transition from religious to lay staffing and lay leadership that characterised the decades when Br Bernard was presiding over the changes in settings of expansion and evolution. Br Bernard had played a large role in the Catholic Secondary Principals' Association while he was Principal.

After retiring as the last Brother principal of Fairfield in 1991, Br Bernard embarked on a new phase of active service. In 2002 and 2003, he completed full-time units at the NSW College of Clinical Pastoral Education with a view to engaging in another form of ministry. In 2004, the Patrician Brothers' Province Leader, Br Paul O'Keeffe, and Bishop Kevin Manning of Parramatta, appointed Br Bernard to be a member of the Diocesan Chaplaincy services at Parklea Correction Centre. His capacity to listen and to meet people "where they were at" in life's journey equipped him well for his chaplaincy service. He found his ministry among the marginalised in prison very rewarding and remained on the roster at Parklea Correctional Correction Centre until a few months prior to his rather sudden death on 17 July 2018.

Br Bernard's extrovert nature and his general positive view of life assured him strong bonds of collegiality with his co-chaplains and with Centre staff who, along with some past inmates, were well represented at his funeral. Earlier in 2018, an attractive plaque was presented to him by the Centre Management with the following wording:

> *To Brother Bernard Bulfin*
> *In Appreciation*
> *of your loyal and dedicated service*
> *To both inmates and staff*
> *At Parklea Correctional Centre*
> *2018*

Br Bernard's overflowing funeral attracted more than 800 mourners to Holy Cross College, Ryde. Retired Irish-Australian Bishop David Cremin wrote that was 'one of the finest farewells I have witnessed yesterday for our beloved Bernie'. Condolences were received from across Australia, Ireland, India, Papua New Guinea, and the United States of America – such was the respect in which Br Bernard was held. Congregational Leader of the Patrician Brother, Br Peter Ryan, summed up the man:

> We have lost a giant in Bernard. He was courageous to the last. We recall his zest for life and interest in people – his perpetual curiosity about every imaginable thing. A journeyman all his life in every respect but grounded in solid faith that released unbounded optimism and a positive view about anyone he should meet along the way.

Thus, the curtain had drawn on a remarkable life of Christian vocation. From a small Tipperary village, a young Irishman had come to Australia and dedicated himself with extraordinary zeal to elevating and making holy the human condition through the ministries of Catholic education and prison ministry for almost sixty years. He loved Australia and its lifestyle. He lived life to the full, was the essence of kindness, and always the one to affirm effort and achievement. From the beginning, he was a passionate supporter of the Parramatta Eels National Rugby League team, initiated by the happy coincidence that the Parramatta colours were blue and gold, the same as those of his native Tipperary.

Above all, his life mirrored an era of unprecedented transition in the story of Catholic schools in Australia, rising from humble beginnings to the highly resourced and professional status into which the sector has evolved. Brother Bernard Bulfin from Tipperary stands out among the generations of Irish religious sisters and brothers who played an integral part in the evolution of the story of Catholic schools in Australia.

Select Bibliography

https://rip.ie/death-notice/br.-bernard-edmond-noel-bulfin-thurles-tipperary/360671

An Insight into the life of Brother Bernard Bulfin. You Tube Video. Holy Cross College, Ryde, 20 July 2018.

Sweetman, Brother Stephen, *Go into the Vineyard – A History of the Patrician Brothers' Australian and PNG Province, 1883-2008.*

Tribute to Bro Bernard for 25 years of service to Patrician Brothers' College, Blacktown and the community. Thanksgiving Mass Booklet, 28 November 1984.

Aquilina, Hon. John. Former NSW Education Minister and Blacktown Mayor. Tribute to Bernard Bulfin on his 2001 retirement from school leadership, made in NSW Legislative Assembly, *Hansard* 23 October, 2001 https://www.parliament.nsw.gov.au/Hansard/Pages/HansardResult.aspx#/docid/HANSARD-1323879322-86327

Patrician Brothers Congregational Archives and CV profiles of Brothers.

Veronica Therese Ryan, rsj (1936–2008)

Walking with Indigenous Australians

Mary Cresp rsj

Veronica was born the daughter of Dennis and Elizabeth Ryan (née Farrell) in Quirindi, NSW, on 12 May1936. She attended St Joseph's primary school, Quirindi, followed by St Joseph's Juniorate, Hunters Hill, for her secondary schooling. She entered the Sisters of St Joseph at Mount Street, North Sydney, on 23 January 1954 and was professed there three years later. After completing teacher training at the Congregation's St Joseph's Training School, Mount Street, North Sydney, she was appointed to a variety of country and city schools in New South Wales. A significant assignment in the mid 1960s was as principal of St Joseph's School, Walgett, where about a third of the pupils were Aboriginal. It was there she realised the need for educational programs that supported Indigenous culture and values.

In 1974, Veronica volunteered for ministry in the Kimberley where the Sisters of St Joseph ran schools in a number of centres. As Principal at Kununurra, and against opposition from the white population, she employed Aboriginal teacher-aides, tutoring and enrolling them in formal study courses in anticipation of the time when, as she wrote in a letter in 1976, 'a suitable training programme will be devised whereby Aboriginal people will become qualified teachers'.

In the meantime, Veronica extended her own tertiary studies with a Diploma of Teaching in 1979 at the Western Australian College of Advanced Education (later Edith Cowan University). Veronica moved to Warmun in 1982. The Ngalangangpum school there was unique in that it had been started three years before on a system of "Two-way education" – the local language, culture and history being taught by the elders, supplementing the regular school curriculum taught by mainstream teachers. Under Veronica's principalship, the system was extended and much work done to have the local Kija language written as well as spoken, as documented in her co-authored book, *Walking Together in the Kimberley*.

A feature of Veronica's life was her ability to relate practical experience with academic expertise. She formed strong bonds with the women of Warmun, sharing their lives and taking part in cultural activities that earned reciprocal trust and friendship. At the same time she constantly updated her qualifications in linguistics, education and theology at various institutions, which all contributed to a Bachelor of Education in 1989 at Armidale University. From the same establishment she gained a Masters in Intercultural Studies in 1991, where her thesis, *Aboriginal Women in the Face of Change*, grew directly out of daily experience and was later distilled into a book, *From Digging Sticks to Writing Sticks*.

With Veronica's Catholic Education Office appointment as Coordinator of Aboriginal Education in 1990, the effort to raise awareness of the needs of Aboriginal students attending Catholic schools throughout Western Australia took on sharp focus. A number of Aboriginal Teaching Assistants and some elders helped Veronica develop an Aboriginal Studies Program to inform staffs in Catholic Schools about the history, culture and values of Aboriginal groups.

In 1994, under the leadership of Veronica and Pat Rhatigan SJG, the Catholic Education Aboriginal Committee produced *The Aboriginal and Torres Strait Islander Education Policy*. Its key principle ensures the incorporation of Aboriginal Studies in all Catholic schools. Veronica also produced a Religious Education program, *The Kimberley Companion*, comprising seventy-two booklets, adding a culturally appropriate component to the teaching of religion in the Broome diocese.

In 1998, Veronica took the opportunity to enhance her expertise with study-leave in Canada, where she visited communities and attended courses in Indigenous Religious Education at St Paul's University, Ottawa, and the Jesuit-run Religious Education for Native Americans at Plains, South Dakota. On her return to Australia, her influence spread further with her involvement in various national bodies such as NATSICC[73] and the Josephite Aboriginal Planning Committee. In 2004, she was made a Fellow of the Australian College of Educators.

Veronica's responsibilities, especially as CEO for the Broome Religious Education Project, involved much travel. Since the Sisters were no longer teaching in the Wyndham school, Veronica decided in 2002 to make Wyndham her base, to provide an ongoing link between the Sisters and people. It was among these people that, on 2 December 2008, she suffered a heart attack and died. In her death, she was ministered to by the friends to whom she had given her all – a true instance of partnership.

Veronica's journey into understanding the culture, language and rituals that are proper to different groups of Aboriginal peoples went side by side with a deep appreciation and respect for each person. Her thirty-four years of ministry were spent mostly in the company of Indigenous Australians. During those years, she became as described by her nephew Peter Ryan in her eulogy 'an icon of compassion, strength, hope, inspiration and determination to everyone she touched'. Andrew West's article in the *Sydney Morning Herald* describing her death bore the heading, 'Education trailblazer in remote north-west' and quoted a co-worker in the WA Catholic Education Office who described her as being 'deft at handling the often-delicate politics of the church and the indigenous communities'. The comments bore testimony to Veronica's own reflections on her ministry penned in 2007:

> Years ago, it took time to recognise the workings of the Holy Spirit in what at first seemed unlikely places. May that same Spirit continue to guide (us in our) desire to walk with Indigenous Australians who are so much in need of 'God's justice and hospitality'.

---

[73] The National Aboriginal and Torres Strait Catholic Council, an advisory Commission of the Australian Bishops' Conference.

Selected Writings

Ryan, Veronica, rsj. Compiler. *Walking Together in the Kimberley*, Sydney: Sisters of St Joseph of the Sacred Heart, 2004.

Ryan, Veronica, rsj. *From Digging Sticks to Writing Sticks*, Perth: Catholic Education Office of W.A., 2001.

Ryan, Veronica, rsj. "How Change Has Shaped Josephite Lives for Mission in the Kimberley". North Sydney: St Joseph's Archives, 2007.

Ryan, Veronica, rsj. "Letter to Sisters of St Joseph", Kununurra Community, North Sydney: St Joseph's Archives, 1976.

Select Bibliography

Obituary, "Education trailblazer in remote north-west," *Sydney Morning Herald*, 23 December 2008.

Ryan, Peter. *Eulogy*. North Sydney: St Joseph's Archives, 2008.

West, Andrew. "Education trailblazer in remote north-west", in *Sydney Morning Herald*, 23 December 2008.

Bishop Barry Collins (1938–2000)

Priest-Inspector of Schools, Religious Education Director, Country Bishop

Seamus O'Grady

Barry Collins was born on 10 November 1938 in Waitara, New South Wales. He was the only son in the family of Arthur (Choppy) Collins and Marie (Mollie) Collins (nee Asser) with three sisters, Elaine, Ann and Barbara. From his First Communion, Barry loved the Mass and often attended daily. His primary schooling was at Our Lady of the Rosary, Waitara where he was a good student, by-passing Grade 5. His desire to enter the junior seminary was discouraged by the advice his mother received from the Sisters of Mercy. His secondary education took place at St Pius X, Chatswood, where he showed leadership and planning skills as a Cadet Officer. Still only 16, he finally went to the seminary at Springwood.

On 30 November 1960, Barry was ordained a Deacon at St Patrick's College, Manly. He was then ordained to the priesthood for the Archdiocese of Sydney in St Mary's Cathedral on 15 July 1961 by Cardinal Norman Gilroy. Barry's interest in Catholic education was quickly recognised by the then-Director, Monsignor John Slowey, who appointed him in 1965 as one of eight Priest-Inspectors of Catholic schools. At the time, there were around 250 Catholic schools in the Archdiocese of Sydney. Priest-Inspectors worked part-time at this important task while attending to their regular duties in the parishes. They shared a small office in CUSA House, Elizabeth Street, Sydney.

Barry completed his BA Dip Ed while juggling his parochial work with his role in the Catholic Education Office. In the early 1970s, he was appointed Assistant Director of Schools. In that capacity he provided the Director of Schools, Monsignor Slowey, with unwavering support, loyalty and friendship.

In 1972, he participated in the Armidale Conference that set down the administrative structure that resulted in the co-ordination of diocesan CEOs, State Commission and the National Catholic Education Commission.

In 1973, during a period of unprecedented change flowing from the Commonwealth Government' implementation of the Karmel Report, Barry served as Acting Director of Schools, which he did whenever Monsignor Slowey undertook his study tours.

In the wake of the Second Vatican Council, crises arose regarding the context, content and methodology of Religious Education. Monsignor Slowey resolved that his senior colleagues would have a sound grasp of catechetics and sent Barry to study at Boston College in the USA where he came under the influence of such catechetical luminaries as Tom Groome, Mary Boys and Richard McBrien.

At the beginning of 1979, the Vicar of Education, Archbishop James Carroll informed Monsignor Slowey that Religious Education 'needed a more systematic approach', that teachers required more assistance, and that there was a need to produce curriculum guidelines for Religious Education and indicated that Fr Collins should be appointed Director of Religious Education for the Archdiocese of Sydney. While there was some friction between the men about this appointment, Fr Collins proved an ideal candidate and for the next thirteen years worked unstintingly to strengthen Religious education in Catholic schools.

In September 1982, he published a Core Statement of Religious Education for Primary Schools Kindergarten to Year 6, *A Journey in Faith*, which was well received by teachers. His leadership saw the emergence of a new position in Catholic schools, the Religious Education Co-ordinator. In 1985, he established the Certificate A Course for teachers anxious to improve their religious education qualifications. And the appointment of Religious Education Consultants and Advisers to the staff of the CEO was an innovation of which Barry was particularly proud.

In later years, as Director of Religious Education, Barry was responsible for the development of *Celebrating Our Journey*, the Religious Education Curriculum for primary schools, and contributed to the development of the secondary curriculum, *Faithful to God: Faithful to People*.

Barry was not an intellectual in the strict sense, but he was an enthusiast and a wide reader and open to new ideas. He was not an ideologue. He was a good leader at the CEO. He protected his staff at a time when religious education was often an area of tension and he gave them room to do the things they were good at. He was not openly political either but was wily. Those who knew him knew his opinions. He often accomplished things by going slowly and making the most of the staff he had. He protected his staff from critics who blamed the CEO for failing to produce Religious Education curricula to their liking. He was confronted by fundamentalist or anxious Catholics, Roman officials and people who came to parent meetings on religious education only to make trouble. Barry was always scrupulously kind but there was no doubt where he stood.

Barry continued in this role throughout the 80s when the Office moved from Broadway to Leichhardt (1983) until 1991, while continuing to serve as parish priest of Mortlake, a Sydney suburb.

Barry Collins was first and foremost a priest. He was a kind of unofficial chaplain to the CEO. He would frequently say Mass in the chapel. He retained a strong pastoral interest in the teachers and colleagues at the Office. He joined in the sorrows, joys, grievances and sufferings of ordinary families. He regarded the CEO as his second parish.

In 1971, Barry was appointed Chaplain to the Federation of Parents and Friends Association of Catholic Schools, the Archdiocesan parent body. For twenty-four years he attended their meetings, celebrated Masses and was their gentle and encouraging pastor and father confessor.

In March 1994, Pope John Paul II appointed him Bishop of the Diocese of Wilcannia-Forbes in Western NSW. He was ordained bishop at Holy Family Church in Parkes, NSW, by Cardinal Edward Clancy assisted by Bishops Doug Warren and David Cremin.

The Diocese of Wilcannia-Forbes was the poorest diocese in Australia and Bishop Collins continued the work of Bishop Warren, particularly in the area of education while regularly visiting the far-flung parishes across the diocese. The kilometres he clocked up with his car were extraordinary not to mention the tiredness such journeys exacted on his health.

At the time of his appointment, there was serious drought. He soon became aware of the stress and depression within communities of the diocese and was concerned how the Church could respond. Coming from Sydney, he was well aware of the works of CatholicCare and he saw the obvious need for similar services in western NSW. In 1996, he sought the help of Sr Margaret Flynn, a Loreto sister and psychologist, asking her to move to the diocese and establish CatholicCare, which from a difficult beginning now has offices in Bourke, Forbes, Narromine and Broken Hill.

Bishop Collins was an active member of the NSW Catholic Education Commission where he sought to change entrenched government funding allocation by pointing out that Wilcannia-Forbes 'did not want charity but justice'.

Sadly, it was at a Commission meeting as members awaited his arrival for the annual photograph to be taken, that news of his death came through. He died peacefully in his sleep on 15 November 2000, aged 62. The funeral Liturgy in Parkes saw over thirty bishops and one hundred priests join family and friends to celebrate the life of a man many knew and loved. Bishop Barry Collins is buried in the Forbes Cemetery.

In life, Barry was quietly spoken, intelligent, gifted, passionate about the gospel and thoughtful in little things like having morning tea conversations with his staff. He had a gentle sense of humour and never held himself above those he met.

Selected Writing

Collins, Barry. "A country bishop looks towards 2000. [Overcoming the potential shortage of priests in country parishes]" in *The Australasian Catholic Record*, v.73, no.4, Oct 1996, 394-400.

Collins, Barry. Editor. *A Journey in Faith*, A Core Statement of Religious Education, Primary Schools Kindergarten – Year 6, Sydney: Catholic Education Office, September 1982.

Collins, Barry, et al. *Faithful to God, faithful to people*: Religious education for secondary schools. Sydney: Catholic Education Office, 1984.

Select Bibliography

D'Orsa, Dr Jim.*Monsignor Slowey – Servant of Education, Facilitator of Change*. Sydney: Catholic Education Office, November 1999.

The Hierarchy of the Catholic Church, http://www.catholic-hierarchy.org/bishop/bcollinsb.html

_____*A Brief History of the Formation of the Wilcannia-Forbes Diocese and the Development of Catholic Education*, https://www.wf.catholic.org.au/our-diocese/our-history/.

Canavan, Br Kelvin, fms. *A Tribute from Catholic Education, in Spirit Across the Plains*, Diocese of Wilcannia Forbes, Volume 4 No 5, December 2000.

CatholicCare, Wilcannia Forbes, Our Story, https://ccwf.org.au/about-us/our-story.

Article by Enda in Catholica, Catholic spirituality for adults, 18 October 2016

Valedictory speech by Graham English, December 1991.

Eulogy by Elaine Hume (sister) at Funeral Mass, Parkes, 22 November 2000.

Barry Francis Dwyer (1938–2009)

An educator who kindled the Catholic imagination of children and young people

Graham English and Anne Benjamin

Barry Dwyer is remembered with affection and admiration as a teacher, writer, story teller, and agent of change who never let his achievements and standing as an educator, both within Australian Catholic education and beyond, override his humility and humanity.

Barry was born at Maroubra on 18 December 1938 to Clement Edwin Dwyer and Joan Clare Dwyer (nee Dawson). Both his parents were Sydney-born and proudly directly descended from two convicts on the First Fleet.

After his primary education at St Michael's Primary School, Daceyville, Barry completed the first three years of secondary school at De la Salle School, Coogee, and then the final two years at St Columba's Seminary, Springwood. At some point, he decided that priesthood was not for him. In January 1961, he married Janet Frances Bennett. The couple had four children, David, Joseph, Rosemary and Marianne and later, nine grandchildren, whom Barry would good-humouredly refer to as his "G&T grandchildren" at a time when "gifted and talented education" was coming into some prominence.

After leaving Springwood, Barry trained as a primary school teacher at Sydney Teachers College, graduating in 1958. His special interests were literacy, literature, history and the media. He began teaching at public primary schools, Waverley Public, Engadine and others while completing a Bachelor of Arts at Sydney University in the evenings, something common among teachers at that time. He majored in English and History. In 1963, he spent a year training to be a school counsellor with the Department of Education. He later completed a Master of Letters (Psychology) at the University of Armidale. He was an inveterate reader. Barry's teaching, all based in and around Sydney NSW, included Waverley Public School (1958), Mortdale Public School (1962), Schools Counsellor, Berkeley, Port Kembla area of southern Wollongong (1964), English/History teacher and Careers advisor, Berkeley High School (1967), History Master, Hurstville Boys High(1967-1969), Lecturer in Education, Sydney Teachers' College(1971).

After nearly twenty years in public education, he brought his experience, talents and questioning into Catholic Education. For the next thirty-three years, he shared his vision, passion and uncommon good sense in the following roles: 1976: Principal Lecturer, Good Samaritan Teachers College, Glebe, NSW; 1979: Education Consultant, Sydney Catholic Education Office; 1983: Director, Eastern Region, Sydney Catholic Education Office; 1994: Area Administrator, Catholic Education Office, Parramatta, NSW.

From 1997, Barry commenced part-time duties at the Catholic Education Office Parramatta, working on curriculum documents, writing speeches and other projects for the Executive Director. He was still engaged in this work at the time of his death.

Through his insights, delightful skill as a communicator and the respect he had earned, Barry was a frequent speaker at conferences and in-service for educators. These included conferences of Catholic Principals' Associations; teachers conferences in the dioceses of Adelaide, Ballarat, Canberra Goulburn, Maitland-Newcastle, Melbourne, Perth, Ballarat and others; the 1991 National Conference of the Australian College of Education; in 2000, he was invited to run a conference in Killarney, Ireland, on Catholic Education as well as writing for a number of educational publishers.

He was an active Catholic especially in his home parish of Gymea in Sydney's south where he enthusiastically led the momentum for major improvements to the parish school. He embraced the changes of the Second Vatican Council (1962-1965) and the hope that the laity would take a bigger part in the Church.

Barry was an innovator, an enthusiast, a good communicator and a questioner. He was a man ahead of his time. All these made him a fine educator though they did not always make him popular with those in authority, especially when he moved from state education to the Catholic system. He was not satisfied with some of the models of leadership and organisation in Catholic education that had for a hundred years been conducted by religious congregations. He wanted cultural change. He was passionate about many things. A major focus for several years was abolishing corporal punishment in schools. Barry wanted to change the culture of Catholic Education. His great mantra was: *prune the curriculum.*

In his 2005 Ann D Clark lecture in Parramatta, Barry spoke of the greatest gift that Catholic schooling possesses being

> the ability to kindle the Catholic imagination of children and young people, to introduce them to profound and ageless mysteries and a worldview that will give their lives meaning and purpose.

Barry was strongly committed to communicating with parents about the education of their children in an accessible and transparent way. His writing style was clear and straight forward and devoid of "educationalese" – jargon.

In the early 1970s, Barry began writing a weekly education column for *The Catholic Weekly* which continued for many years. He also had a column in *The Sun Herald* in the early 1980s. He also wrote a children's book *The Voyage of the Bee* based on the history of his convict ancestors.

In recognition of his services to education, Barry received awards. As a founding member of PETA (Primary English Teachers Association) and president for ten years, he was made a Life Member in 2003. He was awarded a Fellow of the Australian College of Education in 2003, and in 1998 received the Brother John Taylor Award for excellence in Catholic Education by the NSW Catholic Education Commission.

Despite these accolades and his immense experience, Barry was always a great team-player and happily took on tasks as requested. A former colleague recalls him as a joy and delight to work with. He was a great story-teller.

While on summer holidays, Barry died suddenly in Sydney on 25 January 2009. His funeral at St Catherine's, Gymea, was largely attended.

Select Publications

Dwyer, Barry, Roger Milliss & Bruce Thomson. *Mastering the Media*. Melbourne: Longman Cheshire, 1971.

Dwyer, Barry. *Social Change in Twentieth Century Australia*. Terry Hills, NSW: Reed Education, 1974.

Dwyer, Barry & Dwyer, Janet. *K-6 Best Years of Their Lives? A Practical guide and Discussion Statement for Parents and Teachers on the Primary School Child at School and at Home*. Gordon, NSW: Primary English Teaching Association, 1979.

Dwyer, Barry. *You Can Write*. Melbourne: Oxford University Press, 1984.

Dwyer, Barry. *Primary School and Your Child: a parent's guide to primary education*. Melbourne: Oxford University Press, 1984.

Dwyer, Barry & R. D. Walshe. *Learning to Read the Media: a teacher's guide to media education*. Sydney: Primary English Teaching Association, 1984.

Dwyer, Barry. *Catholic Schools at the Crossroads*. Blackburn, Vic: Dove Communications, 1986.

Dwyer, Barry & Graham English. *Catholics in Australia: Our Story* (Student & Teachers' Books). Melbourne: Collins Dove, 1988.

Dwyer, Barry & Graham English. *Faith of Our Fathers and Mothers: A Catholic Story*. Burwood Vic: Collins Dove, 1990.

Dwyer, Barry. *Catholic Schools: Creating a New Culture*. Newtown, NSW: E. J. Dwyer, 1993.

Dwyer, Barry. *The Catholic School: A Guide for Parents*. Mulgrave Vic: John Garratt Publishing, 2002.

Dwyer, Barry. *Parents, Teachers, Partners*. Rozelle: Primary English Teaching Association, 1989.

Select Bibliography

Whitby, Greg. Eulogy. Gymea: St Catherine Labouré Church, 30 January, 2009.

Gleeson, D. J. *This beautiful part of the Lord's Vineyard: Gymea's Catholic community, 1893-2019*. Gymea: St Catherine's Parish, 2019.

Veitch, Harriet, "Teacher told children to question media's impact: Barry Dwyer, 1938-2009", *Sydney Morning Herald*, 9 March 2009.

Authors' personal recollections.

Ann-Marie Webb sm (1943-2008)

Stalwart of Catholic education[74]

Gail Reneker sm

Ann-Marie Webb, Marist educator, was born on 23 June 1943 at Cootamundra, NSW to Kenneth James Webb and Alice Veronica (nee Warren). Ann-Marie's father was initially involved in the management of department stores and then moved into real estate and property management. Her mother had been a nurse. Ann-Marie's primary schooling was completed in schools across NSW: Cronulla (1948), Murwillumbah (1949-50), Leeton (1951-52), Bowral (1953) and St Patrick's, Kogarah (1954). She commenced her secondary school studies at St Vincent's Potts Point (1955-1956) and completed them at Monte Sant' Angelo, North Sydney (1957-1959). Her tertiary studies included a Teacher's Diploma, from the Catholic Teachers' College (Sub Primary); Teachers' Guild of NSW (Secondary); Bachelor of Economics from the University of New England, Master's degree in Educational Administration from the University of New England and two summer schools at the Institute of Pastoral Studies, Loyola University, Chicago. She engaged with the wider educational community through her membership of the Australian College of Education (MACE).

In 1963, having completed Sub-Primary Teacher training and one year of teaching at St Joseph's Enfield (Burwood Heights), Ann-Marie entered the Congregation of Marist Sisters and was professed on 23 January 1965 taking the name Sister Gerard Majella. She was appointed to Cerdon College, Merrylands, where she worked from 1966 to 1974: her outstanding teaching gifts were soon recognised and deeply appreciated especially by those to whom she taught Maths. She was promoted to be Principal of Marist Sisters' College, Woolwich from

1975-1979. In 1980, Ann-Marie returned to Cerdon College as Principal, a position she held with finesse till June 1994.

Ann-Marie's reputation as an educator extended far and wide and won her positions on National and State Boards. These included her role on Parramatta Diocesan Education Committee and Schools' Board, representing the NSW Catholic Education Commission on the Board of Studies Registration and Accreditation Committee, Chairperson of the Parramatta Diocese's Secondary Principals' Association and her being the nominee for the Australian Conference of Leaders of Religious Institutes on the National Education Commission for a four-year term.

Her position on the Standing Committee in the Association of Marist Schools (AMSA) saw her working nationally not only with the Marist Sisters' schools, but also with those of the Marist Fathers and Marist Brothers. As an "Animator of Marist Charism in Education" for the Marist Sisters Province of Australia, she collaborated with Principals and worked closely with the Religious Education and Pastoral Care Departments in supporting the development of the Marist charism in staff and students in Marist schools and in particular those of the two Marist Sisters' schools in Sydney.

Within the Marist Sisters' Congregation, Ann-Marie held a range of positions of authority. She was a Provincial councillor from 1980 to 1989 and was appointed Provincial of Australia for the Marist Sisters in June 1994, a position she held until 2000. She represented the Province of Australia at a number of the Congregation's General Chapters as well as serving in various other capacities.

To these roles Ann-Marie brought gifts of intelligence, insight, acumen and logical thought. One of her special strengths was her capacity to challenge. While she was tolerant and affable, Ann-Marie had the courage to speak out in situations where many others might choose to remain silent. She had the ability to confront, without being confrontational. Ann-Marie was also blessed with an expansive mind. When confronted with issues to be resolved, or plans to be developed, she would consider them with a clarity not constrained by fear or preconception. She was generous in spirit, lively and outgoing which showed in her warm and pleasant bearing.

Ann-Marie had a genuine love for people. Her ability to relate to people from all walks of life engendered in persons young and old, a sense of their worth and dignity as persons and a self-confidence in themselves. Her commitment to education was imbued with her stated belief that 'education is all about people' and with the privilege she felt in her call to contribute to its life-giving role in the lives of young people. Her peer principals recall her attention to courtesy and graciousness in acknowledging colleagues with a detailed attention to the presentation of gifts. At the core of this commitment was her faith in and love of God and her deep awareness of being called to live and serve as a Marist.

This 'stalwart of Catholic Education' was diagnosed with cancer on the Feast of the Assumption 2008 and died just three weeks later at the Mater Hospital in North Sydney on 2 September 2008.

Select Bibliography

Archival File, Ann-Marie Webb, Marist Sisters Archives Australia.

Cerdon College Merrylands. "About Us: Our Story." Accessed 26 October 2018. http://www.cerdonmerrylands.catholic.edu.au

Webb, A-Marie, *A Study of the Influence of Socio-Economic Status on Pupil Control Ideology, Master of Educational Administration dissertation.* Armidale: University of New England, 1979.

Webb, A-M. "Why Me?", *Marist Contact, The Society of Mary.* July 2004.

REFLECTION

Catholic Education: A Dangerous memory?

+ Vincent Long

Introduction

"Who is close to me is close to the fire; who is far from me is far from the Kingdom."[75] This apocryphal saying of Jesus was recorded by the early church Father, Origen. It graphically reminds us Australian Catholics that it is dangerous to be close to Jesus for it threatens to set us afire, to consume us. Only in the face of this danger does the vision of the Kingdom of God that has come near in Jesus light up.

Perhaps, in our times, do we sometimes find this challenge too daunting? Do we really want to let Jesus 'light us up'? Isn't it much easier for us to just settle into a comfortable 'amnesia' in our affluence? Then, we can just simply ignore what is demanded of us as Catholic educators for the 21st century and get on with 'business as usual'.

However, there is an alternative!

Just maybe we need to listen again to theologians like the recently deceased eminent German theologian Johannes Baptist Metz, who called the story of Jesus' passion and death, a 'dangerous memory'.[76] Daily in the Eucharist, this same Jesus pleads us with us: 'Remember me!'

The 'dangerous memory' of Jesus of Nazareth confronts us with the terrible realities of misunderstanding, injustice and innocent suffering. And his memory places before us the surprising possibility that God can and does accomplish great things even in the midst of terrible sufferings.

---

[75] Peter Kirby, "Gospel of Thomas Saying #82" Gospel of Thomas Commentary, (2012). http://www.earlychristianwritings.com/thomas/gospelthomas82.html.
[76] See especially: Johannes Baptist Metz, trans. J. Matthew. Ashley, *A Passion for God: the mystical-political dimension of Christianity.* (New York: Paulist Press, 1998).

So how are we Catholics, especially Catholic educators, in this Great Southern Land of the Holy Spirit, going to keep alive the 'dangerous memory' of Jesus of Nazareth? How will our faith have children for a new future?[77]

Where have we come from? Our 'dangerous memories' as Catholic Educators

Our first critical task is to remember our Catholic identity: who we are as Catholic Christians.

We stand boldly in the tradition of the prophets. We must never forget that one of the deepest strands in the biblical tradition is the desire of the Jewish people to be an *alternative* society to the oppressive systems of domination.[78] These systems were designed by empires to enslave their subjects via forced labour, tributes, taxes and other means of exploitation. The people of God – being a small nation – had a fair share of exploitation. Their experience of empire domination – from Egypt to Assyria, from Babylon to Rome – fed into a radically countercultural vision. Therefore, in contrast to the gods of the empire, who serve the will of the king, the Hebrews worshiped Yahweh who they understood to be free, the critic of kings, and the advocate of vulnerable, oppressed people.

The prophets often speak about the importance of being a community of faith, which is countercultural or antithetical to the dominant social system. This was particularly so when their identity was under threat by the totalising power of the empire.

The prophets did not simply reiterate the past. They re-engaged the remembered faith tradition in the light of contemporary experience. This, by the way, is the basis of the Leuven Project that is being trialled

---

[77] See Walter Brueggemann, "Will Our Faith Have Children?" *Word & World* 3:3 (1983).
[78] The classic study of this is Walter Brueggemann's, *The Prophetic Imagination*, 40th Anniversary edition (Minneapolis: Fortress Press, 2018).

at some selected schools in some Dioceses.[79] The faith tradition is re-contextualised with fresh insights distilled from lived experience. Thus, for example, when the Exodus story was re-engaged in the context of Babylonian Exile, it became a story of emancipation not from the Pharaoh of Egypt but the Pharaoh of Persia. In this way, the prophets were able to provide an alternative vision to that of the dominant system.

God, in Christ, summons us Australian Catholics to live and relate to each other in a way that is different to the kind of ruthless, competitive, inhumane, dog-eat-dog, survival-of-the-fittest economy that we are being seduced into. We are called to practise an ethic of concern, care, support for one another, so that no one is excluded from the table or left behind; we are challenged to be a community of hospitality, compassion and neighbourliness, which is an alternative model to the economy of extraction, self-interest and accumulation. And if we are followers of Jesus of Nazareth, we must be peace-makers who forgive and act as agents of reconciliation.[80]

As Australian Catholic educators, we too need to demonstrate how to be countercultural, not by adopting a fortress mentality and fearful attitude, but by showing a kinder, more inclusive, more caring alternative society under God's rule. Christians today must respond to imperial ideologies which manifest in expressions of things such as hate, discrimination, fear, oppression, power, violence, exploitation and cruelty. We must have the courage to be a community of hospitality, compassion and neighbourliness that serves as an alternative to the dominant narrative.

We seek to reframe the harsh, unjust and inhumane realities that many people experience into an alternative vision of hope, and promote those values that will lead to the fulfillment of that vision. Thus, whether the issue is the Indigenous peoples, refugees, ecology, gender, or other issues, we must show our students the way to a Gospel-centred culture

---

[79] A good introduction to the Leuven project can be found at https://www.schoolidentity.net/introduction/
[80] See Robert Schreiter, *Ministry of Reconciliation*, (New York: Orbis Books, 1998).

of love and compassion, solidarity and service in the world where there is so much fear, indifference and marginalisation.

Where are we going?: "Keeping alive the 'dangerous memory"

We should never forget the history of our Catholic education in Australia. There has truly been so much to be proud of.

Even from the early days, the concern to provide a religious education for Catholic families in the colony galvanised lay people, priests and the bishops of Australia.[81] Their vision was brought to life initially by lay men and women who worked for love rather than for money and then by religious men and women who responded courageously to the invitation to give opportunity to young Catholics. These were mostly poor, socially disadvantaged and, in the post-war period, immigrant children. This special attention to them in Catholic education has not been diminished with the transition from religious to lay leadership. A strong commitment to professional development, especially in respect of the mission, identity and ethos of Catholic schools, continues to guide us to meet the challenges of the 21st Century.

Indeed, Australian Catholic education has been hailed as a jewel in our crown and the envy of other nations.

Yet who can deny that in Australia today we seem to have reached a critical juncture? A *Kairos* moment of decision. Not only are we afflicted by such things as the decline in Sunday worship, the fall in religious practice, the decline in vocations to the priesthood and religious life, we also face the biggest challenge to date, which is the loss of our moral credibility and trust capital due to the sexual abuse crisis.

There needs to be an attitudinal change at every level. This must be a conversion of mind and heart that conforms us to the spirit of the Gospel, puts new wine into new wineskins, not a superficial change or, worse, a retreat into restorationism. There needs, too, to be an attitudinal change at every level: between other faith traditions and

---

[81] The authoritative study on the early history of Catholic education in Australia remains: Ronald Fogarty, *Catholic education in Australia, 1806-1950*, (Melbourne: Melbourne University Press, 1959).

Christian churches and with dioceses, clergy, religious and laity. Of course, this must begin with the Bishops themselves and all leadership of the Church itself. Prophetic conversion from a narrow clericalism which separates us from the lives of the ordinary people of God is imperative.

This was what the early lay teachers did. This is what Saint Mary MacKillop did when she rallied her sisters behind the poor and vulnerable in colonial Australia. She took a prophetic stance, not simply in providing affordable quality Catholic education and health care to the poor masses, but fundamentally in meeting the great cultural challenges of their times.[82]

'Never see a need without doing something about it.'[83] In acting out of a strong passion for the Kingdom and a visceral compassion for the suffering, she brought about a fresh hope for others. Like her, we Australian Catholics are called to be channels of hope and to meet the challenges of our times. In what ways can we follow her prophetic vision and apply it to our context?

Who are today's people who are without hope and how can we reframe the harsh realities that they experience into a hopeful future?

So where to now?

There is a sense that we Australian Catholics are being cut loose from the safe and secure moorings of the past. As we launch ourselves anew into the deep, we grow in the awareness of the 'dangerous memory' of Jesus of Nazareth.

We are just beginning to glimpse what needs to die and what needs to rise. We must learn to live as a minority in the midst of a secular society. We must learn to influence it not as lords and masters but as fellow pilgrims. We must learn to engage with others and to act as leaven in a critical and disbelieving world. All Catholic leaders are meant to be that crucial yeast in critical times. We are meant to transform each

---

[82] See Paul Gardiner, *An Extraordinary Australian: Mary MacKillop: The Authorised Biography*, (Morehouse Publishing Co.1995).

[83] St Mary MacKillop.

of our schools into a refuge for the poor, an oasis for the weary and a hospital for the wounded.

Catholic education is not meant to be a numbers game. It is our substance, and not our size that makes the difference. Hence, this time of diminishment of the institutional church can be a blessing in disguise as it makes us less reliant on ourselves and more reliant on the power of God. Diminishment allows us the precious opportunity to identify with the 'remnant faithful', to learn the power of vulnerable trust. It is not a time for cynicism or nostalgia. It is a time for deepening of commitment, of grounding in our core values.

I am not an expert in Catholic education in Australia. However, I believe that, although Catholic schools are both successful and popular generally, many Catholic school leaders will agree that their mission towards the socially disadvantaged in the community with the passion of the Gospel continues to be an unmet challenge.

There is certainly no room for complacency. Our Pope Francis puts his challenge to Catholic educators and he pulls no punches as he speaks to our Australian Catholic reality powerfully:

> Education has become too selective and elitist. It seems that only those people or persons who are at a certain level or have a certain capacity have the right to an education. This is shameful. It is a reality which takes us in a direction of human selectivity. Instead of bridging the gap between people, it widens it. It creates a barrier between poor and rich.
>
> The greatest failure for an education is to educate within the walls: the walls of selective culture, the walls of a culture of security, the walls of a social class.
>
> We cannot go on like this with a selective type of education. No one should be denied. We must leave the

places where we are as educators and go to the outskirts, to the poor.[84]

How do we as Australian Catholic educators who are people of commitment, passion and imagination address Pope Francis's challenge of outreach to the poor, the marginalised and vulnerable children? How can we respond to the challenge of Pope Francis in going to the new 'peripheries': the socio-economically disadvantaged, the families without values and without faith, the broken and dysfunctional, in order to offer nearness and proximity? How do our school communities embody the powerlessness and the compassion of Christ? How do we balance the need for recognition and success on the one hand, and the fundamental Christian ethos of care for the weakest on the other?

Let's follow the 'dangerous memory of Jesus' and educate our children:

- less in a role of power, dominance and privilege but more a position of vulnerability and powerlessness;

- less in an enclosure for the virtuous but more an oasis for the weary and downtrodden;

- less in an experience of exclusion and elitism but more an encounter of radical love, inclusiveness and solidarity;

- less in an attitude of 'we are right, and you are wrong' and more of an attitude of openness to truth wherever and whoever it is to be found;

---

[84] Pope Francis, Remarks at World, Congress *Education Today and Tomorrow: A Passion that Is Renewed*, (Rome, November 18-21, 2015), organised by the Congregation for Catholic Education.

- less in a leadership of control and more a *diakonia* of a humble servant exemplified by Christ at the Last Supper;

- less in a language of condemnation but more a language of affirmation and compassion.

So, let's continue our pilgrim path forward and dream of a renewed mission for our Church.

Conclusion: A Dream for Catholic education

I dream of a Catholic Church in Australia that dares to break new ground with a view to being radically faithful to the inclusive vision of Jesus. I dream of a future Catholic education system that continues to break new ground with a view to being radically faithful to the 'dangerous memory' of Jesus.

For Jesus has a habit of challenging ingrained stereotyped attitudes, subverting the tyranny of the majority, breaking social taboos, pushing the boundaries of love and redefining its meaning. His interactions with women, with tax collectors and other types of social outcast are nothing short of being revolutionary and boundary breaking.

If Catholic schools are premised on the fundamental dignity of each and every person, how can we be places where this sense of ecclesial inclusiveness is fully expressed? In what ways can we advance Jesus' radical vision of love, inclusion and human flourishing in our communities?

Have we really taken seriously the call of Pope Francis in *Laudato Si*'[85] to educate ourselves and our school and parish communities for ecological conversion? As Australia burns, is this challenge being faced with renewed passion and resources?

Certainly, we must continue to face honestly that the Catholic Church in this country will face diminishment and decline as a

---

[85] Pope Francis, *Laudato Sí*, "On the care for our common home", (2015) http://w2.vatican.va/content/francesco/en/encyclicals/documents/papa-francesco_20150524_enciclica-laudato-si.html.

result of combined forces such as the secularisation of our society, the institutional malaise and, of course, the impact of the Royal Commission.[86] There will continue to be collateral damage that will impact adversely on Catholic education.

And that's alright as long as we, like the midwives during the slavery in Egypt, know how to deliver and nurture new life in the face of painful transition. When we come close to the 'fire' of Jesus and his 'dangerous memory', we are also a people of hope.

May Australian Catholic education continue to be reborn in ways beyond the traditional structures. Like the river that has changed its course, we have a choice to make. It is not in yearning for or holding on to the known and the familiar but in reimagining the future and venturing into the unknown chaos like the old Exodus that we shall find new life. 'Tell the people of Israel to march on'.

Let's draw close once again to the fire of Jesus. For 'who is close to me is close to the fire; who is far from me is far from the Kingdom.'

Select Bibliography

Brueggemann, Walter. "Will Our Faith Have Children?" in *Word & World* 3:3, 1983.

Brueggemann, Walter. *The Prophetic Imagination*, 40th anniv. ed. Minneapolis: Fortress Press, 2018.

CECV. "Enhancing Catholic School Identity Project" Leuven Project on Catholic Education Commission of Victoria website. Updated February 2016. https://www.schoolidentity.net/introduction/

Fogarty, Ronald. *Catholic Education in Australia, 1806-1950* 2 Vols. Melbourne: Melbourne University Press, 1959.

Gardiner, Paul. *An Extraordinary Australian: Mary MacKillop: The Authorised Biography*, Sydney: Morehouse Publishing Co. 1995

---

[86] See the fine analysis of Richard Lennan, "Beyond Scandal and Shame? Ecclesiology and the Longing for a Transformed Church," *Theological Studies* 80: 3 (2019) 590-610

Gospel of Thomas. "Gospel of Thomas Saying #82" in *Gospel of Thomas Commentary*, 2012. http://www.earlychristianwritings.com/thomas/gospelthomas82.html

Johannes Baptist Metz, Johannes. Translated by J. Matthew Ashley, *A Passion for God: the mystical-political dimension of Christianity*. New York: Paulist Press, 1998.

Lennan, Richard. "Beyond Scandal and Shame? Ecclesiology and the Longing for a Transformed Church", *Theological Studies* 80:3 (2019): 590-610.

Pope Francis, *Laudato Sí*, "On the care for our common home", (2015) http://w2.vatican.va/content/francesco/en/encyclicals/documents/papa-francesco_20150524_enciclica-laudato-si.html

Pope Francis, Remarks at World Congress *Education Today and Tomorrow: A Passion that Is Renewed*, organised by the Congregation for Catholic Education, 2015.

Schreiter, Robert. *Ministry of Reconciliation*, New York: Orbis Books, 1998.

Epilogue

Brian Croke

Past

Two centuries ago, Catholic schooling in the new Australian colonies was a frail barque easily tossed around on choppy seas. Thanks to its long succession of inspired and selfless sailors and captains, designers and deckhands, many of whom you will find in this book, it now sets sail on its third century as a secure and well-equipped ocean vessel. It needs to be secure and well equipped to deal with the shoals and rough seas that lie ahead, some of which are already telescopically visible from the deck. Lying in its wake now are the original challenges of sheer survival in a harsh physical and social landscape (Chapter 3).

Most of the Anglo-Irish colonies that opted to form Australia from 1901 were a community divided by religious denomination, of which the Irish Catholics were a determined and generally poor minority with limited schooling opportunities. Also left behind now are the years of struggle from the 1880s to the 1960s to guarantee the bishops' great experiment of importing religious congregations from Ireland, England and Europe in order to maintain the Catholic school dream (Chapter 4). Many of them focused on founding separate boys' and girls' secondary schools, leaving the already vast enterprise of St Mary Mackillop's home-grown nuns to maintain the primary schools, especially in rural areas.

The years after World War II saw a rapid growth in student numbers, accelerated by a high level of British and European migration, a growth in ambition with parents wanting more education for their children than they had enjoyed themselves. The inability of local church authorities and religious congregations to meet the demand led to a financial crisis, although the demand inspired many orders to expand the university education of their brightest members (Chapter 5).

Slowly, from the 1950s, in different states, different forms of government assistance emerged. Support for building and upgrading schools came first, mainly through subsidising interest paid on loans, because that was the most urgent need. Next came grants for recurrent purposes, mainly subsidising lay teacher salaries. Only with Commonwealth and State financial assistance could Catholic schools hope to lower their class sizes, to provide salaries to match those of other schools, especially government schools, and to at least replace the declining number of religious in schools after the mid-1960s. Only with Government financial assistance could the Australian bishops guarantee the quality of education expected by the Catholic parents, to whom the bishops allowed no choice for their children but a Catholic school. The Australian Catholic school's generally unspoken goal of social and occupational mobility for a working class Irish community was soon achieved, made possible by the successive generations of outstanding educators, many of whom are featured in this book. Catholic Prime Ministers and Premiers, to take just one criterion, have long passed.

Present

Having been steered safely clear of the various rocky shoals of the past by many of the people featured in this book, and legions of others, Australian Catholic schools can nowadays be cast as a success story, notwithstanding ever-present challenges (Chapter 6). Across Australia, in city and country, Catholic schools now educate 20% of young Australians who are mainly taught by experienced and qualified teachers in modern facilities. Moreover, the vast bulk of the modern Catholic school's operating expenses are met by Australian and State/territory governments.

The still significant differences across the nation in quality of Catholic education, in provision, and in parental capacity to support the local Catholic school, are all explained by their history. They have been underpinned by a political and social doctrine of choice. That is, in the 1960s and 1970s primarily, the Australian community and the governments it elected at state and federal level all considered it was only fair for Catholics to have a Catholic school to choose for their children. Having fought so hard for the principle of choice, the church is now in no position to object if fewer Catholics make that choice each year and if, instead, it is non-Catholic families who increasingly choose Catholic schools. Indeed, Catholic schools are an increasing choice for Muslim and Hindu families because they are not secular, and for those of no religion at all for their own reasons.

Yet, for all its success, Catholic education in Australia has failed to tell its own story well. One magnificent work stands out, namely Brother Ronald Fogarty's 2-volume Catholic Education in Australia 1806-1950, published in 1959. Br Ronald was clearly an historian of the foremost rank: an indefatigable and accomplished researcher, and a clear writer with a magnificent breadth of vision. His story ends in 1950 and to this day has found no successor. Instead, the history of Catholic schooling for the past seventy years is only available by peeping through the windows of other works.

Thus, we find partial glimpses in histories of education, in histories of the Catholic church in Australia, the histories of particular religious orders involved in schools, and in biographies of individual clerics who played an influential role in education. Above all, we have some histories of individual schools and parishes, even dioceses, from which to begin to understand the broader picture, although they tend to be hastily produced for a particular anniversary. In the end, it has to be said that Australian Catholic education finds itself without a real sense of history, and therefore without that capacity to critique and reform itself which flows from historical self-awareness.

The *Biographical Dictionary of Australian Catholic Educators* (BDACE) goes some way towards filling this gap, but it is no substitute for the histories of Australian schooling over the past seventy years that still need to be researched and written. However, the BDACE does provides an opportunity both to (1) enrich and expand the story from 1806 to 1950 (as told by Br Ronald, back in the 1950s), and (2) begin to tell the story after 1950, during which the school almost exclusively staffed by Catholics, attended by baptised Catholic students, the children of Catholic parents who attended Catholic schools themselves, developed into the school which has 35% of its students and, in the case of secondary, over 30% of its staff, who are not Catholic and have no family affiliation with the church. These figures vary across states and territories, as well as dioceses, but there are states and dioceses where Catholic students are already a minority in Catholic schools. At the same time, the fastest growing segments of the student population have been Students with a Disability and Aboriginal and Torres Strait Islander students.

Meanwhile, increasing numbers of those Catholic families, which, in previous generations, automatically chose the Catholic school, now choose to send their children elsewhere. The proportion of Catholic students in high-fee paying independent schools, for instance, continues to grow annually, as does the number in specialist and academically selective government secondary schools. This presents a new challenge to church leaders and to leaders of Catholic Education alike. Were it not for non-Catholic students, Catholic school enrolments would have declined significantly over the past twenty years or so. This trend has gathered momentum recently when the reputation of the church is lower than at any time in living memory and with its authority figures, bishops and priests, likewise diminished. Catholic parents strongly support their ability to choose the school that best meets their child's needs. Such a scenario was certainly not foreseen, or foreseeable, during the struggles for government financial aid in the 1960s.

Future

One can never know the future with any accuracy, but certain lineaments of the future for Australian Catholic schooling can be teased out, if not anticipated, from present developments or astute observation of the past. These are the new challenges for today's and tomorrow's Australian Catholic educators. They can be summed up as part of the wider quest to define freedom of religion and religious practice in Australian society. For the Catholic school, that means having the authority to decide what is taught, how it is taught, who teaches it, who may be enrolled in the school, how the school may be resourced, and how it may relate to the Catholic community that founded it. Already, or in the near future, lie contests around all these dimensions of Catholic schooling.

The Catholic community, including several of the individuals whose lives form part of this book, led by their bishops and encouraged by their political allies, won the financial support of the Commonwealth and State/Territory governments for Catholic schools in the 1960s and 1970s. The schools, and religion more broadly, were then considered a force for good in Australian society and one to be encouraged, not hindered. The nation also realised that it could not afford to have some schools inferior in resources and outcomes compared to others, a perennial concern but no longer an exclusively Catholic school one. This same commitment to Catholic schools and articulation of the good they can provide for Australian society will be called for from today's and tomorrow's Catholic educators.

Most students spend a total of thirteen years at school, sometimes at the same school. This was not the case with previous generations for whom only a minority was schooled beyond the primary years. Slowly, but occasionally with spurts, more and more Catholic school students stayed longer at school so that now the majority complete their schooling. They are very unlikely to have seen, let alone experienced a religious nun or brother, in their entire school lives.

Most of their teachers are themselves parents too. They are also unlikely to have been taught by an unqualified teacher at any time or sat in an unreasonably large class. However, the extent to which they understand or practise the faith imparted to them during their Catholic schooling is another matter, but a highly legitimate one. The essential ecclesial dimension of the Catholic school, its role in the wider evangelising community of the church, risks becoming dysfunctional. Yet, the school cannot by itself counteract the influence of family and society. Herein lies a fundamental issue for reflection and action by all present and future Catholic educators.

There are signs that the *Royal Commission into Institutional Responses to Sexual Abuse* has already had a negative influence on Catholic school enrolments, which should not surprise. After all, it has had a profound impact on the life and faith of Australian Catholics, many of whom were damaged by abuse at the hands of their teachers, but mostly at the thought that this could have happened at all in a Catholic setting, and the structures were powerless to stop it. For the significant proportion of non-Catholic parents who enrol their children in Catholic schools, it is a far easier decision to go elsewhere.

In addition, the likely future will unfurl a series of challenges which are more 'internal', that is, focused on what the Catholic school stands for, what it does, how it relates to the church more broadly, how it manages its essential goal of transmitting the faith. All of this is against a societal backdrop that is increasingly secular, intolerant of religious privileges, and with a Catholic community as a shrinking minority hankering for the sort of leadership that will take it beyond the status quo, while the Commonwealth and State Government funders of Catholic schooling increase expectations and demands.

Without having to specify timescale, some immediate challenges for all those currently involved in Catholic education or planning to be, are identifiable:

1. Corrosion of integrity of Catholic school's goals and operational principles:

- Australia, already a pluralist society, confronts a drive towards radical secularism, given the reality that "no religion "is the fastest growing belief system of our Commonwealth (as revealed in the most recent 2016 National Census);

- Rapid decline in proportion of Catholics (22.6% in 2016 census) and of school age children who are Catholic (19% in 2016 census);

- Fewer migrants choosing Catholic schools reflects diversified sources of migrants;

- Survey data, and annual school enrolment data, demonstrate a weakened support among Catholics for Catholic schools;

- The national same-sex marriage plebiscite in 2017/18 witnessed both a hostility towards religious views and religious people, and a level of support among Catholics, particularly those of school age.

2. Government interference, mandate and objection

- The recommendations of the report of the *Royal Commission into Institutional Responses to Sexual Abuse* and how governments might prescribe new rules for managing schools and students;

- Recommendations and requirements from the Australian government's *Religious Freedom Review* (2019-21), including preservation of anti-discrimination provisions in current legislation;

- The traditional argument that Catholic schools never seek to discriminate anyway will only elicit the reply that as the current provisions are unnecessary and ineffective, then they should be withdrawn;

- Government mandated 'open enrolment' and 'open employment' policies now become more likely.

3. Separation of 'Church' and 'State'

- When Australia moves to become a republic, if not before, it can be expected that the whole issue of the relation between church and state will be reopened in the prelude;

- In any event, it is also possible that the Constitutional challenge to Commonwealth grants for religious schools of the 1970s (DOGS case) will be recontested, as sometime proposed;

- Since the Commonwealth and State in effect already fund the teaching of religion in Catholic schools, this could lead to a definable separation (religious/non-religious) within the curriculum and teaching allocations, with only the non-religious part as government-supported.

4. Governance and Accountability

- Australia has developed a very centralised and top-down model and tradition of schooling, and the funding of schooling, including Catholic schooling since the 1970s;

- Catholic diocesan systems have formed into relatively tight bureaucracies and increasingly all the religious orders have created, or are creating, more centralised bodies with paid staff and with at least some responsibility for many of the tasks undertaken by Catholic education offices for diocesan schools;

- With high levels of central organisation comes high expectations of accountability and compliance and the capacity to leverage any new requirements;

- As more and more time and energy are directed towards financial and other compliance requirements, the core work of the faith-based school will become harder to maintain.

Learning from the BDACE

Modelled on other biographical dictionaries for individual nations, or disciplines, the BDACE aims to display a rich resource of individual experience of the reality of Catholic schooling over the past two centuries, especially over the past seventy years for which it is possible to obtain first-hand information from living sources. It allows us to see, for the first time in most cases, exactly what a single individual could achieve in a single lifetime of dedication and commitment. The individuals whose lives are described in this publication, and a great many more who are not, have all played their part in the story of Australian Catholic education over the past two centuries. Together, they provide an instructive example of how they influenced those around them in Catholic education – students, teachers, parents. Theirs is an immediate, but also a lasting, legacy to the present day.

The *BDACE*, therefore, provides a solid source of reflection for all those currently involved in the important enterprise of Australian Catholic schooling. Hopefully, it will inspire current and future generations of Catholic educators by directing their attention to what lies at the core of Catholic education, as reflected in the lives of individual educators, over the past 200 years: (1) the message and mandate of Jesus as teacher, and the heritage of his church; (2) the power of education for children of this nation as shown by the women and men of faith who have provided, often heroically and at great personal sacrifice and hardship, a Catholic education of mind and *spirit*. They all well illustrate the Prophet Daniel's claim: *'And those who have taught many people to do what is right will shine like the stars for all eternity'* (Daniel 12:3).

Appendix A
Additional biographies

Additional biographies submitted for inclusion in the *Biographical Dictionary of Australian Catholic Educators* (as at 14 July 2020).

Biography *Biographer/contact*

1. Barry, Mary (Mother Gonzaga) ibvm — Robin Scott
2. Bell, Fr James Ernest sm — Peter McMurrich sm
3. Bowe, Johanna (Judy) (Sr Mary Benignus) RSM — Shirley Garland RSM
4. Boylan, Mother M. Columba op — Angela Moloney op
5. Byrne, Thomas — Charles McGee
6. Claverie, Lucie Lorna McKinley (M. Gabriel) osc — Louise Hume osc
7. Collins, Hannah Mary (Sr Mary Vincent) RSM — Mary P Lowcock RSM
8. Coolahan, Msgr Francis Joseph — Marie Hughes rsj
9. Costello, Agnes (Mother Mary de Salles) RSM — Stancia Cawte
10. Creede, Sr Moira pbvm — Mary Franzman pbvm
11. Dilley, Msgr Vincent Francis — Marie Hughes rsj
12. Donnelly, Sr Isabel RSM — Colleen Rhodes RSM
13. Dwyer, Grace (Sr Mary Vivian) RSM — Helen Delaney RSM
14. Egan, Mary Josephine (Sr Mary Vincent) RSM — Gabrielle Foley RSM
15. Elliott, Monica Josephine (Sr Mary Vincent) RSM — Stancia Cawte
16. Flaherty, Mary Josephine (Mother M. Raphael) RSM — Jennifer Hartley RSM
17. Frizelle, Katherine (M. Dorothea) ibvm — Robin Scott
18. Gallagher, Mary Agatha (Sr Philomena) sgs — Elizabeth Murray sgs
19. Grogan, Patricia Mary (Sr Patricia) fcj — Julie Chamberlin
20. Hartigan, Moira (Sr Mary Ephrem) RSM — Helen Delaney RSM
21. Hayes, Nellie Florence (Sr Mary de Salles) RSM — Mary P Lowcock RSM
22. Kelty, Br Justin Linus cfc — John O'Halloran cfc
23. Kennedy, M. Margaret Mary fcj — Julia Chamberlin
24. Kenny, Mary Anne (Mother Xavier) csb — Kathleen Butler csb

Biography	Biographer/contact
25. Lardner, Anne Veronica (Mother Veronica) fcj	Julie Chamberlin
26. Lennon, Dorris (Sr M. Cyril) RSM	Colleen Rhodes RSM
27. McCarthy, Frumence (Sr Mary Marcian) RSM	Helen Delaney RSM
28. McDonald, Flora Mary (Sr M. Genevieve) RSM	James McDonald
29. McOscar, Doreen (Sr Felician) sm	Gail Reneker sm
30. Mills, Gwladys Evelyn (Sr Mary John) RSM	Stancia Cawte
31. Moran, Sheila Mary (Sr Mary Cecilia) RSM	Jennifer Hartley RSM
32. Murphy, Bishop Patrick Laurence	Mark Askew
33. Nowotny, Joan (Mother Miriam) ibvm	Christine Burke ibvm
34. Nugent, Anna Maria (Sr Mary Bernadine) RSM	Mary P Lowcock RSM
35. O'Doherty, Annie (Mother Oliver) ibvm	Robin Scott
36. O'Driscoll, Bedelia (Mother M. Aloysius) RSM	Gabrielle Foley RSM
37. O'Neill, Br Fintan fsp	Stephen Sweetman fsp
38. Prytz, Violet Gerda (Sr Gerda) fcj	Julie Chamberlin
39. Quinn, Mary (Sr Mary Gabriel) RSM	Mary P Lowcock RSM
40. Ritchie, Marie Genevieve (Sr Carmela) sgs	Elizabeth Murray sgs
41. Sexton, Patricia Joan (Sr Joan) sgs	Lia Haran sgs
42. Slowey, Msgr John	Jim D'Orsa
43. Stock, Anna (Mother Stanislaus) fcj	Julie Chamberlin
44. Walker, Mary (Mother Dorothea) ibvm	Robin Scott
45. Walsh, Kathleen (Sr Mary Perpetua) RSM	Helen Delaney RSM
46. Webber, Fr John Garvey sm	Marist Fathers
47. Welbourne, Adele Eileen (Sr Louise) op	Elizabeth Hellwig
48. White, Mary (Mother Mary Agnes Vincent) RSM	Stancia Cawte

Summary

These 48 biographies have been filed. A further 12 are in process.

Appendix B
Entries by canonical status

Entries in the *Australian Dictionary of Biography* (ADB) and the *Biographical Dictionary of Australian Catholic Educators* (BDACE) by canonical status.[87]

		ADB	BDACE
1	Cardinals	2	0
2	Archbishops	19[88]	0
3	Bishops	17[89]	2
4	Priests (Diocesan)	7	3
5	Augustinian Priests	0[90]	0
6	Benedictine Priests/Monks	1[91]	0
7	Carmelite Priests	0	0
8	Franciscan Priests/Monks	0[92]	0
9	Jesuit Priests	4[93]	0
10	Marist Priests	1	2
11	MSC Priests	0	0
12	Passionist Priests	1[94]	0

---

[87] As at 7 April 2020.
[88] Includes Polding, Vaughan & Reynolds (Benedictines) and James Goold (Augustinian)
[89] Includes Salvado & Torres (Benedictines New Norcia and Geoghegan & Torreggiani (Franciscans).
[90] James Goold included in Archbishops.
[91] Three Archbishops included above and 1 ex-Benedictine Joseph Moore.
[92] Two included in Bishops.
[93] Including former Jesuit Michael Arthur Scott.
[94] Former Passionist Fr Julian Tennison Woods.

		ADB	BDACE
13	Vincentian Priests	1	0
14	Christian Brothers	8	2
15	De la Salle Brothers	1	0
16	Marist Brothers	3[95]	1
17	Patrician Brothers	0	2
18	Brigidine Sisters	2	2
19	Charity Sisters (of)	6	0
20	Daughters/Our Lady of Sacred Heart	0	0
21	Dominican Sisters	4	3
22	Faithful Companions of Jesus Sisters	0	6
23	Good Samaritan Sisters	3	3
24	Holy Faith Sisters	0	0
25	Josephite Sisters	3	0
26	Loreto Sisters	4	6
27	Marist Sisters	0	1
28	Mercy Sisters	11[96]	10
29	Missionary Sisters of Service	0	1
30	Poor Clare Sisters	0	1
31	Presentation Sisters	1	2
32	Sacré Coeur Sisters	2	0
33	St Joseph of Orange Sisters	0	0
34	Ursuline Sisters	1	1
35	Lay Men	3	3
36	Lay Women	1	3
	TOTALS	108	54

---

[95] Including former Marist James Devaney.
[96] Including former Mercy Margaret Moses.

Appendix C

Video interviews

Video-interviews of Australian Catholic Educators (Living Legends) (as at 15 January 2020).

1. Aengus Kavanagh fsp (Sydney) (interviewed by SOG[97] 9/08/16)
2. Ambrose Payne fsc (Sydney) (interviewed by SOG 24/08/16)
3. Kelvin Canavan fms (Sydney) (interviewed by SOG 20/10/16)
4. Bishop Geoff Robinson (Sydney) (interviewed by SOG 26/10/16)
5. Norman Hart fms (Sydney) (interviewed by SOG 27/10/16)
6. Geoffrey Joy (Canberra) (interviewed by SOG 4/11/16)
7. Natalie McNamara (Sydney) (interviewed by SOG 21/03/17)
8. Susan Pascoe (Victoria) (interviewed by SOG in Sydney 16/03/17)
9. Mike Byrne QCEC (Qld)) (interviewed by AB[98] 10/04/17)
10. Joe McCorley (Qld) (interviewed by AB 10/04/17)
11. Margaret McDonald sgs (Qld) (interviewed by AB 11/04/17)
12. Dr Kevin Treston (Qld) (interviewed by AB 11/04/17)
13. Mons Tom Doyle (Melbourne) (interviewed by SOG 18/04/17)
14. David Hutton (Qld) (interviewed by AB 12/05/17)
15. Judith Lawson op (Sydney) (Interviewed by SOG 7/06/17)
16. Rev. Jim Littleton msc (Sydney) (interviewed by AB 16/08/17)
17. Leesa Jeffcoat (Qld) (Interviewed by AB 23/08/2017)
18. Alan Druery (Qld) (Interviewed by AB 23/08/2017)

---

[97] SOG abbreviation for project editor Seamus O'Grady.
[98] AB abbreviation for project director.

19. Tony D'Arbon fms (Sydney) (Interviewed by AB September 2017)
20. Rosemary Crumlin RSM (Melbourne) (Interviewed by SOG 19/09/2017)
21. Peter Annett (Melbourne) (Interviewed by SOG 19/09/2017)
22. Rev. Hugh Brown ocarm (Melbourne) (Interviewed by SOG 20/09/2017)
23. Vin Faulkner (Melbourne) (Interviewed by SOG 20/09/2017)
24. Dan Stewart cfc (Sydney) (Interviewed by AB 1/10/2017)
25. Dr Anne O'Brien (audio) (Melbourne) (Interviewed by SOG 9/11/2017)
26. Michael Green fms (Sydney) (Interviewed by SOG 15/11/2017)
27. Pat Malone rsj (Sydney) (interviewed by AB 17/05/2018)
28. Deidre Jordan RSM (Adelaide) (interviewed by SOG 24/05/2018)
29. Judy Redden RSM (Adelaide) (Interviewed by SOG 24/05/2018)
30. Angela Moloney op (Adelaide) (Interviewed by SOG 25/05/2018)
31. Jillian Havey op (Adelaide) (Interviewed by SOG 25/05/2018)
32. Julian McDonald cfc (Rome) (Interviewed by SOG 19/10/2018)
33. Monica Sinclair RSM (Newcastle) (Interviewed by AB 26/04/2019)
34. Patricia Lake RSM (Newcastle) (interviewed by AB 26/04/2019)
35. Dorothy Campion RSM (Newcastle) (interviewed by AB 26/04/2019)
36. Dr Bill Sultman (North Sydney) (Interviewed by AB 30/04/2019)
37. Barbara McDonough RSM (Parramatta) (Interviewed by SOG 18/06/2019)
38. Denise Desmarchelier ibvm (Melbourne) (interviewed by SOG 9/09/2019)
39. Bill Wilding cfc (Melbourne) (Interviewed by SOG 9/09/2019)
40. Maryanne Confoy rsc (Melbourne) (Interviewed by SOG 10/09/2019)
41. Mark O'Loughlin cfc (Melbourne) (Interviewed by SOG 10/09/2019)
42. Helga Neidhart rsc (Melbourne) (Interviewed by SOG 10/09/2019)
43. Archbishop Frank Carroll (Wagga Wagga) (Interviewed by SOG 8/01/2020).

www.ingramcontent.com/pod-product-compliance
Lightning Source LLC
Chambersburg PA
CBHW010244010526
44107CB00063B/2681